The Surprise of Excellence
Modern Essays on Max Beerbohm

Thomas Photos, Oxford

"Max" accepting with resignation his place among the classics

From the drawing by Ronald Searle in the commemorative
volume presented to Sir Max Beerbohm on his eightieth
birthday

The Surprise of Excellence

Modern Essays on Max Beerbohm

EDITED, WITH AN INTRODUCTION, BY J. G. RIEWALD

ARCHON BOOKS 1974

Library of Congress Cataloging in Publication Data

Riewald, Jacobus Gerhardus, comp.
   The surprise of excellence.

   Bibliography: p.
   1. Beerbohm, Sir Max, 1872-1956—Criticism and interpretation. I. Title.
PR6003.E4Z782   824′.9′12   74-5181
ISBN 0-208-01443-8

© 1974 by J. G. Riewald. First published 1974 as an Archon Book, an imprint
of The Shoe String Press, Inc., Hamden, Connecticut
06514. All rights reserved. *Printed in the United States of America*

CONTENTS

INTRODUCTION

When, in 1921, the author and caricaturist Bohun Lynch confessed to Beerbohm that he intended to write a "little book" on him, Max refused to collaborate in any way: "I won't supply you with any photograph of myself at *any* age, nor with any scrap of corrected MS., nor with any caricature of myself for a frontispiece . . . , nor with *any* of the things you seem to think might be of interest. You must forage around for yourself. I won't even try to prevent you from using anything you may find. I eschew all responsibility whatsoever. I disclaim the horrid privilege of seeing proof-sheets. I won't read a single word till your book is published."

A few years later, when another Beerbohm student presented himself in the shape of a prospective bibliographer, Max's attitude was hardly more cooperative. Replying to the inquiries of A. J. A. Symons in connection with the latter's grandiose project for a bibliography of books of the 1890s, he wrote: "Under the vast piles of masonry that you have reared over me, how can I lift a little finger? How can I even draw my last breath? I am suffocated. I have no last breath to draw. That curse on you which would be the natural accompaniment of that breath cannot be uttered. You have nothing to fear from me. And little to hope."

However, contrary to popular belief, Beerbohm does not belong to that band of genuine artists who invariably refuse to offer the slightest assistance to prospective biographers and bibliographers. Though for the most part of his life his policy in this matter was one of adamantine non-cooperation, his attitude became less rigorous as the years went by. After receiving the typescript of my own "very large" book, he reacted in the following manner: "I shall be grateful if you will write and tell me in what form you propose to use your work. I cannot suppose that it is a mere labour of love. On the other hand I cannot conceive that Holland is greatly interested in me. Nor, by the same token, can I hope that my own native land knows, or wishes to know, one millionth fraction as much about me as is known by *you*! So please write to me." When I wrote him that it was my intention to publish my work in book form, he replied that he wished he could be of some assistance in the matter of my book, and continued: "But this I *cannot* be. The instinct of self-preservation prevents me. I don't know how it might be in Holland, but I know that in *England* the critics (who have always been very indulgent to me) would be instantly down on me if I had aided and abetted you in your magnum opus." He then went on to quote a lengthy passage from Bohun Lynch's book, *Max Beerbohm in Perspective*, what he had written to him, and concluded: "Well, dear Doctor Riewald, what was true all those years ago is as true as ever to-day. I am as far as ever from great—and am moreover as worldly-wise. And thus I cannot do anything that might be construed as the aforesaid aiding and abetting."

Nonetheless, after my book had been accepted for publication, Max graciously supplied me with what he had denied his first biographer: "I will gladly write," he promised, "some kind of little note to you, which could be used prefatorily, and supply a typical page of MS.; and I am sure I could find some self-caricature for reproduction." But in a further letter he reverted to what he had implied before: "I cannot, however, make any additions to, or corrections of, anything in your work. To do so would be incompatible with my resolve not to *collaborate* in any way!" Accordingly, how great was my surprise when, a fortnight later, he appeared to have changed his mind: "In my previous letter I wrote that I could not make any additions or corrections in your work. But I have been looking through the biographical part (Life, Man, Writer) and have found there rather numerous inaccuracies which I should not like to remain there." He wondered whether my publisher would undertake not to proceed with the printing until I had visited him in Rapallo and gone through, with him, the corrigible points. The visit took place early in November 1952. Max and Elisabeth Jungmann received me at the Villino Chiaro on two successive days. We discussed the passages in the typescript which he had marked in colored pencil—and a host of other things besides—, but I did not feel at liberty to make any essential changes in the text. Max was not in the least offended. *Sir Max Beerbohm, Man and Writer: A Critical Analysis with a Brief Life and a Bibliography* came out in the summer of 1953; the copy which the publishers had sent Max arrived exactly on his eighty-first birthday, August 24. Naturally I was relieved and elated when, a week later, I got a letter from him in which, among other things, he wrote: "About the manner and the matter of my writings I know now, thanks to you, very much more than I ever knew—though I shall never rival you as an expert! I hope the magnum, or rather maximum, opus will have some at least of the success that it deserves." He returned to the subject in the spring of the next year, when he wrote me: "Your book has been greatly appreciated by many people whom I know; and I myself, besides being proud of your opinion of me, find your work very useful for enabling me to fix dates in my life which otherwise would have left me trying vainly to guess!"

Perhaps the main reason for Beerbohm's reluctance to "aid and abet" prospective biographers, bibliographers, and bio-bibliographers is disclosed in his letter to Bohun Lynch from which I quoted above. "My life," he writes, "(though to me it has been, and is, extremely interesting) is without a single point of general interest." That Max had no confidence at all in the biographical method, is clear, not only from his attitude to people who had expressed to him a wish to write about him, but also from his own critical *oeuvre*. In the controversy between the adherents of the biographical approach and those of the intrinsic study of art Max has always been on the side of the angels. He firmly believed that the study of art should concentrate on the works themselves, not on the life of the artist. He therefore counseled his younger contemporary to address himself to his writings and drawings, and, notwithstanding the fact that Bernard Shaw had once referred to him as "the incomparable," to *compare* him with other essayists and caricaturists.

Of course Beerbohm's advice to the first serious student of his work to compare him with other essayists and caricaturists was given tongue in cheek. For, after all, Shaw was right. As an essayist, fantasist, and caricaturist Beerbohm really *is* incomparable, and attempts made by critics to define his genius by applying the comparative method to his work have not been notoriously successful. As Professor McElderry writes in his contribution to this anthology, Beerbohm "achieved in caricature what he achieved in writing, a manner and a point of view that were unique in the literal sense. There has been only one Max." Small wonder, then, that many of the critics and scholars represented in this volume have chosen to apply themselves to the analysis and interpretation of his writings and drawings, rather than anatomize his life which, in any but the most personal acceptation of the term, was quite uneventful.

Understandably the uniqueness of Beerbohm's art in either medium is at least partly due to his firm resolve not to transcend his limitations. Max himself has always been aware of the precise scope of his talent: "My gifts are small," he observed when he was at the height of his fame. "I've used them very well and discreetly, never straining them; and the result is that I've made a charming little reputation." Modern critics and scholars have confirmed this view of himself. To quote two recent examples only: in his essay "Max Beerbohm and the Wings of Henry James," reprinted here, Professor Felstiner characterizes Beerbohm as "a precocious artist with narrow but highly developed skills." Lord David Cecil talking to Patrick Garland in the *Listener* of December 24, 1970, expresses the same view in different words: "Here was somebody who'd discovered what he could do, and very seldom tried to do something which was outside the range of his talent. But when he did do something he did it as well as he possibly could, so that it kept an extraordinarily high level." It may be said that Beerbohm's limitations subserved his mastery, so that within his self-imposed frame he frequently achieved excellence, perfection even, both as a writer and a draughtsman. As a result his classic status now seems assured. *Zuleika Dobson* has been included in the Penguin Modern and in the Signet Classics, while *Seven Men and Two Others* has been available in the World's Classics for several years.

It was Stanley Kauffmann who, in the *New Republic* of April 10, 1965, suggested the feasibility of an anthology of writings about Beerbohm, "for," he said, "he evoked much that is good." Twenty of the best and most representative writings that he evoked during the last thirty years or so are here brought together within the covers of a single volume. Most of the pieces included are complete essays, a few are selected parts from full-length studies of Max Beerbohm. While some of them are of a critical or scholarly nature, others illuminate the man rather than the works. A few of the latter, recording the authors' encounters with Max, are essentially interviews or personal reminiscences by important contemporaries who knew him. Creative artists as well as literary critics and scholars, both British and American, are represented. Seven of the contributors are professional scholars, four literary critics; two are novelists, one is a playwright, one a poet, one an art critic; the others are less easy to define. Twelve of the items were written by Americans, seven by British authors, one by a Dutchman.

Among the authors represented in this collection it is Derek Stanford who explicitly emphasizes the quality of excellence in Beerbohm's prose. "'The surprise of that excellence,'" he writes, "serves well to describe the impact which Sir Max's style has upon us, administering its novel, small, unflagging shocks." Professor Dupee discovers this same quality in the perfect unity of style and matter that characterizes Beerbohm's fiction: "In his fiction, if ever in literature, style and substance live in wedded bliss, the perfect midget couple. The English sentence is for him distinctly 'an unit,' to quote one of his instructively correct phrases. He explores the possibilities of the sentence as thoroughly as Pope did those of the heroic couplet. All known devices of rhetoric and syntax are set to performing for us with unobtrusive gaiety." Lord David Cecil, referring to *Zuleika Dobson* as "the truest picture of Oxford in fiction," goes on to say that "it is written in a style which is a masterpiece of sustained virtuosity." Though he considers *Seven Men and Two Others* "an even subtler triumph," he concludes that "as a blend of comedy and prettiness *Zuleika Dobson* has no equal in English literature but *The Rape of the Lock*." The same comparison is made by Harold Nicolson: "In no similar work that I have read (with the possible exception of *The Rape of the Lock*) is there so dexterous an alternation of the element of expectation with the element of surprise. The book, if one attends to it at all carefully, is a masterpiece of design, . . . a consummate piece of artistry." According to Dupee, "Beerbohm had the rococo imagination—so much so that *Zuleika* is closer in spirit to *The Rape of the Lock* than it is to the work of fantasists today, with the exception of Nabokov." In this context it may be remembered that William Empson, in his *Seven Types of Ambiguity*, included Beerbohm among the poets on the strength of certain stylistic features of *Zuleika Dobson*, and that E. M. Forster once referred to this novel as "the most consistent achievement of fantasy in our time."

John Felstiner's contribution particularly deals with Beerbohm's parodies and caricatures of Henry James. While granting the brilliancy of a fantasy like "Enoch Soames," he believes that Beerbohm's real excellence lies in parody and caricature, and he singles out "The

Guerdon" for special praise: "Although 'The Mote in the Middle Distance' has been reprinted more than any other parody of Beerbohm's, 'The Guerdon' is finer; almost too fine." Similarly, W. H. Auden contends that "as a parodist, [Max] is probably the finest in English." In this judgment Auden is supported by Lord David Cecil, who regards Beerbohm as a supreme master of parody because he "manages to parody his victim's sense as much as he does his style," and by Professor Kronenberger, who not only refers to him as "the greatest parodist . . . of our time" but also as "the man who has conceivably written the finest familiar essays in the English language." Testifying to the excellence of Beerbohm's writings in general, Professor Cecil concludes that, for him, they are "the finest, richest expression of the spirit of comedy in all twentieth-century English literature."

Not surprisingly, a somewhat neglected aspect of Beerbohm's genius receives abundant praise in John Updike's review of *Max in Verse: Rhymes and Parodies by Max Beerbohm*, which he calls "an enchanted island of a book." Characterizing one of the pieces included in this collection he says that it is "quintessential light verse, a twitting of the starkest prose into perfect form, a marriage of earth with light, and quite magical."

An ambidextrous artist, Beerbohm was, in Sir John Rothenstein's words, "a leisurely perfectionist" in his drawings as well as in his writings. Practising both parody and caricature, he created, as Felstiner says, a small genre by bringing the dynamics of parody into caricature. As might be expected, the excellence of Max's drawings is the subject of many of the other contributing essayists. Evelyn Waugh's reminiscence stands alone in that it illustrates the excellence of Max's manners.

The items in this collection have been arranged chronologically and include some of the most important essays on Max's art written from 1943 to 1970, a period which saw significant changes in Beerbohm criticism. Early Beerbohm critics often contented themselves with mere eulogy because they wrongly believed, as Guy Boas formulates it, that a study of Max Beerbohm was as inapt as a study of the rainbow. More recent critics have provided a different and more complex assessment of his work. According to Felstiner in his penetrating study of Max's parody and caricature, *The Lies of Art*, "critical writing on Beerbohm in the twenties, thirties, and forties contains isolated perceptions, but always in passing, never developed. The tone is mostly discreet, well-turned, and careful not to bore the reader." Readers of this anthology may feel that Felstiner's characterization applies, in part at least, to some of the earlier criticisms. At the same time they will agree that many of the later contributions show a definite gain in analytical power and critical finesse. Yet much still remains to be done in the field of analysing the works themselves in order to account for their magic appeal. From a purely scholarly point of view, what is especially needed is a linguistic study of Beerbohm's prose style.

Most of the pieces collected in this volume come from various journals and books, some of which are not readily available to the student of modern English literature and caricature. A number of them have been rescued from the "inilluminable catacombs" of first publication, while two are here published for the first time. For the present edition a few of the authors included have made minor corrections and changes in the original text of their contributions. Whenever this is the case, it has been recorded in the acknowledgment note. I have updated a few references and added a note here and there. I have also silently corrected one or two spelling mistakes and misprints. For ease-of reference I have provided a table of dates, a select bibliography, notes on the editor and contributors, and an index.

In preparing this anthology my greatest debt naturally is to all those scholars, critics, and authors who have permitted their distinguished essays to appear in this volume. I would also like to express my sincere gratitude to the Netherlands Organization for the Advancement of Pure Research (Z. W. O.) for the grant which enabled me to visit the British Museum to consult the books and journals I needed. Finally, I am grateful to Mr. Ronald Searle and to the Warden and Fellows of Merton College, Oxford, for permitting me to reproduce the drawing " 'Max' accepting with resignation his place among the classics" from the Max Beerbohm Birthday Book, and to Dr. Roger Highfield, Librarian of Merton College, for arranging for the photograph to be made.

J. G. RIEWALD

University of Groningen
Netherlands
January 1974

John Rothenstein

INTRODUCTION TO *The Poets' Corner*

Max Beerbohm is a leisurely perfectionist who ever since his earliest years has avoided all uncongenial work; so it is that the nine published volumes of his drawings and the nine published volumes of his essays and stories, which represent the greater part of his life's work, contain only his maturest and most personal reflections upon the subjects which have aroused his interest. Anybody who peruses these eighteen volumes (which, being slender as well as infinitely entertaining, require no effort whatsoever) can hardly fail to form a vivid and precise idea of Max's character, intellect, outlook on life, opinion of his contemporaries and of the problems of the day, and of his appearance; even a notion of his voice and manner. These eighteen volumes constitute, in effect, a portrait of a man as complete in its way as Boswell's *Johnson*. It is, appropriately, a less massive work, yet it reveals, although indirectly, as much of the essential Max as the other of the essential Johnson.

To add anything of value to such a portrait would be difficult at any time, but to introduce Max to the immense public which reads Penguin Books is a particularly difficult undertaking. For Max has no love for the public, and has an antipathy for the democratic, collectivist age into which he has lived. A drawing, for instance, such as that in which he makes a proletarian boy exclaim, before a portrait of a supercilious aristocrat, "That's the sort of

John Rothenstein, "Max." From *The Poets' Corner by Sir Max Beerbohm*. With an Introduction by John Rothenstein (London & New York: The King Penguin Books, 1943), pp. 5-13. Reprinted, with minor corrections and changes, by permission of Sir John Rothenstein.

1

class-consciousness *I'd* like ter have!'' is a challenge to prevailing ideals. But Max's is a challenge which should be met, not with impatience but with gratitude, for few things are more salutary to society than satire.

We are fortunate in having among us two caricaturists of the first order: Low, who mercilessly floodlights the iniquities and follies in what was, until yesterday, the accepted order of things, and adumbrates a saner world-society; and Max, who illumines the virtues of the traditional way of life, and ridicules all change which has not some overwhelming justification.

Low and Max, in most things opposites, differ in nothing so much as the publics to which they appeal. During the half-dozen years prior to 1939, when the struggle against Fascism became a conflict of guns, airplanes and tanks, as well as a conflict of ideas, Low wielded extraordinary power. Both Hitler and Mussolini are reputed to have winced under the lash of his ridicule. Appeasers were afraid he would embroil us with the Axis. He showed the people of England how to distinguish, with a facility disquieting to some, their enemies from their friends. And he lassoed Lord Baldwin with adhesive tape and trussed him up with a neatness which would have done credit to a cowboy. Low shows a singular understanding of the predicament of the ordinary man, beset, as he is everywhere, by imminent and deadly dangers, and weighed down by terrifying responsibilities. And to the ordinary man, as he laughs at Low's cartoons, the world appears a saner, a less unintelligible place.

To Max the idea of addressing the mass of the people would hardly occur. His drawings are so intimate as to be almost soliloquies; but soliloquies easily comprehensible to his friends. For it is his friends who constitute Max's chosen public. Low's technique is adapted to mass-production: his drawings are made expressly to be reproduced in *The Evening Standard*; whereas each one of Max's drawings is an end in itself, even when intended for reproduction in a limited edition.

It is apparent that, measured simply in quantitative terms, Max's impact on the world, compared with Low's, is slight. But Max's influence is not to be measured thus. It is true his appeal is to a limited public, but it is an influential and a fervently admiring public. For of those who have the good fortune to be acquainted with his work, the majority regard it with sustained enthusiasm. How many reputations have blossomed and faded since the appearance, shortly after its author had come down from Oxford, of the diminutive volume of essays entitled *The Works of Max Beerbohm*? And who, we may ask, constitute this enviable public? Today, when dukes' daughters work in factories, and labourers sit in the Cabinet, Max's public is losing its cohesion; before the war it might have been identified with those sections of London society most responsive to ideas.

Some caricaturists are guided by animosity in their choice of subject; others are guided by what they suppose to be public or editorial taste; others accept whatever happens to be at hand. But Max is not much of a hater; he is indifferent to both public and editorial taste, and affected by his environment hardly at all; more than twenty years' residence in Rapallo evoked no Italian caricatures.

The principal impulse behind Max's caricature, even the most savage, I believe to be of *reverence*. "Reverence is a good thing," he says in one of his essays, "and part of its value is that the more we revere a man, the more sharply are we struck by anything in him (and there is always much) that is incongruous with his greatness." The fact that Max has chosen for the subjects of by far the greater number of his caricatures not ephemeral beings, but the vivid, gifted, and civilized personalities of his own and the preceding age would seem to lend support to this explanation of his guiding motive. He has dissected these great personalities and exhibited their infirmities to our sometimes almost horrified delight: the streak of vulgar materialism in Arnold Bennett; of schoolboy morbidity in A. E. Housman; and of crude brassiness in Rudyard Kipling. Yet such expositions, however remorseless, do not call in question the achievements of these men. Portraits drawn with so much insight can hardly fail to influence future historians, but it is improbable that they will diminish by so much as a cubit the stature of any of Max's great contemporaries. This freedom from belittlement markedly distinguishes Max, inveterate satirist though he is, from the historians who rush in where Lytton Strachey trod with care, whose effect is not to enlarge our understanding of heroes by treating their frailties with the same degree of candour as their virtues, but to "debunk" them, to divest them, that is to say, of all their greatness.

I have tried to indicate the part which reverence plays in Max's satire. But what are the qualities which he reveres? He told me once that he considered Byron and Rossetti the most fascinating personalities in nineteenth-century England. Their common qualities were a rich prodigality of nature, which involved them both in a complex of dramatic relationships with a number of the other personalities of their time, a robustness of outlook which Byron's poetry only partly reveals, and Rossetti's poetry and painting largely mask; a fierce independence and a developed sense of the art of living. Contrast is of the essence of the multiple caricature; no contrast recurs so frequently in Max's work as that between the full-blooded, sagacious and realistic person on the one hand, and on the other the desiccated, predominantly cerebral person which he finds of all the least sympathetic. In *The Poets' Corner* there are several variations on this theme: the contrast between the abounding vitality of Browning and the twittering pedantry of his disciples; between the formidable Ibsen and the suppliant Archer, and between the fleshly, puzzled Moore and the pallid, fairy-ridden Yeats. The same contrast appears in the marvellous series of twenty-four watercolour drawings, *Rossetti and His Circle*, an exquisite microcosm of pre-Raphaelite society. In one of these Rossetti inquires of his austere sister, as they are examining a selection of brightly-coloured Liberty silks:

> "What *is* the use, Christina, of having a heart like a singing bird and a water-shoot and all the rest of it, if you insist on getting yourself up like a pew-opener?"

In another it is Rossetti himself, robust and knowing enough beside Christina, who wilts in the florid presence of George Augustus Sala.

The great personality (often in contrast with the mediocre personality), the favourite subject of Max's caricature, is today in eclipse. Outside Axis-dominated lands the raising of the moral, intellectual and material standards of the average man is now regarded as of greater consequence than the maintenance or creation of élites. Therefore it is inevitable that such a man as Max, for whom the individual is everything, and the crowd almost nothing, should be out of harmony with the present age. But he is too intelligent to suppose that the clock can ever be put back. How clearly he recognizes the inevitability of the, to him, repellent developments in the social structure, is apparent from a drawing entitled "Civilization and the Industrial System." Considered simply as a drawing, this is one of the least distinguished he has ever done, but it is of particular interest for the light it throws on the underlying cause of the pessimism by which he has been of recent years increasingly affected:

> *The Industrial System to Civilization*: "No, my dear, you may've ceased to love me; but you took me for better or wuss in younger and 'appier days, and there'll be no getting away for you from me, ever."

Max recognizes also that his want of accord with the contemporary form of society is not due entirely to its repellant aspects. The following admission, for instance, which occurs in one of his essays, shows how aware he is of the element in himself which prevents his being in sympathy with a democratic, collectivist civilization. "A public crowd, because of a lack of broad humanity in me, rather insulates than absorbs me. Amid the guffaws of a thousand strangers I become unnaturally grave." For some years now Max has grown unnaturally grave and unnaturally silent, for he has virtually ceased to draw or write.

But not before his picture of a small but choice segment of society, and one which might justly claim to include the arbiters of the positive aspects of English civilization, had been carried to the utmost point consistent with his narrow but exquisitely analytical vision. Max has always had the most exact knowledge of the limits of his talent, which (and of how few artists can this be said!) he has invariably respected. Had he extended his picture it would be warrantable to assume that its perfection would have been impaired.

[1943]

Guy Boas

The Magic of Max

The life of Sir Max Beerbohm has not been eventful: or, if it has, the adventures have not been made public. Born in London in 1872, the younger son of Julius E. Beerbohm and half-brother of Sir Herbert Beerbohm Tree, he was educated at Charterhouse and at Merton College, Oxford. "Strange as it may seem," he tells us, "I was not unpopular [at school]. It is Oxford that has made me insufferable." In 1910 he married Miss Florence of Memphis, Tennessee, and from then until 1938 settled at Rapallo. Both Oxford and Edinburgh have made him an honorary Doctor, and in 1939 the King made him a Knight, despite the early essay, "Arise, Sir __ __ !," in which he remarks that "Even now, the number of those who are not knighted exceeds the number of those who are."

Glimpses of his youth are few, though it is recorded that when asked, while travelling by train to Croydon, why he suddenly pulled down the blinds, he answered: "S-sh! Lest I should see the Crystal Palace." Having sailed with his half-brother to America in 1895, with a view, we are told, to establishing a monarchy in that country, and having failed to consummate that achievement, Max has devoted the half-century since not to statecraft but to art. At the age of twenty-two, after writing some sketches for the *Oxford Magazine*, at the instigation of Aubrey Beardsley he contributed to the first volume of the *Yellow Book*, a compilation published by Mr. John Lane. His contribution, "A Defence of Cosmetics," was reprinted in his first book, a diminutive volume which appeared in 1896 entitled

Guy Boas, "The Magic of Max," *Blackwood's Magazine*, 260 (November 1946), 341-350. Reprinted by permission of *Blackwood's Magazine*, William Blackwood & Sons Ltd., Edinburgh and London.

The Works of Max Beerbohm. Since then he has published six collections of essays, a book of parodies, and a short novel, *Zuleika Dobson* ("No apple-tree, no wall of peaches, had not been robbed, nor any Tyrian rose-garden, for the glory of Miss Dobson's cheeks. Her neck was imitation marble. Her hands and feet were of very mean proportions.") Some eight volumes have also been published containing reproductions of his caricatures.

Once upon a time he wrote two plays, *The Happy Hypocrite*, produced at the Royalty Theatre by Mrs. Patrick Campbell in 1900, and *A Social Success*, acted by Sir George Alexander at the Palace in 1913. He succeeded Bernard Shaw as dramatic critic on the *Saturday Review*, Shaw hailing his successor as "The Incomparable Max," a compliment which Max was later, though less effusively, to return: "If Mr. Shaw's judgements are scatter-brained, he has, at any rate, brains to scatter." After twelve years as dramatic critic Max recorded: "I feel extraordinarily light and gay in writing this farewell . . . And yet . . . habit is mighty . . . and . . . may yet make me envy my successor." In 1920 he edited a number of tributes to Beerbohm Tree, to which he contributed "From a Brother's Standpoint." In 1943 he delivered the Rede Lecture at Cambridge on Lytton Strachey, and on six occasions between 1935 and 1945 made his voice, though not his elusive person, public by speaking enchantingly on the air. Yes, elusive Max has ever been. "Though I always liked to be invited anywhere," he writes in "Hosts and Guests," "I very often preferred to stay at home. If any one hereafter shall form a collection of the notes written by me in reply to invitations, I am afraid he will gradually suppose me to have been also a great invalid, and a great traveller."

There are a few fingers which have touched the arts so lightly that any critical hand laid upon them seems to be composed of thumbs. A study of Max Beerbohm sounds as inapt as a study of the rainbow. Why should we make a task of what the gods have given us to enjoy? Did Herrick write songs, or Chopin preludes, to have them explained? And did the velvet tone, the feather touch, of Max demand an article on his name in the *Encyclopedia Britannica*? One, nevertheless, is there. But happily it is brief, and at least yields one statement in tune with its subject: "His reputation was maintained when he succeeded G. B. Shaw as dramatic critic to the *Saturday Review* by the judiciously small amount of work which he published." Brevity; that is perhaps the first key to Max, as to the soul of wit. But the nature of that brevity deserves thought. Why, in order to raise himself to a niche of universal esteem, has Max only to write a number of short unlearned essays, as Housman had only to compose two slim books of verse, while, to gain their eminence, Carlyle had to preach the virtue of silence in thirty volumes, and Browning to achieve his apex in a poem of over five hundred pages?

In art, as in space, length is not the only dimension. One author may need a long track on which to extend himself; another, if he is a poet, can distill into a page, a paragraph, a sentence, even a word or two, that which produces overtones and undertones, so that height and depth, not length, achieve distance. *"Arma virumque cano . . . . "* "To be or not to be . . . . " Such pregnancy from the serious writers is frequent. But to find the same wealth of orchestration in a few notes from a composer of light music is more rare and difficult. The result is also surprising. Was the composer of Mozart's gay operas a light composer or a heavy classic? Is the author of "No. 2. The Pines" a brilliant but superficial essayist, or did he penetrate to the mad bravura of Swinburne's soul more deeply than has been done elsewhere? Did the author of "A Clergyman" merely throw off a *jeu d'esprit*, or did he give us the whole essence of Dr. Johnson, which Macaulay took nearly forty close-packed pages to obscure, and did he tell us by means of a purely fictitious incident more truth about the Doctor than anyone except Boswell? The entire nine-page pyramid of Max's revealing fancy is built on three brief sentences in Boswell: *"Johnson:* 'We have no sermons addressed to the passions, that are good for anything. . . .' *A Clergyman:* 'Were not Dodd's sermons addressed to the passions?' *Johnson:* 'They were nothing, Sir, be they addressed to what they may.' The suddenness of it! Bang!—and the rabbit that had popped from its burrow was no more. . . . "

It is remarkable how surely Max anticipated the advice of Lytton Strachey : "If the historian is wise he will adopt a subtle strategy. He will attack his subject in unexpected places: he will fall upon the flank, the rear; he will shoot a sudden, revealing searchlight into obscure recesses, hitherto undivined." But whereas Strachey in falling upon the objects of his attention when they were off their guard was apt to magnify the shortness of their legs or the weakness of their ankles, their warts and their squints, the searchlight of Max reveals their hearts. Though Max greatly admired Strachey—he "rejoiced in *Eminent Victorians"*—the two essayists contrast more than they compare. Strachey brought to his work the challenge of an intensely inquisitive but highly subjective temperament, superior, ironical, aloof. Max surrenders himself with such complete sympathy to his sitters that in the portraits nothing but their entire selves appears, and where is the dapper, jesting figure who portrayed them nobody can tell. Did he vacate the studio on their arrival, and leave reproduction to a magic prism? Did he go out for a stroll, and trust the pen to perform the function of a looking-glass? Or did he at least remain sufficiently near at hand to invoke the sorcery which perhaps tells rather more than the clients were themselves aware of?

Both essays and cartoons argue that the elfin artist cannot entirely have disappeared, for it would take more than a looking-glass to mirror the result. Not even an X-ray unaided could do the job, for even X-ray is a mechanical instrument, and in portraits by Max, as in portraiture by any artist, there must be some essence of the artist himself interpenetrated, however subtly, with that of the subject, otherwise a photograph would serve as well, and be less costly. What, then, are the ingredients of this wizard, which one must look for with a microscopic eye?

One may know a man by his friends. One may know him even better by his enemies. Who, then, are Max's enemies, who excite his hostility or rage? The answer is Nobody. And that in a caricaturist is remarkable. Pope may scream with passion at the thought of Atticus in particular, Swift be convulsed with fury at the thought of mankind in general, but to Max all men are friends, for he is a man himself. No man rouses his antipathy; for so modest is he (or so it appears) that he is only concerned to wonder whether in any respect he may jar on others. When it comes to assessment, it is not he who should be vexed by mankind's limitations, but mankind who should be distressed by his. "In the year 1900 I had been considered a rather clever and amusing young man, but I felt no pang whatsoever at finding myself cut out of my own game by a sudden newcomer, named G. K. Chesterton, who was obviously far more amusing than I." Instances of such humility can be paralleled from the writings of Max in profusion. There is the opening, as frank as it is abrupt, to the essay on "Seeing People Off": "I am not good at it. To do it well seems to me one of the most difficult things in the world." There is the confession from his thoughts on "servants": "Perhaps we are not afraid of menservants if we look out at them from the cradle. None was visible from mine. Only in later years and under external auspices did I come across any of them. And I am as afraid of them as ever." There is the abject study "On Speaking French," in which the essayist not only confesses through ten pages of self-scorn that he can only speak French *"un tout petit peu"* (and hardly at all if another Englishman happens to be listening), but that he cannot even listen to it without catastrophe. "To be shamed as a talker is bad enough; it is even worse to be shamed in the humble refuge of listener. To listen and from time to time murmur *'C'est vrai'* may seem safe enough; yet there is danger even here. I wish I could forget a certain luncheon in the course of which Mme. Chose (that brilliant woman) leaned suddenly across the table to me, and, with great animation, amidst a general hush, launched at me a particularly swift flight of winged words. With pensively narrowed eyes, I uttered my formula when she ceased. This formula she repeated, in a tone even more pensive than mine. *'Mais je ne le connais pas,'* she then loudly exclaimed. *'Je ne connais pas meme le nom. Dites-moi de ce jeune homme.'* She had, as it presently turned out, been asking me which of the younger French novelists was most thought of by English critics; so that her surprise at never having heard of the gifted young Sevre was natural enough." Such engaging self-abasement must be unique among artists, who, for whatever else they are eminent, are not prone to humility.

But if there is no one whom Max dislikes, qualities are not lacking which excite his amusement. And amusement, though it is the kindest of critics, *is* a critic, and a most formidable because a most disarming one. Chief among these qualities which rouse the glint in his eye is pomposity. In an essay entitled "A Point to be Remembered" he discusses the amount of time which a great man should allow to elapse before he appears on the scene to greet the hero-worshipping stripling who has come from London to venerate him. "Heroes tend to live a little way out of London. So much the better. The adventure should smack of pilgrimage." It is important, prescribes the essayist, that the great man should not be found in the room. "A person found in a room, if it be a room strange to the arriver, does not instantly detach himself from his surroundings. He is but a feature of the scene. He does not stand out as against a background, in the grand manner of portraiture, but is fused as in an elaborately rendered 'interior.' It is all the more essential, therefore, that the worshipper shall not have his first sight of hero and room simultaneously. The room must, as it were, be an anteroom, anon converted into a presence-chamber by the hero's entry." The method of the hero's entrance is then stipulated: "He must not, be he never so hale and hearty, bounce in. The young man must not be startled. . . . Let him be framed for an instant or so in the doorway—time for his eyes to produce their peculiar effect. And by the way: if he be a wearer of glasses, he should certainly remove these before coming in. He can put them on again almost immediately. It is the first moment that matters." The exact interval of time which the hero should let elapse between the arrival of his devotee and his own appearance is stressed as of utmost importance. Exact advice cannot be offered, but "I should say, roughly, that in ten minutes the young man would be strung up to the right pitch, and that more than twenty minutes would be too much." The visit of the young Coventry Patmore to Leigh Hunt is then cited as a sad instance of bungling on the part of the hero, who kept young Patmore on tenterhooks for two hours in the little parlour before the great one appeared "rubbing his hands and smiling ethereally," to remark without preface, "'This is a beautiful world, Mr. Patmore.' " The young man was so taken aback by these words that they "eclipsed all memory of what occurred during the remainder of the visit. . . . there was nothing wrong about the words themselves. . . . But they should have been said sooner."

Was ever a more indulgent, yet cathartic eye cast upon scenes fraught with the potential of over-solemnity, with Max peeping from behind a screen, or with even his possible presence disembodied but spiritually vibrant in the atmosphere, could Tennyson or Carlyle, or even Mr. Gladstone or the Queen herself, have hoped to maintain a full panoply of dignity or induce the supreme veneration commonly regarded as their due? The author of "In Memoriam," "Ulysses," and the "Ode to Virgil" could hold his head as high as he had every right to do, but would not a slightly uneasy feeling assail the author of the quatrains "To the Marquess of Dufferin and Ava, the "Ode Sung at the Opening of the International Exhibition," or of that delectable little "Welcome to Her Royal Highness Marie Alexandrovna, Duchess of Edinburgh"? Might not Gladstone have thought less of elevated principles and a little more kindly of General Gordon, might not Carlyle have expounded the battles of Frederick the Great to his wife with a joke or two inserted, and rather less late at night, and might not the Queen have found it less imperative, when somewhat French stories were told at dinner, to signify in the plural an absence of amusement? Inversely, let any solemn moralist lay a hard hand on an erring creature, even on a peccant Royalty, and Max is up in a moment for the defence. George IV may have been a rip, a mendacious son, an unfaithful husband, a heartless father; he may have lain in bed all the morning at Windsor with the blinds down and wasting candles, "with all the sporting papers scattered over his quilt and a decanter of cherry brandy within easy reach": but let Thackeray lay so much as a short pellucid essay upon him, and Max is on his feet to plead. "The Fourth George [Thackeray] chose to hold up for reprobation as a drunken, vapid cad. Every action, every phase of his life that went to disprove this view, he either suppressed or distorted utterly. 'History,' he would seem to have chuckled, 'has nothing to do with the First Gentleman. But I will give him a niche in Natural History. He shall be King of the Beasts.' He made no allowance for the extraordinary conditions under which all monarchs live, none for the unfortunate circumstances by which George, especially, was from the first hampered. He judged him as he judged Barnes Newcome and all the scoundrels he created. More-over, he judged him by the moral standard of the Victorian Age. In fact, he applied to his subject the wrong method, in the wrong manner, and at the wrong time."

Into this counterbreath to Thackeray's counterblast we may read the wholesale Edwardian revolt against the Victorian era. But the angle is in fact more individual than this; for Max carries his toleration into every era and puts his plea for mitigation of sentence at the service of every defendant—so long as he is not accused of pretence. With Max in court the judge is in greater jeopardy than the dock. For the judge may be human, the convict is certainly so. *"Homo sum, humani nihil a me alienum puto"*: Max's life-work is the practice of Terence's adage. Consequently in the measure that his fellow-men appeal to him, with all humanity's warmth of error and glow of guilt, so abstract philosophy, cold, inhuman, immacu-late, chills his heart and baffles, so he would have us think, his intellect.

Max's profession is laughter. Now M. Bergson wrote a monu-mental thesis on the subject of laughter, and no one, one might have supposed, would have been better equipped than Max to profit by this standard work. But such is not the case. "M. Bergson, in his well-known essay [on the theme of Laughter], says . . . well, he says many things; but none of these, though I have just read them, do I clearly remember, nor am I sure that in the act of reading I understood any of them." And the reason Max adduces for his obtuse ingratitude to M. Bergson is no lack of merit in the distinguished philosopher's thesis, but in the inability of his hardly less distinguished reader to appreciate the jewels spread before him. For "if you are by way of weaving theories as to the nature of things in general, and if you want to try those theories on some one who will luminously confirm them or powerfully rend them, I must, with a hang-dog air, warn you that I am not your man. I suffer from a strong suspicion that things in general cannot be accounted for through any formula or set of formulae, and that any one philosophy, howsoever new, is no better than another. That is in itself a sort of philosophy, and I suspect it accordingly; but it has for me the merit of being the only one I can make head or tail of. If you try to expound any other philosophic system to me, you will find not merely that I can detect no flaw in it (except the one great flaw just suggested), but also that I haven't, after a minute or two, the vaguest notion of what you are driving at."

Here is the candour which not only explains the indifference of Max to M. Bergson's instruction, but portrays his attitude to life in general. He did not make the world, he is not responsible for mankind, not even for his own appearance at the evanescent picnic; why, therefore, should he pretend to understand a mystery which he had no part in shaping? A watch is complicated enough even to baffle a watchmaker: what pretensions can the lay purchaser claim to grasp, still less to explain, the works? But if it is only a matter of telling the time, of looking on the dial and calculating whether one is likely to be late for lunch, then it is any man's toy, and Max is as ready as the rest of us to join in the game, and with a praeternatural acumen to put two and two together. For not only can he perceive when two and two make four, but also when they make five.

At this point one should remember that Max is amphibious, that he is equally at home as writer or draughtsman. Who else has attained a similar perfection? No other Englishman comes to mind except Rossetti, and his father was so Italian that he only escaped to England from Naples just in time, after writing an ode in favour of constitutional government—a warning against dabbling in more than one of the arts. Many artists have, of course, wished to be ambidextrous, but it does not appear that their wish was granted, not unless they kept the achievements of the other hand mysteriously secret. Their aspirations have been eloquently described by Robert Browning in one of those many private poems which he wrote to Mrs. Browning but did not withhold from an admiring public. Browning calls it "One Word More," though as the poem is nearly 250 lines the title is in the nature of understatement. Raphael, not convinced that his pictures were an adequate expression of gratitude to his wife, composed a hundred sonnets to her. "Did she love those sonnets all her life?" the poet asks, but does not answer his question. It is disturbing that we have no confirming evidence. The only four examples of Raphael's sonneteering which survive suggest the possibility that his wife hurried him back to the easel. Dante once proposed, for the special delectation of his Beatrice, to paint an angel. But the painting is not extant. Perhaps Beatrice tore it up (though Browning does not suggest this) and told Alighieri to drop the maulstick and get on with the *Divina Commedia*. But where Raphael and Dante could only aspire, Max has succeeded, and Mrs. Max Beerbohm has had the opportunity of admiring her husband's genius either by settling down to read the products or by raising her eyes to perceive them hung round about her on the walls.

The art of making two and two make five may be practised in any medium—the coldness of snow can be forcibly expressed in all its discomfort by consecutive fifths in music—but flat canvas is especially suited to the exercise. Tennyson's "In Memoriam" is a great poem, and even the disintegrating wit of Strachey could not shake the authentic magnitude of Queen Victoria. That Max is at heart sensible of the grandeur of these two figures is certain, for his lifework is as sane as it is sensitive. To depict poet and Queen in their genuine glory is the art of two and two making four; but to sketch "Mr. Tennyson reading 'In Memoriam' to his Sovereign," as Max pictured the scene, is to add the odd but revealing unit. The sparsely furnished room of the palace, redolent of utility furniture in a boarding house, with the two elongated fire-irons in the grate and the heraldic clock on the mantelpiece, is an irregular but lambent comment on the decorative taste of the Victorian age. The black of the widow's weeds, the sympathetic black of the poet's doublet (also his trousers and hair, together with the Bismarckian portrait of the late Prince Consort over the chimney-piece), and the irreverent query whether the widowhood, sincere as it was, was perhaps just a trifle excessive, while in the poise of the Laureate's hand, raised heavenwards as he declaims the elegy, the innocent but supernumerary query is added whether it would not be even easier to admire the transcendent qualities of the bard had not such a just estimate of them already been vouchsafed to him by his own intuition. Likewise we could have thought equally, and with no tinge of disrespect, of Coleridge speaking of metaphysics to his guests at table, had not Max pictured the gargantuan yawns of the exhausted visitors, the sense of indefatigable eloquence on the part of the metaphysician, the paucity of refreshment provided in proportion to the monologue, and, above all, if he had not labelled the vision "Samuel Taylor Coleridge, table-talking." Who can ever relish "The Ancient Mariner" again without a profound feeling of relief that one had never encountered the author at breakfast?

As with art so with politics, how easy when two and two make four: but since in politics the answer hardly ever comes out that way, no wonder that our master finds easy scope for his craft in the political jungle. Cartoon of "Independent Liberalism's desire for some means whereby it and Labour shall not clash in electoral contests." Independent Liberalism is represented by a midget figure, a dapper, pince-nez'd intellectual (with years of Harrow and Balliol in the cut of coat and ascetic features, brainy, doctrinaire, frigid, reasonable, righteous), standing on the enormous hand of a huge labourite, clothed too well for the docks but too unshapely for Westminster, protruding paunch, diminutive forehead, massive bulk, and ferocious, covetous mien. Balliol's conviction is absolute that if he and Dockland can get together the sum can be made to total four, but Dockland's reply ensures a jagged result. "Well, I won't say it mightn't be for what you've called the national good. But you see, Guv'nor, the goods are what I'm out for." "*Toujours la politesse,*" an acknowledgment that for national prosperity Balliol may be right, a salute to superior quality in "Guv'nor," but a blockbusting explosion of naked truth, sincere and egotistical to the point of pathos, "The goods are what I'm out for." How can politics ever equate so long as that complex is unresolved, that hunger is unappeased, that conundrum of just distribution remains unanswered?

So the awkward question is posed by the laughing philosopher, though it is not a laughing question; for it strikes at the roots not only of the eternal failure of Society to establish an equilibrium, but at the core of the mystery of the universe: a reminder that the world is round and not flat, that the human heart which since time began has attempted, but with very indifferent success, to control the universe, is not amenable to logic; that the more man discovers about the cosmos, the more he finds remains to be discovered, that the whole business is in fact an intriguing but utterly baffling escapade, and that the sooner we learn to reconcile ourselves to the fact that two and two make three or five or nine or thirteen (particularly thirteen) but never four, the more likely we are to stop worrying. And it is only the artist with a sense of this cyclical shape of things, or the scientist with a grasp, not of arithmetic but of relativity, who is a guide to us. A Bernard Shaw, a Schopenhauer, a Karl Marx, who would force human thought into rigid intellectual grooves, may give infinite delight, entertainment, and stimulation, but for all their forensic eloquence, though they inform us endlessly about what they think of things, they tell us little about things themselves. While they shape life to their design for it, life whirls past them, kaleidoscopic, fluent, orbicular, leaving the little boat in which they undertook to preserve us spinning helplessly in the vortex. The most comforting artist is he who has wisdom to swim with the current, to clutch at any straw and make the most of it, who looks for no landing-place, and is willing to wait for the answer, if answer there be, on the other side.

And this brings us, perhaps somewhat abruptly, to the bottom of Putney Hill. For at the foot of Putney Hill stood (and still stands, wearing proudly its blue plaque) No. 2, The Pines, and it was to No. 2, The Pines, that in the spring of 1899 the young Mr. Beerbohm went walking on air, to visit Mr. Algernon Swinburne, hallowed resident-guest of Mr. Theodore Watts-Dunton. And it is at the end of the golden report when Max wrote of this encounter that he comes nearest to expressing his deepest thoughts. The essay has a curious little history. In 1914 Mr.—not yet Sir Edmund— Gosse was engaged on a life-study of Swinburne. To assist in the task he bethought him of inviting certain acquaintances who had known or seen the poet to write passages which might be incorporated in the Opus. Among others he invited a contribution from Max, but, as often happens when unusual spirits are conscripted, things did not go quite according to plan. Max contributed, but at such length and in so dazzling a vein that Mr. Gosse felt uneasy whether this pyrotechnic display would fit quite as modestly as it should into the entertainment which he himself was providing. The affair is best described in Max's own beguiling words: "I failed in the attempt to make of my subject a snapshot that was not a grotesque. So I took refuge in an ampler scope. I wrote a reminiscential essay. From that essay I made an extract, which I gave to Mr. Gosse. From that extract he made a quotation in his enchanting biography. The words quoted by him reappear here in the midst of the whole essay as I wrote it. I dare not hope they are unashamed of their humble surroundings."

The reminiscential essay in its entirety is extant in *And Even Now* for all to read should they think that the quotation accepted by Sir Edmund was inadequate. It is among the gems of biography, and perhaps Mr. Gosse was prudent in perceiving that if a too radiant jewel is inserted the rest of the crown may be in danger of assuming the appearance of pasteboard. "In my youth the suburbs were rather looked down on—I never quite knew why. It was held anomalous, and a matter for merriment, that Swinburne lived in one of them. For my part, had I known as a fact that Catullus was still alive, I should have been as ready to imagine him living in Putney as elsewhere. The marvel would have been merely that he lived. And Swinburne's survival struck as surely as could his have struck in me the chord of wonder. . . ." After some thirty pages in which Swinburne dances out of the print in the very similitude of life itself (from his entry "shutting the door behind him as might anybody else, and advancing—a strange small figure in grey, having an air at once noble and roguish, proud and skittish," through lunch when "he smiled only to himself, and to his plateful of meat, and to the small bottle of Bass's pale ale that stood before him— ultimate allowance of one who had erst clashed cymbals in Naxos," to his darting up his library ladder after the meal to fondle archly his favourite volumes) we come to the apocalyptic finale where Max perceives his companion beyond the reach or hurt of time.

"But, scant though my memories are of the moments there [i.e., at The Pines], very full and warm in me is the whole fused memory of the two dear old men that lived there. I wish I had Watts-Dunton's sure faith in meetings beyond the grave. I am glad I do not disbelieve that people may so meet. I like to think that some day in Elysium I shall—not without diffidence—approach those two and reintroduce myself. I can see just how courteously Swinburne will bow over my hand, not at all remembering who I am. Watts-Dunton will remember me after a moment: 'Oh, to be sure, yes indeed! I've a great deal of work on hand just now—a great deal of work, but . . . ,' we shall sit down together on the asphodel, and I cannot but think we shall have whisky-toddy even there. He will not have changed. He will still be shaggy and old and chubby, and will wear the same frock-coat, with the same creases in it. Swinburne, on the other hand, will be quite, quite young, with a full mane of flaming auburn locks, and no clothes to hinder him from plunging back at any moment into the shining Elysian waters from which he will have just emerged. . . . 'He's wonderfully active—active in mind and body,' Watts-Dunton says to me. 'I come to the shore now and then, just to see how he's getting on. . . . Look!—there's Algernon going into the water again! He'll tire himself out, he'll catch cold, he'll—' and here the old man rises and hurries down to the sea's edge. 'Now, Algernon,' he roars, 'I don't want to interfere with you, but I do think, my dear old friend,'—and then, with a guffaw, he breaks off, remembering that his friend is not deaf now nor old, and that here in Elysium, where no ills are, good advice is not needed."

The passage is not only the quintessence of Max, but of biography. One can hardly recall any flashlight more vivid in the whole of our letters. Perhaps this is so because the picture is not a slice out of real life, but an imaginary fancy; for a slice can only be a slice, whereas when a poet gets to work, as he does here (whether he writes verse or prose), the result is the whole cake. Into the description is moulded the whole of "those two dear old men," Watts-Dunton, the cultivated, affectionate busybody, and Algernon Charles Swinburne, the three names onomatopoeically descriptive of that shimmering cascade of fire which fell upon the Victorian era like a burst of rockets on a Government office; and, in addition, there is the whole of Max, stretched for once beyond the confines of epigram, suavity, and worldly charm, saluting the beauty of life, the wonder of genius, the sanctity of affection, and making no attempt to conceal that beneath the twinkle he is in love. A love, not only unmeasured for the beauties of this world, but hesitantly, shyly hopeful that all that is real, not Watts-Dunton's ethnology but his unselfishness, not Swinburne's excesses but *Atalanta in Calydon*, once created cannot be destroyed.

Yet I would not bring our subject to a close in Putney, where Max is in danger of being slightly eclipsed by the brilliance of his own portraiture of Swinburne, but rather I would say Good-bye in a spot where he is all alone.

In the essay named "William and Mary" Max traces his contacts with that young married couple. William had been an undergraduate friend at Oxford—a socialist, a poet, and "one of the principal pariahs of our College." Not long after leaving Oxford, William married, and meeting Max in Cockspur Street, invited him to stay in "a sort of cottage" which was his new home. "I know you'll like my wife. She's—well, she's glorious." Max stayed with William and Mary a number of times, and found the description of Mary correct. "When William was alone with me it was about her that he liked to talk, and that I myself liked to talk too. . . . And if, when I was alone with Mary, I seemed to be sounder than I was on the subject of William's wonderfulness, who shall blame me?" Max was in France when he wrote to Mary, and William answered the letter, telling of Mary's death and that of the child she had died in bearing. Returning to England next day, Max saw William for the last time at the Charing Cross Hotel, before William was killed as a Press Correspondent in the Boer War. "I had a presentiment that he would not return, and a belief that he did not want to return." It was twenty years later that Max, happening to journey that way, pilgrimaged back to the "sort of cottage"—"back towards the past, for that past's sake and honour." Making his way through a wilderness of wet grass and weeds that had been their garden, he stood before the door and perceived a small knob of rusty iron. "My hand drew back, wavered, suddenly closed on the knob. I heard the scrape of the wire—and then, from somewhere within the heart of the shut house, a tinkle. . . . But there was no one to answer it, no footstep to come hither. . . . Well, *I* could answer it; and again my hand closed on the knob, unhesitatingly this time; pulling farther. That was my answer; and the rejoinder to it was more than I had thought to hear—a whole quick sequence of notes, faint but clear, playful, yet poignantly sad, like a trill of laughter echoing out of the past. . . . It was so like something I had known, so recognisable and, oh, recognising, that I was lost in wonder. And long must I have remained standing at that door, for I heard the sound often, often. I must have rung again and again, tenaciously, vehemently, in my folly."

Swinburne was a celebrity, but William and Mary were of common clay: such friends as you or I have known, or, with luck, might easily have known, for this land breeds many of their like. And I prefer to take leave of Max not in the scene of his visiting the great, lest the impression be given that he is only moved to eloquence in distinguished company, but pulling at the rusty bell of William and Mary's cottage among the weeds; tugging at that bell, and also tugging—we need not be ashamed to own it—at our heart-strings.

And lest this last encounter seem too fraught with sorrow to be characteristic, let me return to the essay on "Laughter" to quote a last "Maxim" which leaves things in proportion: "I think that . . . if we were trying to determine from what inner sources mankind derives the greatest pleasure in life, [you] would agree with me that only the emotion of love takes higher rank than the emotion of laughter."

[1946]

Louis Kronenberger

MAX BEERBOHM

We shall shortly celebrate a notable occasion: Sir Max Beerbohm's
seventy-fifth birthday. But a not unnotable one is already at hand:
Sir Max's first book in nearly twenty years. And if one would survey the career of a distinguished writer, a book, I think, provides
a sounder starting-point than a birthday. To find oneself criticized in the very act of being congratulated must be a pretty dampen-
ing experience—much as though a writer should discover, on opening a beautifully wrapped birthday present, that someone had sent
him a grammar.

Mainly on the Air, furthermore, though it unfortunately does
not crown Sir Max's career, considerably illuminates it. It reveals,
quite as much as anything he has ever written, the kind of writer
he is, and the kind of man. Indeed, it pretty sharply reveals that
he is seventy-five. This is not because it shows an old man's infirmities, but because it overflows with an old man's recollections, an
old man's harking back to the loves and landmarks of his youth.
Max,[1] God knows, has never not been a period writer. But always,
in reading him before, one felt not so much a gulf between past and
present as that Max had made time stand still—that Victoria, or at
any rate Edward VII, had not ceased to reign, and world wars not
been fought or waistcoats changed fashion. Max was still, somehow, a dandy of the nineties, a worldling of the 1900's; reading him,

Louis Kronenberger, "Max Beerbohm." From Louis Kronenberger, *The Republic
of Letters* (New York: Alfred A. Knopf, 1955), pp. 224-235. Originally published under the title "The Perfect Trifler," *Saturday Review of Literature* (New York), 21
June 1947, pp. 9-10ff. Copyright © by Louis Kronenberger. Reprinted by permission
of Alfred A. Knopf, Inc.

we saw him framed eternally against a background of *fin-de-siècle* Piccadilly, as Keats's youth is young forever on his Grecian urn. When, in an essay on Strachey a year or two back, Max protested— with as much fervor as an urbane Tory would permit himself— against the Century of the Common Man, what surprised you was not that he saw red at (and in) the phrase, but that he should ever have heard of it. He had seemed out of earshot of it by at least a generation.

But now we find that Max has not been living, placidly oblivious of the present, in a *fin-de-siècle* dream. He is too constantly jarred by the present not to be most uncomfortably aware of it. All the things Max loves—elegance, urbanity, a quill-pen leisureliness, the pleasure to be had of little things, the noiseless flick and delayed smart of irony—are not much valued in our day. All the things he hates—noise, speed, garishness, ugliness, Americanization—are ubiquitous and, as he might say, regnant. Again and again he can only shudder at what he sees, and sigh for what has vanished. But the sigh is really far more significant than the shudder. For one feels it is not so much that the present is all wrong for Sir Max—though of course it is—as that the past is all-important. Each of his complaints is fundamentally a comparison. One suspects that Max was already retrospective in his cradle, and downright reminiscent in his crib. And now Max is really, however ironically, the elderly gentleman who sits in his Tory club-window shaking his head at everything he observes in the street. Very often he is soundly protesting against vulgarity; but surely sometimes he is protesting against life. Yet this is not just Max turned elderly—he has always been someone who preferred a style of living to life itself.

On the literary side, *Mainly on the Air* is pretty slight, even for its author, much of it having been composed, as the book's title indicates, for BBC broadcasts. Yet I have found a second reading of the book more satisfying than a first: one starts off keenly disappointed because so little comes even close to Max's best; then gratefully accepts these pieces for what they are—still rather bright, still unmistakably Beerbohm. Their very titles supply their text—"London Revisited," "Music Halls of My Youth," "The Top Hat," "Advertisements," "Speed." But the best thing in the book, the thing most in the old, happy, essayist vein is "Fenestralia," where Max considers the role that windows have played in literature and history. It is a true carved cherrystone, and not from a sour cherry. Possibly the next best thing in the book, the amusing "T. Fenning Dodworth," is not quite a stranger; it was published, in this country at least, as part of *A Variety of Things*. But we may look upon it, surely, as one more link with the past.

And the past is most of all the nineties. The nineties stamped Max and sent him forth as their most engaging ambassador. It does not matter in the end that what Max wrote in the nineties is very far from his best work. It is simply that as the child of esthetic dandyism he never—however often he chose to treat it with a smile—ceased to cling to it. It was his achievement to commemorate an attitude by lightly mocking it, and to emerge from a period of much ill-fated trifling as the perfect trifler.

"The perfect trifler" may seem a slighting way to describe the man who has conceivably written the finest familiar essays in the English language. But I think the phrase fairly suggests, on the most honorable terms, the scale of Sir Max's work and its quite unregrettable lack of "significance." For it does lack significance, in the sense that Peacock and Congreve, not to speak of Rabelais or Moliere, possess it. Max—though he once confessed himself "no book lover" —is palpably, impenitently bookish. Very likely, as he has often declared, he turns to books only when he is unable to be with people. It does not matter. Sir Max is as literary as a quotation from Horace. It is never life itself, only the cultivated, the artistic, the aristocratic life, that he savors or satirizes; and when he savors it is not to make converts, any more than when he satirizes it is really to protest. His work exists simply to give pleasure of the most delicate kind—simply to distill all that we mean by temperament into something characterized by all that we mean by style.

His sheer spoofing aside, most of Sir Max's work may be summed up as the manipulation of a personality. He began manipulating it when it was not yet formed, and when his style, whatever its merits, was still a little absurd. He began impudently; not with the callow impudence of youth, but as a precocious and sort of parthenogenic man of the world. The art that reveals art came before its most celebrated opposite, if indeed the opposite ever quite came at all; the fun in Max lies not in wondering about his dexterity but in watching it. He is acrobat, not conjurer. At the start, however, he was not entirely deft: in *The Works* and *More* the cleverness is fatiguing, the personality obtrusive, the matter quite often thin. (Even something successful like "Diminuendo" or "An Infamous Brigade" is rather a *jeu d'esprit* than a true essay.) Just as Maltby, in *Seven Men*, sat up all night breaking in his new suits in rotation, so was Max, much earlier, breaking in his mannerisms and effects.

What is cardinal to the manipulation of a personality is a completely expressive style; and that, despite an instinctive finesse, came late. Max's style, being mannered, never needed perfect naturalness; but it did need perfect ease. And as late as *Yet Again* and *Zuleika Dobson* there is too often a slight strain in the writing, as there is a slight stretching in the contents. It was the many years that separate *Yet Again* from *And Even Now* that brought perfection. Finally everything came right: the proportions, the tone, the touch that is both intimate and reserved, the *un*exhibitionistic wit, and the Tory point of view that is worn, not as in too young a man, outrageously; nor defiantly, as in too insecure a one. Above all, the personality has found a prose that exactly suits it. It is a personality raised out of life into art, and one that while seeming to confide continues to elude one. There is the pleasantest sort of frankness; the greatest willingness to confess to all one's prejudices, predilections, oddities. But *is* this Max Beerbohm—or is it merely Max being sly? Has he told the truth or had his little joke; revealed a man or trumped one up? Is this autobiography or art, or both?

It is, at any rate, something remarkably engaging. For a certain kind of reader, the small habits and hankerings of this blameless exquisite can be as fascinating as all the demonic and outrageous and unsanctified adventures of a Byron or Jack London. That, whether or not it projects a real person, is proof of real personality. Perhaps in the factual sense we have never been given the true Max Beerbohm. Artistically it makes no difference—though it is my own guess that Max has usually been altogether candid, exploiting the worldling's knowledge that the truth is the last thing people ever believe.

But beyond the question of fact or fabrication lies the *effect* of personality through style; the juggling, so to speak, of the first person singular. It is probably the most ticklish problem that can confront a writer. Many very distinguished writers—Thomas Mann is perhaps the latest—have failed abysmally in talking about themselves. There is the Scylla of egotism, which must be skirted without crashin against the Charybdis of mousiness. There is the danger of striking a pose, which must again not be circumvented at the cost of a priggish earnestness. Moreover, a writer using the first person must seem neither too familiar nor too aloof; neither smug, again, nor obsequious. There is finally the peril, the besetting peril for the familiar essayist, of coyness. And though Max escapes all the other pitfalls, at times even he becomes rather coy. Yet the redeeming thing is that he does not become so oftener, particularly as his style can be very irritating. Even his mature style trades too freely in inversions, in Latinisms and archaisms, in double negatives, in "do but" and "averse from" and "belike" and "how great soever"—becoming precious, conspicuous, waxen; and I suppose one is riled the more from knowing that Max indulges in all these mannerisms with a quiet smile, with an implied "Of course I know the risks I am taking, the effects I am creating—do you take me for a fool?"

It is personality that animates Max's work, but form and finish that will go far toward preserving it. The essays are not simply serpentine excursions in personality; they are real essays, often perfect essays, that explore a subject without seeming to exhaust it, that move suavely and wittily from point to point, till they reach a sound resting-place and stop. They breathe culture, but never down your neck; they are as light, but certainly not as colorless, as air; they are as beckoning and satisfying as his own Golden Drugget. One sometimes wonders just why Sir Max's best essays so completely transcend everyone else's in our time, and one seems to find the answer in their tone. Somehow the most noticeably precious of our writers is also the most genially conversational; he chats with us as Chesterton never did, as Shaw—for all his greatness—never could. He shows the reader every courtesy, but his greatest concern is for the essay form itself—which shall remain an essay and never become a dissertation, an impromptu, or even an out-and-out memoir.

To achieve that tone a writer must definitely possess a temperament. A mind, no matter how bright or agile, is not enough; not even if a sense of fun and a sense of humor go with it. We are back again, no doubt, in the realm of personality, but with some differences; for personality is not temperament, as many writers who had the one without the other—Milton, say, or Macaulay—will prove. It was well for Max to come of age in the nineties, for with all its faults and extravagances that was the last period in which temperament was highly prized or could wholly prosper. It was the last time that a man could play his own tune in his own house, and not against the chords, and frequently the clangor, of the outside world. It was the last time that the eighteenth century—which for all its sense of form reveled in attractive eccentricity—had any decisive influence. Behind Max stands, quite plainly, Yorick. Since the nineties certain writers have had "sensibility"—a word suggesting the frustation of temperament rather more than the fulfillment—and certain others have had "manner"; but temperament in the purest, most unobstructed sense they have for the most part lacked.

It took Max a long time to master his tune; for all his finest essays are to be found in *And Even Now* (1920). Here is "No. 2. The Pines," that glowing memoir of Swinburne which is saved by its impish touches and sly sidelights from being too reverent. Here is that perfect trifle "A Clergyman." Here, again, is "Hosts and Guests," the model and despair of anyone who would write an essay that is exactly, supremely, an essay. Here, indeed, with very few exceptions, is one good thing after another. Yet, before turning away from Max's essays, one ought to note how in all periods they exhibit—though in late periods most keenly—his wit. That wit was pretty enough in the nineties, when Max could remark that "theatrical reminiscence is the most awful weapon in the armory of old age. I am sure that much of the respect which we pay to an elderly man is due to our suspicion that he could avenge any slight by describing the late Charles Matthews in *Cool as a Cucumber.*" But later Max's wit became deeply wedded to his style, as in the inimitable last sentence of "Hosts and Guests."

Sir Max's only novel is not a great favorite of mine. *Zuleika Dobson* contains delightful things, and excellent judges of literature—E. M. Forster for one—have praised it highly. But for me *Zuleika* is unsteadily poised between fantasy and satire, when indeed it is anything more than a classicist's picnic or an Oxford family joke. As to form, perhaps it might better have been a long novelette: stretched into a novel, it has to be elaborate to avoid seeming thin, and it doesn't avoid seeming thin. As to content, the story it tells does not altogether come off. Possibly I lack the delicate imagination that is needed to enter with a whole heart into Sir Max's conspiracy. But possibly the author himself lacked the robust imagination that is needed to make something of this kind really succeed. In satiric fantasy the author must somehow, with a bold maneuver, steal (rather than woo) the reader's credulity; and however great Sir Max's finesse, it is not finesse—and certainly not archness—that a story like *Zuleika* most needs; it is high spirits, lively turns, audacity. And that is just what it frequently lacks. I can't help thinking that the only character in the book whom Sir Max wrote about with real wicked-ness of understanding was the Duke of Dorset. And the chill, haughty, impervious Duke, though a delightful character for a book that might then have been called *Eight Men*, is not at all the best charac-ter for a book needing gusto and energy. (It could be part of the joke that *Zuleika* lacks these things precisely because Oxford lacks them; but if so, that is carrying the joke, artistically, rather far.) The Duke is a superb subject for satiric portraiture, but a doubtful hero for an extravagant plot.

And, for all its skill, there is also a slight crudeness about *Zuleika* and a slight unpalatability. Max, by failing to dissolve the real in the fantastic, cannot make the drownings, when they come, quite mat-ters of disembodied comedy. And this is as good a place as any (since in *Zuleika* we meet the Rhodes scholar Abimelech V. Oover) to touch upon Max's treatment of America and Americans. His aver-sion, real or assumed, for America would trouble me very little if it did not so consistently coarsen his touch. Certainly nothing lends itself more to burlesque than a certain type of Rhodes scholar. But Abimelech is a burlesque of a burlesque—or rather a parody of a parody, since it is his lingo that chiefly matters. How the greatest parodist alive could have gone so startlingly wrong with the Ameri-can language is not easily explained.

For Sir Max is by all odds the greatest parodist, as he is the great-est essayist, of our time; and the best things in *A Christmas Garland* are almost beyond praise. The parody of Henry James, for example, is not only a wonderful take-off of the style ("the scarred, the poor dear old woebegone and so very beguilingly *not* refractive mirror of the moment"); but the subject-matter—two tots worriedly debating whether they should inspect their Christmas stockings—is, as a travesty of a Jamesian predicament, little short of inspired. And the take-off of George Moore contains perhaps the finest single touch in all parody, when the all-too-Gallic and posturing Moore, seized with "strange thoughts that I cannot express in English," turns Pater's description of the Mona Lisa into French. To be quite perfect, there should be one or two mistakes in the French; though possibly there are.

If one persists in asking oneself why Max's treatment of Abime-lech falls so flat, the answer may well lie in the less effective of the *Christmas Garland* pieces. All Max's finest parodies are at the ex-pense of writers he loves or appreciates: "One can't really under-stand what one doesn't love, and one can't make good fun without real understanding," Maltby tells Max in *Seven Men*, though it might better be Max telling Maltby. The parodies of Wells, say, or Kipling, are extremely clever; but they fall short of the piece on Gosse or James because they are conceived in antipathy. Max bludgeons Wells, but somehow Wells escapes only bruised; but he kills James, in the sense that each man kills the thing he loves.

If Max partly failed with his one novel, he brilliantly succeeded with that other work of fiction, *Seven Men*. These stories make up a book almost as original as it is captivating. In "Enoch Soames" and "Maltby and Braxton" Max has spoofed the literary temperament of the nineties, and of more than the nineties—its affectations and insane vanities, its snobbery and emulousness—with superb skill. In these tales Max found his perfect material, reviving with precision and nostalgia a real world of real people, and then, through fantasy, standing it squarely on its head. "Enoch Soames" is a fine yarn into the bargain. I feel sure that on June 3, 1997 there will be many Maxists posted, in a high state of tension, about the Reading Room of the British Museum; I shall be ninety-two, but I hope to be there myself. And in " 'Savonarola' Brown" Max has woven Shakespeare and seventh-rateness into imperishable nonsense.

Sir Max's theater criticism doubtless suffers from the fact that its author was never deeply drawn to the theater, or powerfully held by it. No one could have been less stage-struck than that reviewer, who confessed he was bored by the play he saw on his tenth birthday. But his critical approach has, besides a certain personal charm, a certain solid usefulness. By not surrendering easily to the theater's "glamour," Max was saved from swallowing a lot of its silliness. He saw the stage for what it was and largely still is: the least impressive, the least adult of contemporary arts. He never, like Shaw, attacked it frontally; he just slowly undermined its pretensions by quietly underlining its stupidities. I suspect that, in the perspective of half a century, we get a sounder estimate of the English theater of his time from Max than we do from his more knowledgeable and responsive colleagues Walkley and Archer. To be sure, Max's temperament led him into errors and inadequacies. He underrated Gorki, for example, and overrated Maeterlinck. There is again no gusto in his criticism; but there is much unprofessional shrewdness, there is fairly much professional observation, there is mild wit and —mixed blessing—an essayist's emphasis on form. Max was not an outstandingly good critic; nor, like Shaw, so superb a journalist and electrical a personality that he himself still holds up where his subject-matter doesn't; but he wrote the sort of antiseptic criticism that, by not succumbing to the moment's emotionalism, has more than the moment's value.

As to Sir Max's general "place" in literature, one can more easily dispute how high it is than how permanent. Of all the writers of their time, it is men like Max and A. E. Housman—men who in their minor way frequently achieved perfection—that we can feel surest will be read with pleasure for many generations to come. They cared more for art than for life, for art, moreover, that has shapeliness rather than size; and the preference greatly limits them in stature. But it should also preserve them in time, in the sense that enamel outwears flesh. In terms of posterity, perfection is much less of a gamble than greatness. How big Max's audience will be a generation, or a century, hence is indeed something else again. Max was always caviar; probably he always will be. But a dozen of his essays and two or three of his stories should survive as long as there is a civilized point of view.

[1947]

Note

1. Alone among writers, he was universally referred to by his first name. Yet the "Max" never denoted familiarity or even, primarily, affection; it was a kind of badge of his uniqueness. One referred to him by his first name much as one does to a king—which may be why it now comes hard to demote him to a knight.

Harold Nicolson

Zuleika Dobson—a REVALUATION

A new edition has just been issued of Sir Max Beerbohm's popular novel, *Zuleika Dobson*. The book was first published in 1911, at a time, that is, when two world wars had not arisen to extirpate the last vestiges of eighteenth-century values, and before the city of Oxford had become a small and eccentric enclosure set in the midst of an expanding industrial area. I can recall that when I first read the book in 1911 I was slightly shocked that anything as sacred as my own university should have been made the scene of so frivolous a fantasy. When as an older man I read it again between the two wars, I realised that Sir Max's reverence for Oxford was as sedate as my own, and that underneath the sparkle of his narrative flowed a deep tide of love and homesickness. And when I read it for the third time recently, I was astonished by its vitality, and filled with admiration for the delicacy of its style and the perfection of its composition. How comes it that this story should in thirty-six years have lost nothing of its early freshness and that we can read it again today with undiminished amusement and delight?

Before I embark upon an appreciation of the story, I feel that it is important, although difficult, to establish the date at which the events recorded are supposed to have taken place. The internal evidence with which the author supplies us is in many ways self-contradictory. In one passage he confides that the mass-suicide of the un-

Harold Nicolson, *"Zuleika Dobson*—a Revaluation," *The Listener*, 25 September 1947, pp. 521-522. Reprinted by permission of Nigel Nicolson.

dergraduates of Oxford University took place "a few years" before 1911: in another he discloses that this tragic episode occurred "in the midst of the Edwardian Era." This would seem to fix the date of the occurrences as the month of June, 1905. There are, however, certain references in the text which indicate that Sir Max had an even more remote period in his mind. He speaks repeatedly of the rooms of the undergraduates and the fellows being lit by candles, whereas by 1905 electric, or at least gas, light had been introduced into all but the more penurious colleges. On his very first page, moreover, Sir Max describes the undergraduates who were waiting at the railway station as "gay figures in tweed or flannel." The use of the word "or" in place of the word "and" suggests (and I think rightly) that these young men were not dressed in tweed coats and flannel trousers but that they either wore tweed suits, with coat and trouser to match, or that they wore white flannels, perhaps accompanied by a blazer and a cricket cap. Now by the summer of 1905 the fashion of wearing flannel trousers with a sports coat was, if my memory serves me aright, just creeping in, whereas the fashions of wearing cricket caps and blazers was, if my memory serves me right, just creeping out. The point is not without critical significance, since it implies that Sir Max Beerbohm, in choosing the summer of 1905 as the setting for his story, was in fact picturing the Oxford, not of the first decade of this century, but of the last two decades of the last. It is this dual focus, perhaps, which gives to his narrative so exquisite a *fin de siècle* flavour.

The story itself is familiar to most listeners. Its theme, as the author asserts, is "Love as Death's decoy, and Youth following her." This phrase, which occurs on page 191, is not among the most crystalline which Sir Max Beerbohm has coined. He should have said, either "and Youth following it," meaning the decoy; or "and Youth following him," meaning the God of Love. We must forgive this lapse from clarity, since the young Beerbohm, at the moment he was coining this phrase, was floating as a disembodied ghost above the vapours of Christ Church meadows, and was rightly disconcerted by the "fume and fret of tragedy" which he had been enabled to portend. His story moreover was meant to be a fantasy and not an allegory; the delicate wings of Sir Max's genius are in fact not suited to the pins and strings of allegory; nor should we force ourselves to discover meanings and implications which were not intended. All the same, I do regret that Sir Max Beerbohm, in this vital passage,

31

should have used the word "her" when he must have meant to use the words "him" or "it".

It would be better therefore not to seek for themes, allegories or lessons, and to take the story as the simple narrative that it is. Miss Zuleika Dobson descends upon Oxford on a visit to her grandfather, the Warden of Judas. Her allure is that of a tigress burning bright, with the result that only three days after her arrival all the undergraduates of Oxford, except one, leap into the river and are drowned. The solitary survivor, a man of the name of Noakes, commits his suicide on the fourth day by jumping from the window of his lodgings into Broad Street. Afflicted by sudden remorse, by the sudden loss of companionship, Zuleika Dobson decides for a moment to take the veil. But on second thoughts she feels it would be more beneficial to charter a special train for Cambridge.

Such is the delicate thread upon which Sir Max Beerbohm has been able to string many acute observations on life and character, frequent passages of lyrical beauty, and two complete and really striking portraits of his central characters, Zuleika Dobson herself and the young Duke of Dorset. Let me examine the refined venom with which Sir Max Beerbohm has portrayed these two characters.

Zuleika Dobson was the daughter of an impoverished curate and of a circus rider of skill and beauty. Her parents died when she was a girl and since her grandfather, the Warden of Judas, disapproved of the marriage and its result, she was obliged, as an orphan, to seek her own living. Her early career as a governess was as uncongenial to herself as it was to her successive employers; the sons of the house invariably succumbed to her then nascent charms; and in the end she stole from the freckled brother of one who was to be her last pupil a little box of conjuring tricks, armed with which she launched herself alone upon an unexpectant world.

It is characteristic of Sir Max Beerbohm's aversion from overemphasis that he does not represent Zuleika Dobson as a very good conjuror or even as a woman of surpassing beauty. She was a bad conjuror and the patter with which she accompanied her tricks caused her admirers (and all became her admirers and all were fervent) to hang their heads in shame. Her features were not regular, and although her eyes were enormous, so also was her mouth. But she possessed, and she exploited, an attraction for men such as would have made Cleopatra veil her face in envy and have induced Helen to descend with muttered imprecation the stone stairway of the Skaian gate. Thus armed and thus accoutred, Zuleika Dobson embarked upon a career which set flame to two hemispheres. The whole of Paris, at her advent, went wild with excitement; the students of German universities organized torchlight processions below her hotel windows; famous matadors sacrificed their lives for her in an orgy of self-immolation; Austrian archdukes knelt before her and yearned for morganatic marriage; American millionaires lavished upon her their fortunes and their private trains; and a scion of the House of Romanov presented her with a replica of her conjuring apparatus cast in solid gold. From all this Zuleika Dobson derived much money, many diamonds, but small contentment. Even her conjuring tricks failed to satisfy her. "She was, indeed," comments Sir Max Beerbohm, "far too human a creature to care for art."

She was consumed, moreover, by that most irritating of all human defects, an abiding sense of self-pity. She had no women friends; she hated dogs; her attitude towards men was as eccentric as that of the praying mantis. Her appetite for admiration was insatiable; her triumph over the male heart was immediate and universal; yet she was bored by her own success, she no longer wished to be omnisubjugant. Her cruelty was as instinctive as that of the hyena; in comparison to Zuleika Dobson a pride of peacocks would have seemed but a knob of widgeons; display and domination became for her as necessary as the air she breathed. Yet always as she passed from city to city with her malachite box of gold conjuring apparatus, with her *Bradshaw* and her *A.B.C.* encrusted with tourmalines and agates, always she would be haunted by the demon of self-pity. Her health was as indestructible as were her emotions. And ardently she sought and sought in vain to find the man who would be blind to her charm, who would resist her seduction, who would fail—at least at first— to fall in love with her. Such was Zuleika's tragedy; and as year by year she journeyed from city to city with her wardrobe and her French maid, as the armies of her adorers increased to millions, this longing to find a man who would or could resist her became an obsession. Thus it happened that when on that June afternoon of 1905 she drove in the Warden's landau along the Cornmarket, and when the Duke of Dorset riding by in his straw hat enlivened by a Bullingdon ribbon (here, incidentally, is another anachronism— even Dukes in 1905 had ceased almost to wear boaters when riding)

—when as I said the Duke of Dorset averted his gaze from her when riding past, she believed for one moment of ecstasy that she had found the man whom she had been seeking all these years.

The Duke of Dorset, for his part, was a successful young man. There were few things which, at the age of twenty-two, he did not possess or had not accomplished. He was immensely beautiful, immensely rich; he had gained all the scholarships which Oxford offered and further high academic honours were in his grasp; he excelled at games; he could play the piano so beautifully as to rouse Chopin from his grave; he could write Greek lyrics and invectives in the manner of Alcaeus, and Italian sonnets which might have been mistaken for those of Petrarch; he owned numerous castles, a house upon the Riviera, a house on the Champs Elysées, a yacht, and a villa at Baise; and while still an undergraduate he had been created, on the basis of a single fulminating speech in the House of Lords, a Knight of the Garter. It was in fact, as you remember, in his garter robes that he committed suicide; that rich blue mantle floated above him down the Isis, or down the Thames, I cannot be sure which.

Apart from these startling possessions and achievements, this "orgulous and splendent" man, with his seignorial features, was, and wished to appear, the master-dandy. He was the type of which Barbey d'Aurevilly had for so long dreamed and had always failed to imagine. Such was his prestige at Oxford that when he walked through the Turl in full garter robes "there was none," to quote Sir Max Beerbohm, "to deem him caparisoned too much." He was arrogant, insulting, supercilious, not wholly insufferable. "His," confesses Sir Max Beerbohm, "was the Oxford manner"—a manner which, I suppose, can be said, by some, to cover a multitude of sins. But the point about the Duke of Dorset was that he was sinless, virginal, untouched. When he glanced away from Zuleika Dobson his gesture was a spontaneous reflex, occasioned by his loathing of all unmarried women. And when he, as all the others, surrendered to her charms it was with a sense of deep personal disloyalty and humiliation.

Such, in general outline, is the theme, and such are the two main characters, of *Zuleika Dobson*. Obviously Sir Max Beerbohm, in spite of his intricate genuflexions to Clio, was not writing history.

Nor was he composing either a pure novel or an allegory. He was devising a fantasy, which of all branches of literature is the most treacherous and the most delicate. The slightest alteration of key, the faintest suggestion of over-emphasis, a single clumsy movement of the hand or mind, will degrade a fantasy into a burlesque. The charm of *Zuleika Dobson* is that it never (or only twice) degenerates into a burlesque. Now to poise upon so thin a rope, and over such an immediate abyss, requires a most acute awareness of balance, an exquisite sensitivity of touch. I regard *Zuleika Dobson*, if not as a supreme work of art, then certainly as an extreme expression of artistry. One admires the skill. It is the skill of the thing which will keep this little book eternally alive. And of what exactly is that skill composed?

In the first place, style. By that I mean, not wording only, but also composition. In no similar work that I have read (with the possible exception of *The Rape of the Lock*) is there so dexterous an alternation of the element of expectation with the element of surprise. The book, if one attends to it at all carefully, is a masterpiece of design. With what unerring deftness is the direct narrative interchanged with the indirect narrative, how ingenious are the pauses and the interruptions, with what cunning has Sir Max Beerbohm mingled the real with the fantastic! For instance, in front of the Duke's lodgings at No. 45 Broad Street (now, alas! destroyed by the new Bodleian annexe—a construction which some find horrible and some find gay) stood and still stand the busts of the Roman Emperors with their cavernous disintegrating eyes. Admirably has Sir Max Beerbohm used these friable effigies as a chorus to his tragedy. They weep, they mumble, they observe. And their comments, as is well within the tradition of choruses, are almost invariably beside the point. At a culminating stage of the *desis* of his tragedy, Sir Max Beerbohm (and it is one of the passages where he approaches closest to burlesque) afflicts the Duke of Dorset with a cold in the head: he sneezes hard. With admirable ingenuity Sir Max extricates himself from this uneasy lapse, by introducing another reality in the shape of Mr. Druce, the Oxford chemist familiar to generations of alumni. With really astonishing skill be expands, he extends, he transmutes this chemist's shop into something slightly above life-size; the glass jars in the window swell and coruscate into domes of many-coloured glass; the atmosphere of the recognisable and the familiar is lifted by this device up into the stratosphere of fantasy. It is, I repeat, a consummate piece of artistry.

Yet these symbols and associations would not exercise their imaginative effect were it not that Sir Max Beerbohm has been able throughout, and wholly consciously, to maintain the same ruminative level of his voice. When he changes the key (as with the useful comments of the Duke's housekeeper, Mrs. Batch) he apologises for the intrusion of such cacophony upon his measured, modulated, tones. It is the constant rhythm of his sentences which give continuity to these fantastic episodes. It is the drone and music of his flute which lull us into the so necessary suspension of disbelief.

The student of English prose will of course find in *Zuleika Dobson* many curious echoes of the *Yellow Book* mode. He will note such cadences as "It was made of ivory, and of fluted ivory were the slim columns it swung between." And he will delight in such a sentence as an exhibit of the manner of the 'nineties. He will observe also, as an illustration of period, the author's somewhat belated preoccupation with the names of hard-stones and jewels. And he will delight in Sir Max Beerbohm's more personal pastime of introducing into his paragraphs words which are recorded in the dictionary (if recorded at all) under the sub-heading *Obs*. Lovely, and perhaps useful words, such as ebon, gallimaufry, opetide, disseizin, deliquium, jacamar, peripety, and octoradiant star. I like that sort of thing: I do it (but not quite so much) myself. These are but baubles which it amused, and has always amused, Max Beerbohm to attach to the damask of his style. Only a man devoid of all sense of tone or movement, devoid of all sense of the flux and reflux of our English tongue, could fail to observe the ingenuity, the assiduity—nay the utter hard work—which has gone to the perfecting of Sir Max Beerbohm's lovely cadenced style.

The same, or much the same, could, I suppose be said about Jeremy Taylor or of Browne on *Urn Burial*. But there is another note, a special note, a note which was new at the time and which today still strikes us as authentic, which renders Sir Max Beerbohm's writings so perennially fresh. It is the note of intimacy. The reader feels that he is being trusted with the most embarrassing, although utterly discreet, confidences of an elderly and most distinguished man. You remember the passage on page 185 of the first edition which begins with the sweet phrase: "Ever since I can remember, I have been beset by a recurring doubt as to whether I be, or be not, quite a gentleman." In 1911 such a sentence echoed as the sound of a hunting horn in some distant wood. Even today it evokes in many a smile of affectionate gratitude.

In the end, if he will allow me to say so, our admiration for Sir Max Beerbohm's urbane manner melts into a cloud of affection. Is it that, in my love for Oxford, I find in all his writings, and in this book in particular, an echo of a similar love, and an expression of the Oxford manner as it ought to be—a manner, never supercilious, but bland always, always tolerant, receptive, inquisitive, fastidious and humane? I do not think it is always that. The serious ingenuity of Max Beerbohm's writings may perhaps reflect in its many facets some glories which Oxford, as I dare to believe, alone can give. But essentially he is a mirror of our English—I do not say British—type of observation. And if you are feeling irritated by all this, please remember that Zuleika Dobson, having polished Oxford off completely, did take a special train to Cambridge; that thereafter she drove her car of Juggernaut through Aberdeen and Edinburgh, through Belfast and Dublin, through Wales and the West Country; and that she completed her progress with a quick and deadly visitation of the Combined English Universities.

[1947]

Edmund Wilson

AN ANALYSIS OF MAX BEERBOHM

This reviewer is a little late in getting around to Max Beerbohm's *Mainly on the Air,* which was brought out as long ago as last year; but it may be pleaded that the book itself is not strictly up to date, containing as it does three pieces that first appeared in the early twenties and two that have been published before in earlier volumes of Max's essays. The other pieces, with one or two exceptions, are not—agreeable reading though they make—quite of the author's best. About half of the thin book is made up of B.B.C. broadcasts—three from the thirties, three from the forties—which deal mainly with the London of Max Beerbohm's youth (music halls, glimpses of Gladstone, the old quiet London squares), and most of the non-broadcast pieces are in a similar mild reminiscent vein (top hats and Charterhouse school-days). So the occasion, not important in itself, may conveniently serve as a pretext for a general discussion of the author.

The book has been already so used by Mr. Louis Kronenberger in an admirable little essay called "The Perfect Trifler," in the *Saturday Review of Literature.*[1] Mr. Kronenberger begins by assuming that Max is already a classic, and he tries to discriminate the qualities that are likely to ensure his permanence. I agree with Mr. Kronenberger that Max Beerbohm is likely to be read much longer than certain of his British comtemporaries who at one time attracted as

Edmund Wilson, "An Analysis of Max Beerbohm." From Edmund Wilson, *Classics and Commercials: A Literary Chronicle of the Forties* (New York: Farrar, Straus, 1950), pp. 431-441. Originally published under the title "Analysis of Max Beerbohm," *The New Yorker,* 1 May 1948, pp. 80-86. Copyright ©1950 by Edmund Wilson. Reprinted by permission of Farrar, Straus & Giroux, Inc.

much attention. Chesterton and Belloc, for example, seem today merely literary journalists advertising their barbarous prejudices with the rattle of a coarse verbal cleverness. Their prose is unreadable now, when Max Beerbohm's seems even better than it did when it first appeared. Though I am not much given to rereading books, I have often reread Max Beerbohm, and my respect for his writing has immensely increased since the early nineteen-hundreds, when it was natural to see him as a mere minor sparkler suspended in rather an anomalous position between the constellation of Wilde, Beardsley, Whistler, the *Yellow Book* and the Rhymers' Club, and that of Shaw, Bennett, Wells, Chesterton, Galsworthy and Barrie. But for an expert appreciation of his writing, I refer you to Mr. Kronenberger. What I want to try to do here is go a little behind Max's engaging mask and analyze the point of view which gets expression in his writings and his caricatures, and which it seems to me that Mr. Kronenberger has made to look somewhat simpler than it is.

The truth is that Max is quite complex, and that complexity and the intelligence it generates are what—given his double talent, a complexity in itself—have made him interesting beyond what one might expect from work that seems at first sight so playful. We learn from the memorial volume edited by Max for his half-brother, the actor Sir Herbert Beerbohm Tree, that their father, who was born in Memel, was "of German and Dutch and Lithuanian extraction," and that he "settled in England when he was twenty-three," where he became a successful grain merchant in London and married a lady with an English name. His three sons by this first marriage were sent to be educated in Germany, at the same college where the father had studied. Thereafter one of them went to Cape Colony and decided to spend the rest of his life there, another explored Patagonia and wrote a book on the subject, and the third took to the stage (adopting the name of Tree, derived from the original *baum* of Beerbohm), where he enjoyed, if any actor ever did, a life of fantasy that blithely soared above his actual milieu and era. When, later, their mother died, their father married her sister, and Max was born when his father was sixty-one. (There has always perhaps been about Max something of the *enfant de vieux*, with his frailness, his elfin aspect and that poise and air of experience that caused Wilde to say about him, in his twenties, that he had mastered the secret of perpetual old age.) These are the only data available in regard to Max Beerbohm's antecedents, but they suggest a mixture of foreign with English blood, and an element unassimilated by England that inevitably gravitated away from her. Max himself did not study abroad; he was sent to Charterhouse and Oxford, and seems to have grown up entirely in England; yet, though odd, it did not seem unnatural that, when he married in 1910, this master of English style, who had absorbed so much of Oxford and London, this popular English caricaturist, who had depended on first-hand observation of Parliament, the Court and the theater, should, at the age of thirty-eight, have taken his wife to live in Italy, and should only have returned, under pressure of events, just before the second World War. There had always been perceptible in his work an alien point of view not amenable to English standards.

This alien side of Max Beerbohm declares itself most fully and frankly in the album of drawings called *Rossetti and His Circle,* published in 1922, when Max had lived more than a decade in the country of Rossetti's origins. "Byron, Disraeli, and Rossetti," he explains to us in his preface, "these seem to me the most interesting men that England had in the nineteenth century. . . . To be interesting, a man must be complex and elusive. And I rather fancy it must be a great advantage for him to have been born outside his proper time and place." As for the drawings themselves, they are mainly a set of variations on the theme of Rossetti's relation, not to his romantic art, but to the influences of Victorian England that try to distract him from it. You see him—preoccupied, obstinate, brooding, unkempt, ill-dressed—resisting importunity and pressure: the blighting smugness of the academic Jowett, the slick eloquence of the fashionable Leighton, Meredith's self-conscious nature cult, Mill's shy, pale and gentle rationalism, the bohemianism of Sala and Browning's society ladies.

For the alien element in Max is at least as exotic as Rossetti. He says somewhere in his theatrical criticism that the rococo is his favorite style; but this element, when he gives it its head, does not stop with being rococo. In its gemminess, its artificiality, its excrescences of grotesque fancy, it sometimes becomes positively Byzantine. The Englishman in Max, on the other hand, is moderate and unassertive, dominated by common sense—and not merely correct and prosaic, but even occasionally a bit of a Philistine. It was the Byzantine that made him love the nineties and led him to find Beardsley enchanting; it was the Englishman that kept him steady, so that, almost alone of his group, he survived the *fin de siècle* without tragedy, breakdown or scandal—and he walked out of the pages of the *Yellow Book* and into those of the *Saturday Review* as politely and unperturbedly as he might have gone to dine at Simpson's after absinthe at the Café Royal. It was the Byzantine that pricked him to cultivate his early preciosity of style; the Englishman that taught him the trick, which it has amused him to practise so often, of letting this preciosity down, with deprecating and comic effect, by a descent into the flatly colloquial.

This mixture of contrasting tendencies appears in all Max Beerbohm's work, sometimes with confusing results. In the title of *Zuleika Dobson* there is a simple juxtaposition of the exotic and the British; but in the novel itself the two are entangled in a curious way. I agree with Mr. Kronenberger—though I know we are in a minority—that there is something unsatisfactory and, as he says, "unpalatable" about this book. The trouble, I believe, is due to the fact that in this case the two sets of colors, instead of being blended in a fabric, have got into a kind of snarl. What is the pattern or the point of *Zuleika*? Is it a satire or parody or nonsense or what? It is full of amusing things and patches of clever writing, but it has also tiresome stretches of the thought and conversations of characters who do not even have the two-dimensional kind of life—like that of the people of Congreve or Firbank—that is possible within a comic convention. Max Beerbohm may be trying to satirize the admiration of Oxford for a duke, but, just as he frankly himself adores Oxford, so he seems fascinated, less frankly, by his duke, who sets the fashion for all the other undergraduates. (One remembers Max's eulogy of Ouida; and his attitude toward the Duke is closely related to his attitude toward royalty, a subject with which he was preoccupied in his first two collections of essays and to which, in both his writings and his drawings, he has constantly returned. Though he has made a good deal of fun of English monarchs and their households, one feels that he has been somewhat beglamored by them. The waspishness he sometimes displayed at the expense of George V and his family—whom he saluted with satirical verses at the time of the coronation and later caricatured so sharply that a protest from an official source compelled Max to remove certain drawings from one of his exhibitions—seems largely to have been prompted by resentment at their failure to be glamorous enough.) But though it is

English to love a duke, the Duke of Dorset projected by Beerbohm is Byzantine and apocalyptic. The hyperbole of magnificence here has its effectiveness, poetic and comic, but it is surely not of Oxford. The wholesale suicide at the end of the book is also apocalyptic, but it seems to me completely unreal, completely unamusing. An exotic imagination has lost touch with an English subject.

And Max Beerbohm's imagination has in itself never been very strong. It is, in general—to my taste, at any rate—in this department of fairy-tale fantasy that he is usually least successful. Neither *Zuleika* nor *The Happy Hypocrite* is a favorite of mine among his works; and *The Dreadful Dragon of Hay Hill* is perhaps the only really bad thing that he has allowed to get into a book. These stories force unworkable conceits; they get queerly out of range of Max's taste. He is much better when—in "Enoch Soames" or "Not That I Would Boast"—he sticks closer to a real background. Yet this is not enough, with Max, to produce one of his first-rate stories: the feeblest of the *Seven Men* are the ones that are least fantastic. Max's talent for impersonation, extraordinary in its way, is almost exclusively literary—that is, he can give you a poem, a play, a letter, a speech in Parliament, but he is unable to give you people—the heroine of *Zuleika,* for example—whose style can have no basis in reading. When Zuleika begins to talk like a book, she has to explain that she has picked up the habit from a certain Mr. Beerbohm, "who once sat next to me at dinner." The two short stories mentioned above are the virtuoso pieces of a parodist, as is the best thing in *Mainly on the Air,* a portrait of a sententious old fraud called "T. Fenning Dodworth;" and *Zuleika,* it seems to me, succeeds best when the comedy is verbal, when it arrives at its own kind of parody by exploiting a preciosity that is half burlesque.

There is another set of contrasts in Max's work which should probably be approached in another way. The alien in Max Beerbohm has, one guesses, adapted himself to England at some cost to his better intelligence, but he takes his revenge in indirect ways and at unexpected moments. He has learned the most perfect manners. "Before all things, from first to last," he wrote, or quoted, on the flyleaf of his first book, "I am utterly purposed that I will not offend." Yet his writing is full of hoaxes: he loves to disconcert the reader with bogus historical characters and invented literary references, as he is reported, in private life, to be addicted to such practical jokes as pasting indecent words into the text of John Drinkwater's poems and leaving the book on the night-table of his guest-room.

These irreverent pranks by an imp at the expense of a perfect little gentleman, like the dandiacal aberrations of the foreigner in Max who is bored with his bowler hat, contribute to the series of surprises that are so much more spontaneous in Max's work and so much more piquant, than the mechanical paradoxes of Chesterton or even, sometimes, than the systematic efforts of Shaw to "put the obvious in terms of the scandalous." And Max's digs that have a background of demureness leave, in some cases, real scars. It is true, as Mr. Kronenberger says, that Max Beerbohm, in his later years has been a little in danger of slipping into the role of the professional old fogy. Yet he has not been always a conservative, nor has he always been a gentle "trifler." It was no doubt an exaggeration for Bernard Shaw to say, in 1917, that Max was "the most savage Radical caricaturist since Gillray," and that *Zuleika* was "only his play, not his work." But the series of political cartoons, done during the Boer War and called *The Second Childhood of John Bull*, as well as many of his other drawings between then and the first World War, would go a long way to bear this out. Max gave at that time the impression of being something of a middle-class liberal. In any case, there was sometimes in his caricatures, less often in his writings, an unmistakable accent of anger. His impudence was by no means so childlike as his caricatures of himself, wide-eyed and wispy-limbed, seemed calculated to make one expect; but his animus was never derived from political or moral principle: it was simply an intense dislike of certain vulgarities, stupidities, impostures. What one feels is irrepressible contempt in his drawings of Sir Edward Carson, in his caricature of "Mr. Charles Whibley consoling Mr. Augustine Birrell for the loss of the Education Bill by a discourse on the uselessness of teaching anything whatsoever, sacred or profane, to children of the not aristocratic class," and its effect is none the less deadly because the dig appears to be humorous and made, as it were, in passing.

The series called "Tales of Three Nations," done in 1923, in which Max cartoons the shifting relations, between Napoleon's

time and our twenties, of Germany, France and England, shows
a point of view quite free from nationalism and a consistent sympathy with the underdog. He was frightened, however, by the
Russian Revolution, and it provoked some of his bitterest pictures.
He seems always to have been biassed against Russia and one
suspects that here a British provincialism combined with some
Baltic inheritance to produce an unreasonable prejudice. But, aside
from the vagaries of the Russians, the turn that things were taking
dismayed him. In *A Survey* (1921), he explained, in an epistle to
Britannia, that he "used to laugh at the Court and at the persons
around it; and this distressed you rather. I never laughed with you
at Labour. Labour didn't seem to me quite important enough yet.
But Labour is very important now, very strong indeed; as you have
found. And I gathered, this year . . . that you thought me guilty
of not the very best of taste in failing to bow my knee to your new
Baal." In *Observations* (1925), his last volume of topical caricatures,
he has a drawing of Civilization wedded to the hideous Industrial
System: "You took me for better or wuss in younger and 'appier
days, and there'll be no getting away for you from me, ever"; and
another, of the Governing Classes booted, bewigged, epauletted
and equipped with a silk hat and an umbrella, assailed by a demon-
eared Communism brandishing a knife and a torch. It is really
the whole modern world that Max Beerbohm despises and dreads;
but he has never worked out a consistent line for dealing with
contemporary problems. His point of view is instinctively that of
the cultivated merchant class. He may admire the feudal nobility,
but he is not necessarily sympathetic with them. He prizes the
security and freedom of the old-fashioned middle-class gentleman,
but he hates all the horrors and rigors, on the masters' side as
well as the workers', which have eventually resulted from the
system upon which these advantages were based. The difficulties
of his position are disarmingly exposed in his essay on servants
in *And Even Now*—it appears that he does not like to be waited
on and would be glad to see domestic service abolished—in which
he calls himself a Tory anarchist.

This is deplorable from the point of view of the man who thinks
that "art is a weapon" on one side or other of the class war; but it

has not prevented Max Beerbohm from being one of the great critics of his time. Max the critic has a personality somewhat different, though never quite distinct, from Max the storyteller and personal essayist. The writer that emerges, for example, in the two volumes of theatrical notices contributed to the *Saturday Review* has stripped himself, after the pieces of the first few months, of the coyness which Mr. Kronenberger rightly complains of as Max's worst vice. Max tells us that this weekly journalism, which his friends thought a waste of time, actually helped him to improve his writing. In the course of his twelve years of service, he had reduced the arabesques of his earlier style to the sobriety of his later prose; and one meets here, as in no other department of his work, the mind that gives a base to the whole: very flexible, very free from prejudice (he has dropped his undergraduate poses), but completely sure of itself (though he has sometimes to revise his first verdicts), very definite and firm in its judgments, and very direct and courageous in registering unpopular opinions. In its different way, this body of writing is as remarkable as the dramatic criticism of Max's predecessor Shaw—who suggested him to fill his own place on the basis of the young man's attacks on Shaw's *Plays Pleasant and Unpleasant.* Max's caricatures of contemporaries, which are a criticism of public life, also give us the tougher Beerbohm (though, for some reason, the forewords to the albums are sometimes pitched in his coyest lisp). But the field in which his critical faculty is happiest and most at home is that of literature, and here the parodies of *A Christmas Garland*—the most searching, except Proust's, of our time—have their place in a body of comment which has undoubtedly left a deeper imprint than the lightness of its tone ever promised.

It is now a long time, however, since Max Beerbohm the literary critic has played his bright pocket-torch on the present. One gets the impression that Lytton Strachey has been the last contemporary writer in whom he has felt any real interest. One would like to know, by word or picture, what he thinks of T.S. Eliot, Virginia Woolf, Hemingway, Priestley, Maugham. The only ray of light that has reached me on Max's opinion of Joyce has been by way of an anecdote which, since it brings out the discrepancies of our subject, may furnish this piece with an appropriate close. One of the younger English writers had shown Max a copy of *Finnegans*

Wake. The veteran of the *Yellow Book* period, who had defended in his earlier days some startling unconventional work, examined this outlandish production; then, "I don't think," he said, "he'll be knighted for that." Max himself *had* just been knighted.

[1948]

Editor's note

1. Reprinted in this book.

J. G. Riewald

MAX BEERBOHM AND OSCAR WILDE

It might, at first sight, seem remarkable that the name of Oscar Wilde, the dominating literary figure of the Nineties, does not occur among the writers expressly parodied by Beerbohm. The fact that Wilde had been exhaustively parodied by Robert Hichens can hardly have been a reason for Max not to attempt a version of his own. His real motive for excluding Wilde is, I think, to be sought in his fine sense of decorum. In 1912, after Meredith's death, Max apologized for reprinting the skit he had made of that author's work while he lived.[1] It must have been this same delicacy of feeling that prevented him from expressly parodying, in 1896 or later, an author who had practically ceased to exist in 1895. Yet it can be proved that much of Beerbohm's early work was influenced by Wilde. The exact nature of this influence, however, is often difficult to assess. It ranges from unconscious and conscious imitation to pastiche, and from pastiche to parody, overt or veiled, or even unconscious, and it may affect either the subject-matter, or the style, or both. As the vexed and much eschewed question of Beerbohm's place in the so-called "Decadent" movement practically resolves itself into the alternative problem of his literary relation to Oscar Wilde, the Father of the movement, a first attempt to elucidate this affinity will not be out of place here.

An interesting clue to the solution of this problem is provided

J. G. Riewald, "Max Beerbohm and Oscar Wilde." From J. G. Riewald, *Sir Max Beerbohm, Man and Writer: A Critical Analysis with a Brief Life and a Bibliography*. With a Prefatory Letter by Sir Max Beerbohm (The Hague: Martinus Nijhoff, 1953, and Brattleboro, Vermont: The Stephen Greene Press, 1961), pp. 129-141. Reprinted by permission of Martinus Nijhoff.

by Beerbohm himself in "Gibiesse Oblige," a dramatic criticism written in 1898, when the influence of Wilde was already on the wane. In this article Beerbohm posits that every great man in art begins by *imitating* one or another of his forerunners.[2] An even more illuminating utterance is found in a criticism written in 1904, a few years after Wilde had ceased to stir his imitative or parodistic faculties. In this essay, called "A Play and a Mimic," Max is very eloquent on the subject of mimicry and the related subjects of parody and caricature. Parody, he insists, is to literature what mimicry is to acting and caricature to painting—"a subsidiary art", and a speciality of youth. "Read any undergraduate journal," he goes on, "and you will find that it is mainly composed of *parody, unconscious and conscious.*"[3]

I have no hesitation in declaring that these two essays, in which Max insists that the destiny of every writer begins with parody and imitation, contain the key to the mystery of his own literary relation to Oscar Wilde. This relation partly resembles Wilde's own relation to Maturin, Keats, Hood, Mrs. Browning, Tennyson, Jean Ingelow, Morris, "Lanoe Falconer", Stevenson, Poe, Whistler, Balzac, Huysmans, Andersen, and others,[4] and may be summarized in Stevenson's phrase about the "sedulous ape." But in Beerbohm's case the relation was of a dual nature. While it is true to say that, as an undergraduate, he began by parodying Wilde, it is equally true that he ended by imitating him. Roughly speaking, the parody belongs to the two years preceding the fall of Wilde; the imitations to the two years after, while the transition is marked by *The Happy Hypocrite*, published in 1896, and by parts of *Zuleika Dobson*, which was conceived in 1896, and discontinued shortly afterwards. But the whole process did not take more than four years. After "The Story of the Small Boy and the Barley Sugar" and "Yai and the Moon", which were both written in 1897, examples of direct Wildean influence become exceedingly rare; to all intents and purposes the majority of them should be classed as cases of "unconscious" imitation.

The young Max certainly fulfilled the two conditions necessary for a successful imitation or parody of Wilde—a natural susceptibility to the idiosyncrasies of his thought and style, and a sympathetic understanding of his personality. The incident, related by Bohun Lynch,[5] of the youthful Max pulling down the blinds of his compartment lest he should see the Crystal Palace, shows that, in those days, he was no stranger to Wilde's aestheticism. We also know that, as an undergraduate, he admired the *Intentions* and "that splendid, sinister work" *Dorian Gray*,[6] while later, as a dramatic critic, he never left off praising his dramas. But perhaps the most striking proof of the spiritual kinship between Wilde and Beerbohm is to be found in their ideas on individualism (Wilde speaks of "the immoral ideal of uniformity of type"[7]), education ("To instruct is a dreary function;"[8] cf. Wilde's "But oh! my dear Ernest, to sit next to a man who has spent his life in trying to educate others!"[9]), realism ("As a method Realism is a complete failure"[10]), and the antagonism between art and experience. Professor Hillebrand has pointed out that, for Beerbohm as well as for Pater and Wilde, art was the product of passionate observation, not of actual experience[11] —a circumstance which would seem to account for the comparatively modest place allotted to life itself as a source of inspiration in the work of these artists. We know, for instance, that Pater always felt happier when criticizing life as revealed in a work of art than when dealing with life itself. Beerbohm's concern with the world of books and plays and pictures, and of their makers, is a parallel case in point. But whereas aesthetes such as Pater, Wilde and Arthur Symons looked upon life as a form of art, and even treated it as such, Beerbohm never lost sight of the essential difference between the two. Life, according to him, had no formal curves and harmonies and, therefore, was not an art.[12] And though, in the case of Max himself, the interest of the question is purely academic, because he never set out to describe life as such, the remark shows that, in this respect at least, Beerbohm's critical acumen was superior to that of the aesthetes. Finally it should be remembered that Beerbohm appreciated Wilde as a man. At the Cafe Royal he had been among the most sympathetic acclaimers of Oscar, who, in his turn, was fascinated by Beerbohm's enigmatic personality; and it is not known that Max ever changed his feelings.

I

Apart from the discarded "A Peep into the Past" (which was a

good-natured satire[13]) the earliest literary evidence of Wilde's
influence on Max Beerbohm is found in "The Incomparable Beauty
of Modern Dress," the first essay he ever published, and in the
essays which he collected in *The Works* in 1896. It occurs in the
form of parody and imitation, either conscious or unconscious.
A fine example of what he himself calls "unconscious" parody
is provided by the following sentence, which dates from 1896:
". . . but scarce did they dare to look upon her countenance, for
it was as the face of an Angel."[14] Though this is meant as a
parody of Marie Corelli, it is a literal echo of Wilde's "But no
man dared look upon his face, for it was like the face of an angel."[15] But in many cases the parody is indistinguishable from the
imitation. When, for instance, he writes that "To the aesthetic
temperament nothing seems ugly. There are degrees of beauty—
that is all"[16], the parody is unmistakable (cf. Wilde's notorious
"There is no such thing as a moral or an immoral book. Books are
well written, or badly written. That is all"[17]). Our doubts in-
crease when we hear that "expression is but too often the ruin of
a face"[18] (cf. Wilde's "Intellect is in itself a mode of exaggeration,
and always destroys the harmony of any face"[19]), or when we read
about "younger men, with months of activity before them"[20]
(cf. Wilde's "I am a little jealous of the picture for being a whole
month younger than I am"[21]). But what are we to think of "To
have seen Mr. Hall Caine is to have read his soul. His flowing,
formless cloak is as one of his own novels, twenty-five editions
latent in the folds of it"[22] (cf. Wilde's ". . . when she is in a
very smart gown she looks like an *édition de luxe* of a bad French
novel"[23]), or ". . . women are a sex by themselves, so to speak"[24]
(cf. Wilde's "Work is the curse of the drinking classes"[25])? These
quotations, which all belong to the period 1893-96, are interesting
for three reasons. They not only prove Beerbohm's early preoccupation with Wilde in general, and with *Dorian Gray* in particular;
they also show that, in those years, his reactions to that author
ranged from parody to pastiche, and that, between these categories,
it is not always possible to draw the line. Of course the quotations
of the second group may be looked upon as successful "unconscious" parodies of the relevant passages in Wilde. But at the same
time they are so felicitous and so characteristically Beerbohm that
they seem to acquire a life and vigour of their own, so that they

may be enjoyed apart from the model that inspired them. In other words, they transcend ordinary parody and clearly approach the level of creative imitation, conscious or unconscious, of which the third group provides examples. Incidentally, it may be noted that the quotations seem to point to the fact that, in this case too, parody preceded imitation.

It is necessary at this stage to specify the object of Beerbohm's parody in these early essays. In spite of his natural affinity with Wilde, the parody in at least one of the "Tite Street" essays was concerned not so much with Wilde's stylistic peculiarities as with his ideas on art. Thus the essay on Cosmetics is essentially a parody of Wilde's insistence on the superiority of Art to Life and Nature (in which Max did not believe), not a parody of his style as such. From his review of De Profundis we know that Beerbohm admired the prose of Wilde's Intentions, and of his plays, and of his fairy-stories.[26] But the fact that The Picture of Dorian Gray (which he liked as an undergraduate) is not included in this maturer praise is significant. With this in view it is only natural that the stylistic parody in Beerbohm's essay should be aimed at Wilde's excessive use of paradox, marivaudage, and archaisms—affectations which characterize his Dorian Gray and some of his other writings, but which are almost entirely absent from his fairy-tales. This attitude is typical of the whole period of Wilde's influence on Beerbohm. While the "Tite Street" essays, which belong to the years 1894 and 1895, are a subtle parody of Wilde's ideas and of some of his stylistic peculiarities, the two fairy-tales, which were published at the end of the period—"The Story of the Small Boy and the Barley Sugar" (1897) and "Yai and the Moon" (1897)—are frank imitations of a technique for which Wilde was indebted to Andersen. The transition from the parodistic to the imitative stage may be studied in The Happy Hypocrite, which belongs to the middle years of this period, and which is a curious blend between a Wildean fairy-tale and a parody of Dorian Gray.

Though, on the face of it, this "fairy tale for tired men" would seem to be no more than a very successful imitation of a technique in which Wilde excelled—so successful indeed that even its title has already begun, like that of older works such as Religio Medici, to inspire other authors (cf. Ronald Firbank's Odette: A Fairy Tale for Weary People, London, Grant Richards, 1916)—a closer analysis reveals that it is also a subtle, though for the most part unconscious, parody of the motives employed by Wilde in his *Dorian Gray*.

II

The Picture of Dorian Gray was published in 1891, five years before *The Happy Hypocrite*. It is the story of the young, handsome, and wealthy Dorian Gray, whose magnetic personality enables his friend Basil Hallward to create his masterpiece—a life-size portrait of Dorian. The latter, however, gradually falls under the sway of the decadent, cynical mocker Lord Henry Wotton, who gives him a book of the *A Rebours* type to read, and finally brings about his moral ruin. But, as the sinister result of a wish once passionately expressed, Dorian's face, in spite of his debauchery, preserves its innocence and youth, while his crimes and the advance of the years are duly registered on the carefully hidden portrait. Regardless of conventional morality Dorian, like another Faustus, now plunges into a life of mere pleasure. He begins his career by repudiating his first pure love, Sibyl Vane, a little East End actress, and ends it by murdering his friend Basil Hallward. But, though his cunning, combined with the mask of his eternal youth, shields him from discovery, he does not escape his Nemesis. At last he also wants to make away with the only remaining witness of his shameful double life—the life-size portrait, which the corruption of his soul has now changed into the picture of a horrible old monster; and with the knife that had once stabbed the painter he now stabs his work. But he has reckoned without his host, for the portrait which, as his visible conscience, might have been a positive factor in his life, now assumes the role of avenger, and destroys him. And, Wilde concludes, when the footmen entered the room, "they found, hanging upon the wall, a splendid portrait of their master as they had last seen him, in all the wonder of his exquisite youth and beauty. Lying on the floor was a dead man, in evening dress, with a knife in his heart. He was withered, wrinkled, and loathsome of visage."

Beerbohm's fantastic parable is a subtle variation on this theme. For the background of his *Happy Hypocrite* he took his beloved Regency period—which must have fascinated him in the years

1894-96—and for its hero Lord George Hell, one of the Regent's boon companions, who spends his evenings with La Gambogi, an Italian dancer. Lord George is wicked, and he is proud of his wickedness, until, all of a sudden, he falls in love with the ingenuous Jenny Mere, a *débutante* in a new operette. But Jenny spurns his love, because she can never be the wife of a man whose face is not saintly. In the desperate hours that follow this rebuff, the buck conceives the means of winning Jenny Mere. A fashionable mask-maker in Old Bond Street supplies him with the mask of a saint, which will forever hide his evil countenance. When he leaves the shop, La Gambogi stands watching her lost lover with sinister eye, and orders a spy to track him down. But Lord George does not heed her and, with his heart all sunshine, hurries on to his Jenny, who now accepts him on the strength of his saintly face. He at once marries her under the name of "George Heaven," and brings her to a woodman's cottage, where they have a wonderful honeymoon. And as the days go by he truly repents the evil he has done in the past, and the spectre of the *femme fatale* gradually recedes into the background. However, on the "mensiversary" of their wedding the jealous Signora discovers them in their cottage. Like a panther she springs upon her old lover and tears away the mask, but to her immense dismay she sees that the face under it is as saintly as the mask has been. To Lord George bewailing the imposture he has wrought upon her Jenny says: "Surely, your face is even dearer to me, even fairer, than the semblance that hid it and deceived me. I am not angry." After that she "put her arms round his neck; and he was happier than he had ever been."

The analogy with *Dorian Gray* is obvious. The leading motive of both stories is the Good and the Evil, set off by the mask of hypocrisy. In Wilde's novel this motive is expressed in the following telltale sentences: "Each of us has Heaven and Hell in him" and "In hypocrisy he had worn the mask of goodness." This more or less "decadent" theme must have appealed to Beerbohm's impish imagination, for his story of Lord Hell, alias Lord Heaven, may be interpreted as a delicate, though unintended, parody of it. The fact that Max never allows the parody to interfere with his independence of treatment would seem to strengthen this supposition, and may have been the reason why the unconscious parody has never been recognized as such. But in spite of the difference in treatment the parallelism is unmistakable. In the case of Dorian the "mask of goodness" is the mask of his own radiant youth; in the case of Lord George it is the mask of a saint. This detail is symbolic of their attitudes. While Dorian's life is spent in the pursuit of worldly pleasures, Lord George aims at a higher and more spiritual bliss. The function of their masks varies accordingly. Dorian's fleshly mask of youth not only hides the moral degeneration which reveals itself in the portrait; it also precipitates it. Lord Hell's mask of wax, on the other hand, is a triumphant earnest of the moral regeneration which, owing to a momentary glimpse of uncorrupted virtue granted him in the person of Jenny Mere, has begun to manifest itself under it. Dorian as well as Lord George know that the life they are leading is insincere, and, though their ends differ, they both accept hypocrisy as a means of multiplying their personalities. Furthermore, both Wilde and Beerbohm (who once called his story *a fable with a moral*) acknowledge the regenerating power of pure love and a good intention. "Love makes people good," Sibyl Vane is heard to remark in Wilde's novel. But these words, which are in fact the theme of Beerbohm's story, do not get a chance of realizing themselves in Dorian Gray, because his intentions are evil. At the end of his life, it is true, he tries to remove the traces of vice from the portrait by being good; but even then he remains the typical hypocrite. It is at this point that the story is taken up by Beerbohm. His tale begins where Wilde's novel leaves off. Beerbohm's hero, Lord Hell, is of good will, which is enough to make a Lord Heaven of him. He, whom pure love forced to assume the mask of hypocrisy, becomes the *Happy* Hypocrite, whereas the pleasure-seeking Dorian, whose mask has turned into an instrument of crime, is the typical *Unhappy* Hypocrite.

The parallelism between the novel and the fairy-tale is not restricted to the leading ideas; it also shows itself in the structure. The heroes are both wealthy men, who fall under the spell of a disastrous influence. Both get a chance of redeeming themselves by loving a pure girl. In both cases this girl is an actress, whom they "discover" in the playhouse. Both conceal their surnames from their sweethearts who, not unnaturally, consider themselves unworthy of their lovers. The revenge motive, too, runs parallel. Dorian and Lord George are both persecuted; the former by Sibyl's brother, who seeks to avenge his sister's suicide; the latter, after his metamorphosis, by a spy of the vindictive Signora. Furthermore,

Mr. Isaacs, the manager of Sibyl's little theatre, appears in Beerbohm's story as Mr. Garble who, like his prototype, insists on the girls addressing their lovers as "My Lord", while Mr. Aeneas, "the fashionable mask-maker" of Old Bond Street, takes the place of Mr. Hubbard, "the celebrated frame-maker" of South Audley Street. In the same way Basil Hallward's sudden disappearance, which caused so much excitement, finds its logical, and even verbal counterpart in the sensational disappearance of Lord George Hell. The likeness also appears in the scene between James Vane and the prostitute and that between the Signora and the Dwarf. It even seems to affect the names. For while Sibyl's lover is known to her as "Prince Charming", it is as "King Bogey" that Lord Hell acquires a doubtful reputation in nurseries. But it becomes especially striking towards the end when Dorian's dead body on the floor finds its serene counterpart in Lord George's mask lying upon the lawn, upturned to the sky.

The parallelism even shows itself in such minor details as Dorian's nightly ramble through London after he has left Sibyl Vane, and Lord George's nocturnal peregrination through the same city after Jenny Mere has rejected him. In almost the same words we learn that, at the ensuing dawn, Dorian found himself close to Covent Garden, while Beerbohm's hero, at that hour, was treading the outskirts of a little wood in Kensington. Wilde as well as Beerbohm then go on to describe the morning air, heavy with the scent of flowers, and dwell on the sinister aspect of the sleeping city. Another possible parallel is the description of Dorian's home-coming in the morning ("The bright dawn flooded the room, and swept the fantastic shadows into dusky corners, where they lay shuddering") and that of Lord George's similar *rentree*: "Shadows lay like memories in every corner of the dim hall." The account of the light slanting through the window is equally suggestive.

Analogous structural and stylistic parallelisms exist between Beerbohm's fantastic story and some of Wilde's other writings. Thus the theme of *The Happy Hypocrite*—a saint converting a sinner—is generally reminiscent of Wilde's *La Sainte Courtisane*, while two of its leading motives—a belief that love is stronger than evil, and the idea of the soul being able to metamorphose the face—occur in Wilde's stories. To take one instance only, in "The Fisherman and his Soul" the hero's love proves stronger than the evil with which he is tempted, while the Star-Child, in the story of that name, changes face twice in accordance with the state of his soul. His second metamorphosis, which, in fact, resembles the one related in *The Happy Hypocrite*, even finds its stylistic counterpart in Beerbohm's story. "And lo! his face was even as it had been," Wilde exclaims; and Beerbohm echoes: "But lo! his face was even as his mask had been." The cadences of the writing, too, are definitely Oscarish.

These, and similar parallelisms bring out the affinity between *The Happy Hypocrite* and *Dorian Gray* on the one hand, and that between *The Happy Hypocrite* and Wilde's fairy-stories on the other. But it should be insisted that these affinities are of an entirely different nature. While, as to form, *The Happy Hypocrite* is an imitation of the Wildean fairy-story, it can be shown that, in substance, it is an unconscious parody of the "decadent" atmosphere suggested in *Dorian Gray*—a parody, therefore, done in the fairy-tale technique of which Beerbohm's victim was a master. This enables us to connect it with a definite and important stage in the history of Max's artistic relations with Oscar Wilde—the transition between the parodical and the imitative stage. It need hardly be stressed that this subtle blend of parody and pastiche is far more characteristic of the real Beerbohm than the two or three attempts at pure imitation that followed.

That *The Happy Hypocrite* may be looked upon as an unconscious parody of Wilde's novel is proved by many significant touches. I only select a few. When Dorian, at the end of his criminal double life, persuades himself that he is mending his ways, there appears in the mouth of the portrait "the curved wrinkle of the hypocrite." Beerbohm raises this scene to the level of parody. When Lord George stigmatizes the saint's mask he has just tried on as too "contemplative", Mr. Aeneas promptly makes it into the mask of a saint who loves dearly by putting "a fuller curve" upon the lips. On one occasion, Wilde tells us, two gentlemen left the smoking-room of the Churchill, because Dorian Gray came in. Beerbohm improves upon this as follows: ". . . whenever he [i.e., Lord Hell] entered a room . . . they would make straight for the door and watch him very severely through the key-hole." This "through the key-hole" is conclusive. Furthermore Lord Henry's statement "I adore simple pleasures . . . They are the last refuge of the complex" finds its caricatural illustration in the incident of the once famous *gourmet* eating buns with Jenny Mere—a "pagoda" of buns, to match Lord Henry's "pyramid" of seeded strawberries. Finally there is parody in the way in which Max describes the tearing away of the mask. In *Dorian Gray* the *denouement* is accompanied by a "horrible cry" and a "crash", while the unmasking scene in *The Happy Hypocrite* is enlivened by a "wild cry" and a "loud pop, as though some great cork had been withdrawn". Even the name Jenny Mere seems to contain an allusion to Wilde's predilection for that word in his novel: Sibyl Vane, for Dorian, is "*mere* beauty"; she has, according to him, "not *merely* art", but personality also, while on the fatal evening she is for him "*merely* a commonplace, mediocre actress".

Though there are certain indications that would seem to point to such a conclusion, it is difficult to prove that Beerbohm, in the person of Lord Hell, intended to give us a caricature of Oscar Wilde, the *man*. Of course, it cannot be gainsaid that the latter has drawn his own portrait in the character of Lord Henry Wotton. Considering the close parallelism that I have shown to exist between *Dorian Gray* and *The Happy Hypocrite*, it is, therefore, not impossible that Beerbohm, in his turn, should present us with a picture of Oscar in the person of Lord George Hell. The fact that he makes his hero exactly as old as Wilde was reputed to be when he published his *Dorian Gray*, may be a mere coincidence; for in the play he is "about 45".[27] But there are other clues. A recent biographer described Wilde's figure as inclining to corpulence, and his face as fleshy, humorous, "proconsular," and, at first, repellent.[28] Beerbohm's Lord George is a "vast and fearful gentleman," and "rather like Caligula, with a dash of Sir John Falstaff." Whenever this personage enters a room many people get up and leave. The same thing had happened to Wilde himself, who, moreover, retaliated in much the same way as Lord Hell;[29] for, when the ladies gathered up their skirts as they passed the wicked Lord, "he would lightly appraise their ankles." And then there is Lord George's fondness for fine clothes, and his "sudden disappearance" from the social sphere. Beerbohm's explicit statement that his Lordship was a non-smoker—his only virtue, and that a negative one—only heightens the poignancy of the jest, since everybody knew that Wilde was a tremendous smoker. Finally, the saintly mask capable of transforming the features of a George Hell into those of a George Heaven, may symbolize contemporary hopes about the purifying influence of the punishment Wilde was undergoing. Beerbohm himself refers to this sentiment in his review of *De Profundis*, written in 1905: "Nothing seemed more likely than that Oscar Wilde, smitten down from his rosy-clouded pinnacle, and dragged through the mire, and cast among the flints, would be *diablement changé en route*".[30] It is certainly remarkable that all these indications concern the "decadent" side of Wilde's life and character. In view of my thesis that Beerbohm's fantastic story may be looked upon as a parody of the "decadent" *contents* of *Dorian Gray*, this circumstance would seem to strengthen the conjecture that at least some of the mockery in *The Happy Hypocrite* is directed against the *person* of Oscar Wilde.

III

Zuleika Dobson, which was begun in the Nineties, also shows traces of Wildean influence, both in its subject-matter and in its style. But it is equally difficult here to distinguish between caricature, imitation—conscious or unconscious—and the various grades of parody, because, in the preciosity of its manner, the book is so thoroughly of its period. However, some of the motives, situations, and stylistic devices seem to be linked, in some way or other, with Wilde's tales, and with his novel. A few examples may suffice to illustrate my point.

First of all the story of *Zuleika Dobson* is vaguely reminiscent of *The Picture of Dorian Gray*. Its theme—an honest dandy drowning himself for love of a callous and unworthy amateur juggler—is the reversal of an important motive in *Dorian Gray*—a pure and simple actress poisoning herself for love of a callous and unworthy dandy. In the same way Zuleika's fatal influence on the Duke, which leads him to consummate his love by the "sacrament" of death, calls to mind Lord Henry's sinister power over Dorian who, immediately after Sibyl's death, finds comfort in the thought that, from now on, his love will always be a "sacrament" to him. But under the influence of his evil genius he soon persuades himself to see Sibyl's suicide from a purely artistic point of view.

"It often happens that the real tragedies of life occur in such an inartistic manner that they hurt us by their crude violence, their absolute incoherence, their absurd want of meaning, their entire lack of style," Lord Henry had told him.[31] Beerbohm's "novel", in which the gods arrange everything artistically, and in which everything, down to such a vulgar incident as the outpouring of Zuleika's water-jug on the Duke's face, is stylized, seems to be a subtle parody of Lord Henry's words. At the same time Zuleika's reaction to the wholesale suicide of Oxford undergraduates is a splendid caricature of Dorian's attitude: if the latter, on the evening after the girl's death, is seen to amuse himself at the Opera with another woman, Zuleika, with even more perfect composure, celebrates the destruction of her adorers with a luxurious bath, after which she orders a special train to Cambridge. (The trick of the bath as the "solution" to a critical situation also occurs in *Dorian Gray*.) Finally Dorian's "English"-speaking French valet finds his counterpart in Zuleika's French maid.

Similar factual links seem to exist between *Zuleika Dobson* and some of Wilde's stories. First the exaggerated "deportment" complex of the Duke is strongly reminiscent of the "duty" complex of the hero of "Lord Arthur Savile's Crime." His determination to keep the real reason of his self-sacrifice a secret from the world seems to be a caricature of Arthur Savile's oath that "come what may, he would never let her know what he was doing for her sake, but would keep the secret of his self-sacrifice hidden always in his heart." Arthur's idea that murder requires "a victim as well as a priest" is echoed by Dorset when he says that he is "priest as well as victim." Other passages in *Zuleika Dobson* seem to reflect situations used by Oscar Wilde. After his plunge in the Isis the Duke's career under water is described in words that are almost identical to those used by Lord Henry in *Dorian Gray*. "I see him [viz. Basil Hallward]," Lord Henry exclaims, "lying now on his back under those dull-green waters with the heavy barges floating over him, and long weeds catching in his hair." The Duke's vision of his future fate might be a paraphrase of this: "I, clinging to the weeds of the river's bed, shall see dimly the boats and the oars pass over me." In the same way the incident between Mr. Oover and Humphrey Greddon ("Withdrawing the blade, he wiped it daintily on his cambric handkerchief. There was no blood") recalls a passage in "The Fisherman and his Soul": "The blade whizzed through me, and did me no hurt." Finally, the ghosts at Tankerton, Dorset's estate, remind one of Wilde's famous romance "The Canterville Ghost." Even the name Tanville-Tankerton is suggestive.

In its style, too, *Zuleika Dobson* shows traces of Wildean parody and imitation. The trick of personifying flowers and things, which Max employs here (e.g., on p. 87 and p. 263) as well as in other works, derives from Wilde, who used it freely in his stories and who, in his turn, had borrowed it from Andersen. A passage like " 'Explain yourself!' he commanded. 'Isn't that rather much for a man to ask of a woman?' " (p. 47) could have been written by Wilde himself. On the other hand a sentence like "It was framed in ivory, and of fluted ivory were the slim columns it swung between" (p.7) would seem to be more generally reminiscent of the *Yellow Book* mode.[32] That such curious rhythms cannot always be looked upon as parodies, or even as conscious imitations, is proved by the occurrence of a similar cadence in an essay written thirty years after *Zuleika* had been begun: "And the moustache was jet-black, and jet-black were the eyebrows and the eyelashes."[33] Real stylistic parody, however, is found in what Harold Nicolson erroneously called "the author's somewhat belated preoccupation with the names of hard-stones and jewels."[34] In my opinion this preoccupation is decidedly critical. There can be no doubt that the catalogues of jewels and precious stones which Wilde used to insert in his stories after the example of Huysmans are parodied in such passages as: "On the back of one cover BRADSHAW, in beryls, was encrusted; on the back of the other, A. B. C. GUIDE, in amethysts, beryls, chrysoprases, and garnets" (p.7; note the play upon the initial letters), or "But I am heart-set on you, and to win you there is not a precious stone I would leave unturned. Conceive a *parure* all of white stones—diamonds, white sapphires, white topazes, tourmalines" (p. 57), etc. In the same way the passage beginning "The moon, like a gardenia in the night's buttonhole—but no! why should a writer never be able to mention the moon without likéning her to something else—usually something to which she bears not the faintest resemblance?" (p. 144) is a direct hit at one of Wilde's weaknesses (cf. the latter's "Through the parted curtains of the window I see the moon *like a clipped piece of silver,*"[35] and, in the same essay, "Out of a tawny mane or drift she [i.e., the moon] gleams *like a lion's eye.*"[36]

IV

That Beerbohm's two fairy-tales, "The Story of the Small Boy and the Barley Sugar" and "Yai and the Moon," were influenced by similar stories of Oscar Wilde is proved by a comparison of their subject-matter, their spirit, and their style. It may, I think, be posited that the central theme of many of Wilde's stories, such as "The Birthday of the Infanta," "The Star-Child," "The Nightingale and the Rose," and "The Devoted Friend" is the conflict between one or more aspects of the Good and the corresponding aspects of the Evil. A perfect illustration of this thesis is found in the tale of "The Nightingale and the Rose," in which the Nightingale stands for idealism, altruism, romanticism, and culture, whereas the Student is the embodiment of materialism, selfishness, cold reason, and Bloomsbury. It is exactly these conflicting tendencies that are the subject of Beerbohm's fairy-tales. The theme of "The Story of the Small Boy and the Barley Sugar" is the frustration of unreserved kindness and idealism by base egoism and materialism, whereas "Yai and the Moon" is a dramatization of the clash between Eastern romanticism and culture on the one hand, and Western intellectualism and barbarism on the other. The parallelism is too striking to be attributed to coincidence. It can only be accounted for by Beerbohm's sincere admiration of Wilde's fairy-tales. This admiration must have been all the greater in that it was not· exclusively based on the printed, more ornamental, though often less direct versions of them. We know that the young Max was often among the audience, when the Lord of Language held the table spell-bound by his *histoires parlees*,[37] and his admiration of the best of his fairy-stories was so great that he not only placed them above his highly-praised comedies,[38] but actually adopted the master's technique, not to parody him, as he had done in the earlier essays, but to emulate him. Though, on the one hand, his artistic conscience prevented these imitations from degenerating into pastiche, his "quick sympathies" made them perfectly worthy of their model, because they not only reproduced Wilde's themes, but also his spirit and his own particular variety of the fairy-tale style. In spite of his pretence, in "The Story of the Small Boy and the Barley Sugar," of addressing himself to children—a trick never practised by Wilde—both Wilde's and his own fairy-tales contain something of that cynical bitterness which appeals to the adult reader only. It is found, among many other of Wilde's tales, in "The Nightingale and the Rose," as well as in Beerbohm's "Story of the Small Boy," and in either case it supplies the tale with the "inconclusive" ending that Max once stipulated as the *sine qua non* of all good tragedy. A parallel case is provided by "Yai and the Moon," in which the moon has the same fascination for Yai that it had for Wilde himself. A mere juxtaposition, finally, of any two pages from these stories will convince the reader of Beerbohm's stylistic dependence on Wilde.

That Max went on experimenting in the Wildean fairy-tale after 1897 is proved by a MS story dated June 8, 1899, in which, under the title "Altruism," he tells us of a "very good little boy," who set free a caged bird: "Presently the bird hopped out, and, with an adroit pass of its beak removed one of the boy's eyes."[39] But by this time Max must have discovered where his real strength lay, and the two published tales were to remain the only evidence of an interesting phase in his evolution as a writer.

As I have said, Beerbohm's imitative faculties practically ceased to be stirred by Oscar Wilde after he had written "The Story of the Small Boy and the Barley Sugar" and "Yai and the Moon." Of course there are still echoes, such as his paradoxes, his curious inversions, and his significant use of the word *once,* for whose ironic possibilities he is certainly indebted to Wilde's conversations (cf. Wilde to Frank Harris bragging of his social successes: "Yes, dear Frank, we believe you—you have dined in every house in London, *once,*"[40] and [of Aubrey Beardsley]: "Dear Aubrey, he knows France so well—he has been to Dieppe, once"[41]). But such echoes are rare, and, on account of his spiritual affinity with Wilde, often difficult to pin down as such, so that they should rather be classed as cases of "unconscious" than of conscious imitation. We can say, therefore, that, soon after his two or three attempts in the Wildean fairy-story, Wilde ceased to be an inspiration for him, while, after Wilde's death, his delicacy of feeling forbade him to make Oscar the subject of his parody.

[1953]

Notes

1. "Euphemia Clashthought: An Imitation of Meredith," *A Christmas Garland,* p. 169. Unless otherwise stated, references are to the Collected Edition of the works of Max Beerbohm (London: William Heinemann, 1922-28).

2. *More Theatres: 1898-1903* (London: Rupert Hart-Davis, 1969), p. 18.

3. *Last Theatres: 1904-1910* (London: Rupert Hart-Davis, 1970), p. 66; italics mine. Cf. "Budding genius is always . . . imitative," *Around Theatres* (London: Rupert Hart-Davis, 1953), p. 444.

4. Cf. Lord Alfred Douglas, *Oscar Wilde and Myself* (London: John Long, 1914), passim, and Madeleine L. Cazamian, *Le Roman et les Idées en Angleterre,* II: *L'Anti-intellectualisme et l'Esthétisme (1880-1900)* (Paris: Les Belles Lettres, 1935), p.177.

5. *Max Beerbohm in Perspective* (London: William Heinemann, 1921), p. 10.

6. "The Incomparable Beauty of Modern Dress," *The Spirit Lamp* (Oxford), June 1893, p. 97.

7. "The Soul of Man under Socialism," *The Works of Oscar Wilde* (London: Collins, n. d.), pt. III, p. 424.

8. *Mainly on the Air* (London: William Heinemann, 1946), p. 39.

9. "The Critic as Artist," *The Works of Oscar Wilde*, pt. III, p. 327.

10. "The Decay of Lying," ibid., p. 240.

11. Harold Newcomb Hillebrand, "Max Beerbohm," *The Journal of English and Germanic Philology*, 29 (1920), 260.

12. *Around Theatres* (London: Rupert Hart-Davis, 1953), p. 275.

13. Privately printed New York: Max Harzof (G. A. Baker & Co.), 1923; reprinted in *A Peep into the Past and Other Prose Pieces by Max Beerbohm*, ed. Rupert Hart-Davis (London: William Heinemann, 1972), pp. 3-8.

14. *The Saturday Review* (London), Illustrated Supplement, Christmas 1896, p. 8.

15. "The Young King," *The Works of Oscar Wilde*, pt. I, p. 368.

16. "The Incomparable Beauty of Modern Dress," loc. cit., p. 93.

17. "The Picture of Dorian Gray," Preface, *The Works of Oscar Wilde*, pt. I, p. 9.

18. "The Pervasion of Rouge," *The Works of Max Beerbohm*, p. 100.

19. "The Picture of Dorian Gray," ed. cit., pt. I, p. 13.

20. "Diminuendo," *The Works of Max Beerbohm*, p. 138.

21. "The Picture of Dorian Gray," ed. cit., pt. I, p. 70.

22. "Dandies and Dandies," *The Works of Max Beerbohm*, p.19.

23. "The Picture of Dorian Gray," ed. cit., pt. I, p. 203.

24. "The Pervasion of Rouge," ed. cit., p. 92.

25. Hesketh Pearson, *The Life of Oscar Wilde* (London: Methuen, 1946), p. 192.

26. "A Lord of Language," *A Peep into the Past and Other Prose Pieces by Max Beerbohm* (London: William Heinemann, 1972), pp. 37-40.

27. Cf. "Vague Hints from the Author to the Company," in George Arliss, *Up the Years from Bloomsbury* (Boston: Little, Brown, 1927), pp. 185 ff.

28. Hesketh Pearson, op. cit., pp. 162-163.

29. Cf. ibid., p. 266.

30. "A Lord of Language," loc. cit., p. 38.

31. "The Picture of Dorian Gray," ed. cit., pt. I, p. 119.

32. Harold Nicolson, *"Zuleika Dobson—a* Revaluation," *The Listener* (London), 25 September 1947, p. 522; reprinted in this collection.

J. G. Riewald

33. "Two Glimpses of Andrew Lang," *Life and Letters* (London), June 1928, p. 2; reprinted in *A Peep into the Past and Other Prose Pieces by Max Beerbohm*, ed. cit., pp. 68-76.

34. *"Zuleika Dobson*—a Revaluation," loc. cit., p. 522.

35. "The Critic as Artist," ed. cit., pt. III, p. 281; my italics.

36. p. 287; my italics.

37. "Speed," *Mainly on the Air* (London: William Heinemann, 1946), p. 20.

38. " 'Lady Windermere' and 'Aglavaine'," *Last Theatres: 1904-1910*, ed. cit., p. 102.

39. *Catalogue of Original Sources of Literature and History*, No. 381 (London: Myers & Co., 1948), p. 9.

40. Hesketh Pearson, op. cit., p. 181.

41. William Gaunt, *The Aesthetic Adventure* (London: Jonathan Cape, 1945), p. 165.

David Stevenson

IRONY AND DECEPTION

There are inter-relationships between Beerbohm's caricature and parody but the two stand apart from his other work. Unlike these, irony, the device now under consideration, pervades all of his creative efforts. Because of its adaptability to the iconoclasm and sophisticated effrontery Beerbohm often affected, and because it was in keeping with the jesting spirit of his work, he used it freely. Beerbohm held the general public in low esteem and directed his efforts toward a well-informed and educated group which he regarded as a sort of cabal against the masses of the reading public. Many of his more impudent early works may be regarded as practical jokes which he played on the half-educated public for the amusement of those clever enough to see through them. For such jokes, irony was admirably suited. Unfortunately, this conspiratorial attitude has, with the passage of time, clouded allusions to people and events of the early century and occasionally leads to difficulties of interpretation which cannot be satisfactorily resolved.

Oftentimes, however, Beerbohm's irony is of an obvious type. He ridiculed actors and playwrights, for example, by means of ironic comparisons. Occasionally he elevated the object of criticism, as when he said that nothing short of a miracle could have produced as much trash as was seen on the London stage during the season of 1904-1905.[1] More often the comparison reduced the object criticized to a lower order. These sentences are examples of this type of reduction:

From David Stevenson, "The Critical Principles and Devices of Max Beerbohm," Diss. University of Michigan 1954, pp. 133-149. Reprinted by permission of David Stevenson.

65

As a branch of university cricket, the whole performance was, indeed, beyond praise.[2]

[The actors] were like a hutchful of white rabbits trying to behave like a cageful of lions, and failing.[3]

At present his [Arthur Bourchier's] restraint is rather like that of an arrested motor-car. One seems to hear strange snorts and to feel terrible vibrations.[4]

In the latter two statements, human beings are compared with non-human things. The comparison of the actors with rabbits who were trying to behave like lions is made additionally telling by a double comparison, the first between human beings and animals, and the second between the most humble and the most kingly of beasts. In regard to the third example, it is well to note that the automobile itself was scarcely out of the joke stage in 1901.

Another simple epigrammatic method found in the dramatic criticisms is the reversal of expectations, as when Beerbohm substitutes *inoffensive* for *offensive* in speaking of a libidinous play which was too long. "I would suggest," he writes, that "some of the inoffensive scenes should be cut."[5] Similarly, the statement, "He has aimed low, but even so he has missed,"[6] reverses the cliche, "He has aimed high and missed," which customarily describes a praiseworthy effort. The same technique is used in "Mr. Martin Harvey . . . is proceeding steadily . . . from bad to worse."[7] Here the phrase *is proceeding steadily* is switched from its usual laudatory meaning to a derogatory application. None of these statements, while containing ironic reversals, offer any difficulty of interpretation. The best of them heightened the critical effect of the articles from which they were taken because the reader was amused by the comparison or reversal. The object was, of course, to ridicule the person or play being criticized, and to solicit the support of the reader by amusing him.

Customarily, disregarding epigrammatic statements and such paradoxes as "An Infamous Brigade,"[8] which pretends to condemn fire fighters as destroyers of beauty, Beerbohm was far from obvious in his use of irony. Typical of his attitude toward the reader is his statement, on one of the prefatory pages of *The Works*, that "I am utterly purposed that I will not offend,"[9] after which he proceeded to be as cleverly offensive as he knew how. Throughout

The Works and, to a lesser extent, all of his writings, he questioned authority and accepted standards repeatedly while pretending not to. This division between actual and avowed purpose is the essence of his irony and justified his own description of himself as an ironist.

A related use of irony, which may be considered as purposive deception, is illustrated by one of the early essays, "Poor Romeo!"[10] The essay is an ironic hoax, designed to deceive the unwary reader. Its true import involves a reversal, although the actual clues furnished for the benefit of the astute reader are few—the use of the name of the legendary founder of Bath, Bladud, being the principal key. The essay pretends to be critical, both in method and conclusions, but is actually a purely mischievous piece of virtuosity.

Often Beerbohm's point of view was so subtly implied that the reversal was difficult to detect. His first *Yellow Book* contribution, "A Defence of Cosmetics,"[11] and a later essay, "No. 2. The Pines,"[12] illustrate this ambiguity, which was probably, but not certainly, intentional. That is, in these essays, both ambiguity and questionable sincerity play a part in the ironic technique. One may doubt the sincerity of the author, but have no absolute proof of ironic intent.

"A Defence of Cosmetics" is, on the surface, a simple paradox. It presents artifice, especially as applied to the use of cosmetics, as a positive good and praises artificiality above nature. It was deeply offensive to many readers and drew a storm of protest. Beerbohm, in a rejoinder, claimed that he was maligned. The essay, he said, was a burlesque:

> Indeed, it seems incredible to me that any one on the face of the earth could fail to see that my essay, so grotesque in subject, in opinion so flippant, in style so wildly affected, was meant for a burlesque upon the "precious" school of writers.[13]

To explain his motive further, he added:

> There are signs that our English literature has reached that point, when, like the literatures of all the nations that have been, it must fall at length into the hands of the decadents. The qualities that I have tried in my essay to travesty—paradox and marivaudage, lassitude, a love of horror and all unusual things, a love of argot and archaism and the mysteries of style—

are not these displayed, some by one, some by another of *les jeunes ecrivains?* Who knows but that Artifice is in truth at our gates and that soon she may pass through our streets?[14]

In short, the essay was constructed in such a way that on the first level of meaning it was sufficiently "grotesque in subject, in opinion so flippant, in style so wildly affected" to draw attention to its author. Beerbohm claimed, however, that, on a deeper level, it was a searching criticism of the attitudes and style of the English decadents. In the context of the essays in *The Works*, it is certainly doubtful that Beerbohm's motive was as constructive as he claims. On the other hand, there is an element of truth in his assertion which cannot be ignored. Albert J. Farmer, in his discussion of Beerbohm in *Le Mouvement Esthétique et "Décadent" en Angleterre: 1873-1900*, argues that this essay and "A Note on George the Fourth"[15] are modelled on Wilde.

> . . . si on reprend *A Defence of Cosmetics,* on s aperçoit que cet essai rappelle, par le thème comme par la manière, certains écrits caractéristiques de Wilde, et notamment la brillante *Décadence du Mensonge.* Le badinage plein de paradoxes auquel Beerbohm se complaît s inspire manifestement des procédés du maître; ce sont les affectations de pensée, les maniérismes de style chers à Wilde quil s' efforce de reproduire. Déjà on devine le rôle qu'il s' est assigné dans la "décadence": il en sera l'observateur amusé, le critique narquois. Dilettante, il cheminera en marge du mouvement, qu'il prendre just assez au sérieux pour pouvoir le railler à son aise.[16]

The question becomes complicated: was the essay written to shock and draw attention to its author, to mock "the precious school of writers," or to point out the course English literature was apt to take and to criticize that propensity? Because of the ambiguity, which seems deliberate, equally sound briefs could be drawn up for any of these interpretations.

Comments in a recent autobiography make it clear that an intelligent and informed reader may object to "No. 2. The Pines" in much the same way as the writers to the editor objected to "A Defence of Cosmetics." Alfred Noyes in *Two Worlds for Memory* singles out "No. 2. The Pines" as a deliberate and defamatory distortion of the character of Swinburne. Describing a visit to the home of Swinburne and Watts-Dunton, Noyes writes:

One very definite fact I did observe, and I feel it should be recorded here. Max Beerbohm's description of his own visit to The Pines was an exceedingly clever caricature deliberately designed to be amusing, and very artistically shaped to that end and to that end alone. But in the interest of literary history it should be said that it omits everything of real value and goes woefully astray on many points of demonstrable fact. There was, for instance, far more of Rossetti and William Morris than of the suburban early Victorianism upon which Max Beerbohm insists in a description of the interior of the house. Incidentally, a house crammed to overflowing with books of the Elizabethan period as well as from the Kelmscott Press, falls completely out of the category in which Max Beerbohm tried to place it.[17]

Beerbohm himself explains his motive in writing the essay in quite another fashion:

Early in the year 1914 Mr. Edmund Gosse told me he was asking certain of his friends to write for him a few words apiece in description of Swinburne as they had known or seen him at one time or another; and he was so good as to wish to include in this gathering a few words by myself. I found it hard to be brief without seeming irreverent. I failed in the attempt to make my subject a snapshot that was not a grotesque. So I took refuge in an ampler scope. I wrote a reminiscential essay. From that essay I made an extract, which I gave to Mr. Gosse. From that extract he made a quotation in his enchanting biography. The words quoted by him reappear here in the midst of the whole essay as I wrote it. I dare not hope they are unashamed of their humble surroundings.[18]

Comparison of Beerbohm's stated purpose and Noyes's interpretation with the text of the essay affords no proof either of ironic or sincere intention. One hundred words are used to describe the original Rossettis hanging in the hall of Swinburne's home, for example, but the dining room of the house is described as, "in form and 'fixtures,' an inalienably Mid-Victorian room, and held its stolid own in the riot of Rossettis."[19] Again, Beerbohm describes Swinburne's delight in showing off his library, which is known to have contained many erotica. Beerbohm does not say whether or not the books he saw were of this type, however; he describes one as a first edition "by some lesser Elizabethan or

Jacobean"[20] and identifies another as *The Country Wench*. On the basis of this evidence it would be difficult to decide which statement, Noyes's or Beerbohm's, is accurate. The important point is not where the truth lies, but that, as in "A Defence of Cosmetics," there is an intentional ambiguity of meaning.

Beerbohm's support of an unpopular opinion must not arbitrarily be classified as ironic, since, as I have indicated extensively elsewhere,[21] his actual views were often antithetical to generally accepted opinions. It is true, nevertheless, that many of the theses of his writings are ironic by virtue of their gratuitous and mocking reversal of accepted points of view. "Porro Unum . . . "[22] is perhaps the most bald example of this type of reversal. This essay proposes that the King of England make a goodwill visit to Switzerland, a nation, Beerbohm says, which has produced no painters, no musicians, "only couriers, guides, waiters, and other parasites."[23] The King will be greeted by "a Swiss national anthem, hastily composed for the occasion,"[24] and will hear a speech "in the Swiss language (English, French, German, and Italian, consecutively). . . ."[25] The King will bestow the Victorian Order on all the headwaiters and then depart. Beerbohm continues to insult the Swiss in a similar manner for several pages. His purpose in this essay, it seems apparent, is not serious; he feigns a constructive suggestion as an excuse for a series of clever insults.

Several recurrent themes in Beerbohm's writing are treated in a similar manner, but with less obvious effrontery. Among these are nobility, fashion, popular writing, the raising of children, and popular idolatry of royalty. The latter serves as an example of good-natured irony. In "A Good Prince," Beerbohm describes an encounter in a park with Prince Edward. The Prince, he says, would be called an ignoramus in any age but the present, but is admirably suited to modern times because he has done absolutely nothing to distinguish himself. In person he is "short, even insignificant," and has "an obvious tendency to be obese."[26] This description, which is extended for several hundred words, is a praise-blame inversion of the positive and negative qualities of royalty. As such, it is an insult to the Crown, and, by implication, to those who idolize it. One discovers at the end of the essay, however, that it is a "description" of Edward VIII as an infant. Through a deliberate ambiguity in the time of the incident he pretends to describe, Beerbohm has tricked the reader. Furthermore, he leaves in doubt whether the true intent of the essay is to perpetrate the trick or to describe the qualities of Edward VII as an adult under the guise of describing an infant.

In another essay, "Some Words on Royalty,"[27] Beerbohm pretends to pity the rulers, who do not rule and are deadened by isolation from their fellow men. "Those heavy, handsome, amiable, uninteresting and uninterested faces, are they indeed (not masks but) true mirrors," he asks, "of souls which a remote and esoteric life has gradually impoverished?"[28] He then quotes a fictitious "source" to tell of a king who substituted a mechanical dummy for himself on state occasions. With mock seriousness, Beerbohm implores his readers to find some means of "ameliorating the royal lot."[29] As in "A Good Prince," the intention is to poke fun at royalty under the pretense of praise and thereby to annoy those who are deeply loyal to the Crown.

These essays represent a criticism of contemporary England as manifested in its royalty and are consistent in point of view with the attitudes outlined earlier in this study. The treatment is ironic, however, and one cannot feel that the writer was motivated by any deep bitterness, but only by a prankish desire to make fun of a deep-seated British trait.

The same mild irony occurs in the caricatures and parodies. Many of the captioned drawings gain their humorous effect from a contradiction between what is represented graphically and the statement ascribed to the person drawn.[30] The caricature "Somewhere in the Pacific," which shows Conrad standing on a shore observing a snake which is writhing about a skull, is an example. In the face of this terrible desolation, Conrad says: "What a delightful coast! One catches an illusion that one might forever be almost gay here."[31] Another, more obvious, example shows Dame Europa, wearing a crown and dressed in rags and ermine, talking to a fat and shrewd Brother Jonathan. In the background are crates containing the art treasures of Europe. The caption reads:

Reciprocity

Dame Europa: "And now, young man, now that you've bought up all *my* art products, I shall be happy to acquire all *yours*; and I am willing to pay a generous price."

Brother Jonathan: "Name it, Marm."

71

David Stevenson

DAME EUROPA: "Twopence-halfpenny."
[*Brother Jonathan is slightly hurt, but, like a sensible fellow,
closes with the offer.*][32]

As in much of Beerbohm's prose, the intended meaning of these
examples depends not only upon that which is unsaid but unmistakably implied, but also upon facts which the observer must
supply. In the instances cited, the reader is assumed to know Conrad's
view of life and to have some information about purchases of art
by wealthy Americans. Further, he is assumed to agree with Beerbohm's opinion that America is a land of materialists and has no
art of its own, and that Conrad's pessimism is an exaggeration of
actual conditions, in which he revels. A more subtle example of
irony in caricature is "Rossetti's Courtship. Chatham Place, 1850-
1860."[33] While one who knows nothing about Rossetti would
expect a display of passion in a drawing with that caption, and
a person who knows something about him would anticipate a
show of affection, at the least, the drawing shows the poet and
Elizabeth Siddal standing several feet apart, very bored, contempla-
ting space. A mouse sits quietly on the floor. Both the contrast between what one would ordinarily expect of lovers and what we
know of this love affair, and an exaggeration of the passivity of
Rossetti's ardor are brought out by the drawing.

Beerbohm's fiction is ironic in that the attitude the reader is
expected to take toward a given character or situation is usually
the opposite of that expressed by the narrator: the narrator is an
admirer of the writings of Enoch Soames and "Savonarola" Brown,
but it is clear that Beerbohm is making fun of their poems and plays;
in spite of himself, the narrator is an admirer of a gambler, but
we are supposed to realize that the man is obsessed. More examples
could be listed.

Throughout his essays and fiction, Beerbohm used an ironic
type of candor which supplemented his critical point of view.
While this candor is not, strictly defined, an independent critical
device, it is sufficiently important to an analysis of his method to
warrant description here. It was a form of mask or pose which
served one or the other of two functions. Either it protested that
Beerbohm, although known by his public as a man of intelligence
and wit, was a rather shallow and naive fellow, or it served as a
mild and witty insult to his reader. As examples of pretended

ignorance, one may cite Beerbohm's insistence that he was un-
versed in the drama,[34] that he could not understand Schopenhauer,
William James, or even Bergson.[35] There are many instances of the
use of arrogance which was assumed in order to invert the customary
pretense of modesty and humility. Among these are: "I was a
modest, good-humoured boy [while at Charterhouse]. It is Oxford
that has made me insufferable,"[36] and "A few of us will be buried
in it [Westminster Abbey], but in the meanwhile we don't go to the
Tower, or the Mint, or the Monument."[37] These remarks, like the
ending of "Diminuendo", are intended to give the impression of
overweening conceit and thus to shock the sensibilities of the reader. Such statements are made as asides and serve to protect Beerbohm from the imputation of seriousness, as well as to annoy those
outside his circle and delight those within it.

These statements also underscored an indifference to public
opinion. The same may be said of the comments he often made on
his own style or manner of treatment in a given passage. In one
instance, for example, he said that a rather long paragraph he had
just written was "a piece of quite admirable prose."[38] He often
injected commentaries of this kind which defied any sense of unity
a reader might have, by shifting from impersonal to personal address
in order to comment on his own attitude or to chide the reader for
some idea which Beerbohm thought might have occurred to him.
In "Hosts and Guests," for example, human beings are being
classified under the categories of givers or receivers of hospitality
when the following is injected:

> I have already (see third sentence of foregoing paragraph)
> somewhat prepared you for the shock of a confession which
> candour now forces from me. I am one of the guests. You
> are, however, so shocked that you will read no more of me?
> Bravo! Your refusal indicates that you have not a guestish
> soul. Here am I trying to entertain you, and you will not be
> entertained. You stand shouting that it is more blessed to give
> than to receive. Very well. For my part, I would rather read
> than write, any day. You shall write this essay for me. Be it
> never so humble, I shall give it my best attention and manage
> to say something nice about it.[39]

Similar passages which comment on the style, attitude, or detail
used in a given section are frequent in *Zuleika Dobson*, Beerbohm's
longest and, probably, most complex work. At one point, having

stated two questions which may have occurred to a reader, he says:

> In a way, you have a perfect right to ask both those questions. But their very pertinence shows that you think I might omit things that matter. Please don't interrupt me again.[40]

At another place he inserts this paragraph:

> I am loth to interrupt my narrative at this rather exciting moment—a moment when the quick, tense style, exemplified in the last paragraph but one, is so very desirable. But in justice to the gods I must pause to put in a word of excuse for them. They had imagined that it was in mere irony that the Duke had said he could not die till after the bumping-races; and not until it seemed that he stood ready to make an end of himself had the signal been given by Zeus for the rain to fall. One is taught to refrain from irony, because mankind does tend to take it literally. In the hearing of the gods, who hear all, it is conversely unsafe to make a simple and direct statement. So what is one to do? The dilemma needs a whole volume to itself.[41]

Such comments serve to distract the reader from the action and thus to annoy him. They also keep him from taking the matter at hand seriously. They shock his sensibilities on the score of unity and the proper serious attitude of an author toward himself and his art. In this way they coincide with Beerbohm's ironic levity at the expense of his reader and with his inversion of what might ordinarily be expected of a writer in regard to consistency of tone.

Irony in Beerbohm's work is a critical device which, like parody and burlesque, demands cooperation on the part of the reader. Like them, it also involves a distortion of the actual state of affairs, permitting the truth to be disguised in various types of persiflage, ranging from obvious reversals in epigrammatic form to essays which, like "A Defence of Cosmetics," are so subtly constructed that they present numerous difficulties of interpretation. It allows Beerbohm to exercise his wit in hoaxes and to assume a false modesty and an equally false effrontery for effect. It involves, like the impersonation of parody, a love of wit, which disguises serious opinion, and allows the author to stand apart from his critical points. Above all, it contributes a lightness of tone and an atmosphere of fun into the critical commentary, so that Beerbohm can escape the imputation of seriousness.

[1954]

Notes

1. *Last Theatres: 1904-1910* (London: Rupert Hart-Davis, 1970), p. 182.
2. *Around Theatres* (London: Rupert Hart-Davis, 1953), p. 63. Beerbohm refers to the Benson company's production of *Henry V*.
3. Ibid., p. 131.
4. *More Theatres: 1898-1903* (London: Rupert Hart-Davis, 1969), p. 406.
5. Ibid., p. 259. The play was Belasco's *Zaza*.
6. Ibid., p. 201. The subject is Hall Caine's *The Christian*.
7. Ibid., p. 353. A similar statement is "Mr. Grundy" . . ."is . . . progressing" . . . "backwards," Ibid., p. 431.
8. *More* (London and New York: John Lane, 1899), pp. 65-71.
9. *The Works* (London: John Lane, 1896), p. [v].
10. Ibid., pp. 127-145.
11. In *The Works* this is called "The Pervasion of Rouge".
12. *And Even Now* (London: William Heinemann, 1920), pp. 57-88. This essay was written in 1914.
13. *The Yellow Book*, II (July, 1894), 282.
14. Ibid., p. 284.
15. Reprinted in *The Works*, ed. cit., pp. 59-96, under the title "King George the Fourth."
16. Albert J. Farmer, *Le Mouvement Esthétique et "Décadent" en Angletere: 1873-1900* (Paris: Honoré Champion, 1931), p. 312.
17. Alfred Noyes, *Two Worlds for Memory* (Philadelphia: Lippincott, 1953), p. 45.
18. *And Even Now*, ed. cit.,p. 57.
19. Ibid., p. 62.
20. Ibid., p. 76.
21. Chapter III of this study, pages 51-58. [Not reprinted here.—*Editor's note.*]
22. *Yet Again* (London: Chapman and Hall, 1909).
23. Ibid., p. 38.
24. Ibid., p. 41.
25. Ibid.
26. *The Works*, ed. cit., p. 33.
27. *More.*
28. Ibid., pp. 4-5.

29. Ibid., p. 13.

30. The cartoons "The Second Childhood of John Bull" often illustrate this device.

31. *A Survey* (London: William Heinemann, 1921), frontispiece.

32. *Things New and Old* (London: William Heinemann, 1923), Plate XXXII.

33. *Rossetti and His Circle* (London: William Heinemann, 1922), Plate II.

34. *Around Theatres*, ed. cit., pp. 1-4.

35. "Laughter," *And Even Now*, ed. cit., pp. 303-304.

36. *More*, ed. cit., p. 155.

37. *Yet Again*, ed. cit., p. 228.

38. *More*, ed. cit., p. 7.

39. *And Even Now*, ed. cit., pp. 128-129.

40. *Zuleika Dobson: or, An Oxford Love Story* (London: William Heinemann, 1911), p. 219.

41. Ibid., pp. 288-289.

Derek Stanford

The Writings of Sir Max Beerbohm

To all writing of real excellence—unless its place is with the highest of the high—fashion behaves capriciously. It suffers its "ups-and-downs" of approbation, neither of which strictly correspond with the verdict of a detached judgment. Perhaps the present reception of Sir Max Beerbohm's work shows the working of such a visitation.

On the one hand, we have a number of his titles published recently by Penguin Books,[1] with others scheduled for the same popular fame; while on the other, his position is assessed by a leading younger critic in no too friendly terms. "The best discursive prose," writes Mr. G. S. Fraser in *The Modern Writer and His World*, "within its frail and tiny limits, of the later 1890s and the Edwardian decade is Sir Max Beerbohm's, and Sir Max is a writer who is all 'manner,' and nothing but manner; his style like his personality is artificial, a conscious construction. . . ."

We are probably due, as Mr. T. S. Eliot suggests, for a period of "lower-middle-class culture"; and it is therefore natural that the serious critic should quiz rather strongly what the majority approves. But in this case the irony is double. That Sir Max— once the mascot of a literary *élite*—should reach the paper-bound-reading-public is cause enough for reflection, surely; but that, by so doing, he should bring upon his work the doubts of a younger *cognoscente,* is twice to pay the toll-charge of time.

Because of this—because his writing stands so well to the front

Derek Stanford, "The Writings of Sir Max Beerbohm," *The Month*, NS 13 (June 1955), 352-365. Reprinted by permission of Derek Stanford and the Editor of *The Month*.

in the ranks of common favour, gaining, at the same time, reserved assent only in certain quarters more "advanced"—there exists a need to look below its surface (which Mr. G. S. Fraser takes to be the whole) of this author's style and perspective. And when we do this, I think we descry the delicate outlines of a meaning and purpose, lightly but brilliantly disguised beneath a show of mannerism and wit.

We do not ordinarily consider Sir Max Beerbohm as being a critical author. Apart from the collection of dramatic notices, contained in the two volumes of *Around Theatres*,[2] his work is not critical in substance. Neither is it critical in tone, if by such be understood the voice of reasoned argumentation. Yet if the term is extended to imply the play of discernment and selection, at least three headings propose themselves under which to sound Sir Max's merits as a critic: first, as a judge and scrutinist of his own process of composition; secondly, as an informal commentator on things in general, as one man sees them; and thirdly, as a parodist, remarking on the obverse face of rated talent.

I

In his engaging study of Newman, Mr. Robert Sencourt employs the following illuminative phrase. Speaking of the words of the preacher at St. Mary's, he observes that "they had in them the surprise of that excellence which makes words literature." "The surprise of that excellence" serves well to describe the impact which Sir Max's style has upon us, administering its novel, small, unflagging shocks.

"For my own part," he tells us, "I am . . . a *petit maître*"; and it is this certainty of, this confidence in, his own capacity that has enabled Sir Max to adjudge his proper effects and keep them all to scale. The works of this author are not largely planned; the broader attractions and harmonies and structures of more developed forms are beyond their scope. Because of this—their limited area— the appeals of that "surprise of . . . excellence" must be the more numerous, the more constantly at hand. So it transpires that our main response to this unsleeping prose is a tingling awareness, a pleasurable alarmed apprehension, awaiting the next trill or tinkle of the bell.

One needs only turn to the first page of the author's first book, *The Works* (1896), to locate the presence of this alerted language. The essayist is speaking of the drawings of Grego, a fashionable Regency artist; listen: ". . . the unbridled decorum of Mdll. Hullin and the decorous debauchery of Prince Esterhazy in the distance, make altogether a quite enchanting picture." Now if the essence of criticism lies in the selection and dissociation of terms and ideas, then these words were written by a critic: "unbridled decorum" and "decorous debauchery" are critical conjunctions of a high order—they are not commonly found keeping company together.

All good writers hold the *cliché* suspect. Most are content to avoid its path; but Sir Max takes sport in tracking it down, and standing it, topsy-turvy, on its head—almost. Almost, I say—for the act of inversion which makes for paradox is not quite completed. Instead, the platitude finds itself deposited, upside-down, but a little awry. A commonplace in thought and expression has been challenged; but the juggler's gesture which makes the paradox as frequently as untrustworthy as the truism is not carried through to its automatic end. It stops short a little, this side of contradiction. Thus, Sir Max will blithely insist that "old friends are generally the refuge of the unsociable," or that "the thought of a voluptuary in pain is very terrible." At first the deft reversal of opinion delights us; next, we demur at its pert audacity; and finally concede to it a sort of half-assent. Acclaimed by Shaw as "the incomparable Max," the essayist informs us that it was Oxford which rendered him "insufferable." "The attitude he has all along adopted is that of 'the *insufferable* Max,' " writes Muriel Spark in an article on him; and part of this "insufferability" is the gay measure of shrewd truth within it. Conceived always with "the sentiment of style," and cast in "the very deuce of a pose," Sir Max's writings constitute some of the lighter-hearted progeny of Wisdom.

II

As an essayist, Sir Max is a critic of prejudice; an iconoclast of fallacies both popular and refined.

The distinction between these two types of fixed ideas may, I think, be thus expressed. According to the vulgar insular mind, all

79

foreigners are either rogues or insane: at the other wing-tip of opinion, we discover an equally false "aesthetic" notion that all foreigners are superior to us. Everyone has heard the "halfway" intellectual rhapsodising over Continental "isms," asserting the foreigner's greater erudition, culture, courtesy, and handling of women. And to counter this more precious and "progressive" assertion, it takes an intelligent independent mind. "The English," wrote Coleridge, "have a morbid habit of petting and praising foreigners of any sort, to the unjust disparagement of their own worthies." It is often the truly international intellect that best displays to us our national merits.

The insular cult of the foreigner is one of those "fine" prejudices over which Sir Max lingers with a light and loving ridicule. In "Kolniyatsch"[3] his irony finds two objects for its play: the alien author selected for applause, and the fashionable attitude of exotic worship.

> These foreign fellows [writes Sir Max] are always especially to be commended. By the mere mention of their names you evoke in reader or hearer a vague sense of your superiority and his. . . . Where, for the genuine thrill, would England be but for her good fortune in being able to draw on a seemingly inexhaustible supply of anguished souls from the Continent—infantile wide-eyed Slavs, Titan Teutons, greatly blighted Scandinavians, all of them different, but all of them raving in one common darkness and with one common gesture plucking out their vitals for exportation?

"Kolniyatsch," written in 1913, is a comment on a somewhat frenzied era of translation. This is not to suggest that Sir Max was deaf to the ululation of Slavonic genius; but rather that, with a fund of amusement, he foresaw the danger of primitivism as a spreading artistic tendency.

And concerning his life of "Kolniyatsch"—"a life happily not void of those sensational details which are what we all really care about"—how he exaggerates upon the violent, so that his figure appears to stand out as the acme of antinomianism:

> Kolniyatsch was born, last of a long line of rag-pickers, in 1886. At the age of nine he had already acquired that passionate alcoholism which was to have so great an influence in the

moulding of his character and on the trend of his thought.
Otherwise he does not seem to have shown in childhood any
exceptional promise. It was not before his eighteenth birthday
that he murdered his grandmother and was sent to that asylum
in which he wrote the poems and plays belonging to what we
now call his earlier manner.

The social philanthropic notions which have gained ascendancy
since Sir Max wrote his essays have sensitised the minds of many
of us to the point where we feel the first sentence to be more callous
than comical; but we cannot deny to the passage as a whole the
marks of a successful caricature-drawing, a caricature of "utterness—
of expressionism carried over into ethics, which in the land of the
via media must always have something risible about it. Nor should
we ignore the means by which this parody is created: the way in
which the precocity of "Kolniyatsch" (aged nine) in matters alco-
holic is off-set by his belatedness (according to standards of Slav
genius) in murdering his grandmother in his eighteenth year.
What, we may ask, is the principle, if any, behind Sir Max's
casual "criticism"? At the start, it may look like waywardness,
a personal literary instinct for mischief; but when the "criticism"
is not concerned with making sport of prejudices, either learned
or unlearned, it would seem to derive from an impulse to surprise—
not for the sake of effect alone, but rather for the sake of truth.
Just as Sir Max enjoys the spectacle of a common-place forced
to turn a somersault, so he likewise delights to uncover the often
naughty nakedness of our nature. But badly though this bareness
sometimes shows, it is not for the pleasure of a scandalous exposure
that Sir Max holds precious the denouncements of deceit. His
magnificent re-phrasing of a letter-writer's vade-mecum in "'How
Shall I Word it?'"[4] reveals his pursuit for truth beyond·*esprit*.
"Face to face with all this perfection," writes Sir Max of these
copybook correspondents, "the not perfect reader begins to crave
some little outburst of wrath, of hatred or malice, from one of these
imaginary ladies and gentlemen." An illustration of "some little
outburst" (how splendid the litotes in which he refers to the blister-
ing impact of the following address!) may be discovered in "Letter
to Member of Parliament Unseated at General Election," from
which I quote the opening thirteen lines:

DEAR MR. POPSBY-BURFORD,
Though I am myself an ardent Tory, I cannot but rejoice in the crushing defeat you have just suffered in West Odgetown. There are moments when political conviction is overborne by personal sentiment; and this is one of them. Your loss of the seat that you held is the more striking by reason of the splendid manner in which the northern and eastern divisions of Odgetown have been wrested from the Liberal Party. The great bulk of the newspaper-reading public will be puzzled by your extinction in the midst of our party's triumph. But then, the great mass of the newspaper-reading public has not met you. I have.

There are moments when the control or suppression of our first raw feelings makes for growth of character; others when they lead to hypocrisy and cant. Few things are more fatal to the true promotion of the ethical life than an unrelieved attitude of "Chinese politeness." We must, on occasions, take ourselves for what we are, rather than for what we ought to be; lest dishonesty of spirit claim us for its own, and blunt the recognition of good and bad entirely.

It is of the essence of Sir Max as commentator that a personal reality and point-of-view (elusively recalcitrant to any common system) are ever present in his writings. Initially, we may mistake this attitude for capriciousness, a cult of inspired inconsistency; but in fact it is not of the feminine kind. Its nature stands arrayed in its own distinctiveness when we compare a "fad" of Sir Max with one of André Gide's notorious *actes gratuits*. "If I were reading a First Folio Shakespeare," Sir Max assures us in his essay "Whistler's Writing,"[5] "by my fireside, and if the matchbox were ever so little beyond my reach, I vow I would light my cigarette, with a spill made from the margin of whatever page I was reading." Needless to observe, his assurance here is of a rhetorical and hypothetical order. The offence, which, he tells us, he would glibly commit is not an idle whim of vandalism; but a corrective against excessive bibliolatry, in defence of the proper substance of literature; an assertion of the properties of style, wit, and imagination as against those of paper, binding, and print.

When we contrast this passage by Sir Max with those of André Gide in which he recounts how Michel (in the novel *L'Immoraliste*) collaborates with a farm-hand in poaching on his own estate; or how delighted he is to witness a favourite young Arab boy stealing a pair of shining scissors from him, which he makes no effort to recover; or how, in *Les Caves du Vatican*, the hero Lafcadio, for no other reason than the desire to experience the crime, pushes an inoffensive passenger out of the carriage of a train as it speeds across a deep gorge, the difference between the two ideas of destruction of values becomes apparent. Gide's *mystique* of "unmotivated crime"[6] is a part of his private worship of the impulse; is regressive and recidivistic, and takes no account of society. On the other hand, Sir Max's "barbarian" project is purposive and critical, aiming in its own spritely fashion at a true valuation of the nature of books.

A cult of the anti-cult: that perhaps is how we may sum up the trend or direction of Sir Max's commentary. He has never allowed himself to be trapped in his own elegance as in a prison-cell. Author of a model essay on dandies,[7] he has avoided in his own work any fixed formulation of dandyism, whose rules he might have felt it incumbent to observe. Individualism *ne plus ultra*, as dandyism may be held to be, appears too limited for Sir Max's liking; inveterately he prefers to be himself.

This greater, less stereotyped personality, constantly evident in his writing, is what makes Sir Max, of the "Beardsley generation," the most convincing in tone and opinion. Wilde was weighed down by his "chrysoberyls," Lionel Johnson by his antique erudition, Symons by his excitement over "sin." All of these authors found it difficult to extricate themselves from their original premises, from the hardened shell of their self-ritual.

Unlike them, Sir Max has had the temerity of each fresh prejudice; for although his whole work is a tribute to taste, he has not permitted a standard called good to steal from him the pleasure of his own preferences. And in this fidelity to preference, there resides his own contribution to truth.

III

To hear that one of his books had become "set reading" at an ancient English University would doubtless be calamitous news for Sir Max. With modesty and malice, he has told us that "self-respect and . . . ignorance" prevented him "from the otherwise easy task of being an academic critic";[8] and the thought that these properties were now confided to tender professorial care would probably appear to him as a mortal blow at any legitimate hopes of posterity. With this very natural fear and disappointment, we should readily sympathise; yet the question may be asked if his volume of parodies, *A Christmas Garland* (1912), would not more dextrously advance the aims of the "textual school" of criticism at Cambridge than a deal of dour polysyllabled talk of "operative sensibility," "critical-constructive interplay," and "poetical formulations of antecedently defined attitudes and beliefs." Since the promoters of the "Cambridge approach" are hardly likely to co-opt this suggestion into their scheme for educating the young, our anxiety over Sir Max's disturbance can happily be set at rest. Should it ever be realised, at least Sir Max, in his dismay, would be able to exonerate Oxford, whose English School fights shy of our language once it has assumed recognisable form.

For these few flippancies I must ask pardon, occasioned as they are by my difficulty in stating, with bare-faced directness, what I hold to be the case: that *A Christmas Garland* is one of the most valuable documents of criticism on certain modern writers; on Kipling, George Moore, Henry James, Meredith, Bennett, H. G. Wells, and others. The way in which good parody provides good criticism is obvious; and yet, so ambiguous is the day, that some preliminary remarks may be in keeping.

"The beginning of criticism is to read aright," states Mr. Percy Lubbock in his masterly work *The Craft of Fiction*, "in other words to get into touch with the book as nearly as may be." This counsel, in stressing the need to "cut as closely" to the text as possible, tallies with the chief hortation of the "Cambridge school," with their emphasis on finer, more attentive reading. But however fine the tooth-comb which the textual critic takes (if his employment of it is to the end of criticism, not scholarship), the substance of his findings demand the adhesive of general statements, implying general values.

Of criticism, the only type which stays content with particularising comment is parody—an informal, creative, critical composition. "The beginning of criticism is to read aright"; and Sir Max has confessed to us how he "played the sedulous ape" to "this or that live writer—sometimes, it must be admitted, in the hope of learning rather what to avoid." His sly discipleship instructs as it delights.

Style results from a sense of self expressed by means of a sense of language. If this be so, the parodist stands in need of twin perceptions; one that recognises the thinking-process, and one the writing-process of his subject. Only if he has the access to the thinking-process of the victim, will the parodist be able to criticise the values, as well as the language, of his author. So in "P. C., X, 36," Sir Max hits off those less endearing aspects of the mind of "R*D**RD K*PL*NG."In an encounter between a constable and Santa Claus, he precipitates for us the following Kipling-esque obsessions: exaggerated respect for uniform, avid and guileless attention to the specialist, and a tendency to hero-worship, the latter particularly if combining with the former fetish. But Sir Max's parody carries us further. He shows us the analysed devotion to order imposed, like a tightly-fitting lid, upon a timid hysterical nature. "An' it's trunch, trunch, truncheon does the trick" (*Police Station Ditties*) resolves in one line of music-hall English those sadistic accents so often heard when Kipling descanted upon authority.[9]

Less cutting but equally critical is "Perkins and Mankind" by "H. G. W*LLS." All the coarse over-confident side to that late-progressive's popular scientism is redolent in the names of the high-days and holidays observed in the future Utopian State. "General Cessation High-Tea" is partaken in the "Municipal Eating Rooms"; but the happiest festival of the year is known as "the ceremony of Making Way," by which the older citizens, no longer employable by the State, avail themselves of "the Municipal Lethal Chamber." ("I thought at one time," writes "H. G. W*LLS," "that it would be best for every man to 'make way' on the actual day when he reaches the age-limit. But I see now that this would savour of private enterprise.")

The element of insensitiveness—of a vulgar unawareness of vulgarity—which was present in Wells, is brought out to perfection. Perkins (the hero of the tale) is asking himself "What was the matter with the whole human race? He remembered again those words of Scragson's that had had such a depressing effect on him at the Cambridge Union—'Look here, you know! It's all a huge nasty mess, and we're trying to swab it up with a pocket handkerchief.' Well, he'd given up trying to do that. . . ."

Wells's weakness of taste, of discretion, is parodied in his bright picture of To-morrow, as much as in his censorious reflections on the unscientific defects of To-day. Here he is made to speak of "the beautiful young breed of men and women who, in simple, artistic, antiseptic garments, are disporting themselves so gladly on this day of days" ("General Cessation Day," that is). The way in which "artistic" and "antiseptic" are placed side by side to nullify each other and render the prospect ridiculous, reveals Sir Max's nice feeling for those killing verbal opposites which few possess.

Perhaps the parody which encompasses the greatest number of its subject's "notes" is "Dickens" by "G**RGE M**RE." Everything is here, from Moore's tags in French (consciously exhibited, as it were, like a naughty schoolboy's dragging shoe-laces) and Frenchified construction ("the north-west wind that makes the pollard aspens to quiver"), to his tergiversations and unstable enthusiasms, his unreliable information (Tintoretto is referred to as a Flemish painter), and the parading of his sexual preoccupation ("There are moments when one does not think of girls, are there not, dear reader?").

Moore's flimsy powers of veneration for the masters of the past, as anything more than the changing digits of his latest artistic whims, are reflected in the following passage: "In those days I was kneeling at other altars, I was scrubbing other doorsteps. . . . He [Mr. Wardle of Dickens] is better than all Balzac's figures rolled into one . . . I used to kneel on that doorstep."

The acme of "M**RE's" aesthetic capriciousness, as Sir Max presents him to us, is where the novelist finds that he can no longer express his thoughts on his heroine in English. "Elle est plus vieille que les roches entre lesquelles elle s'est assise," he begins—translating into French Pater's "gala" passage on the Mona Lisa—only to break off with, "I desist, for not through French can be expressed the thoughts that surge in me. French is a stale language. So are all the European languages, one can say in them nothing fresh. . . . The stalest of them all is Erse. . . ."

"Criticism undiluted"—this expression comes from Sir Max's discourse on Lytton Strachey, delivered as the Redé Lecture for 1943; and describes a species of activity in which he engages only with reluctance. On succeeding Bernard Shaw as the dramatic critic of the *Saturday Review*, -in 1898, he made his repugnance for "responsible straight thinking" delightfully and ironically clear. "This absurd post which I have accepted," he wrote, "will interfere with my freedom in life, and is quite likely to spoil and exhaust such talent as I might otherwise be exercising in literary art. However, I will not complain. The Editor of this paper has come to me as Romeo came to the apothecary, and what he wants I give him for the apothecary's reason."[10]

However disagreeable a duty this suggests, the fact remains that Sir Max held this office till 1910—a dozen odd years!—during which he wrote what seems to me the most intelligent, and intelligible, prose that our murky century has produced. This obviously calls for definition; and I should like, for the present purpose, to employ the distinction which Thomas Hobbes made between "natural" and "acquired wit," the first of which I would equate with the term "intelligence" and the second with "intellect." By "natural wit" Hobbes understood that "which is gotten by use only and experience; without method, culture, or instruction"; by "acquired wit," that gained by "method and instruction." The true name of this wit, he tells us, is "reason."

By designating Sir Max's dramatic criticism as *the prose of intelligence*, I do not mean to deny to his writing those properties of culture as we understand the word. When Hobbes describes "natural wit" as that in which culture plays no formative part, he is thinking mainly of a rational culture, a scientific and systematic discipline; something synonymous with logical method; and not of that all-round exercise of the understanding, imagination, and sensibility which we have in mind to-day. Sir Max's definition of "a good critic" is disingenuous almost in its simplicity: "a cultured man with brains and a temperament," as he tells us, very much by the way, in his essay on Ouida.[11] For one kind of "good critic" that well may pass; but, apart from "temperament," it hardly serves to enumerate the elements distinguishing Sir Max in this role. I return to the term "intelligence" in the hope of filling out the formula a little. Nimbleness, manoeuvreability, a quick shrewd sense for the strong points of a case, a native alertness and originality, an indifference to being either in or out of fashion where the merits and worth of an object are in question: these, I think, are the marks of "intelligence" wherever that faculty is exercised in judgment; and these it is that illuminate the prose of Sir Max as a dramatic critic.

"The tart ozone of distinction": that is a phrase which the essayist used to fix the social tone of Covent Garden in the 'nineties; and if each mind may be said to have its savour, that of Sir Max is distinctive, tart, and salted. Here, in his dramatic writings, the wise affectations of the essayist have been sharpened down to a stylish common sense, while the waspish blandness has been exchanged for an urbane forthrightness of manner. A wit not too fine for general understanding; a judgment poised and independent; and a power of utterly personal praise—these are his "quarterings" in this jostled field.

Sir Max's twelve-year tenure of office as dramatic critic may be simply summarised: a persistent understanding of the art of shock-treatment. On starting his employ with the *Saturday Review*, Sir Max played his first disconcerting gambit.[12] "Frankly," he wrote, "I have none of that instinctive love for the theatre which is the first step towards good criticism of drama. I am not fond of the theatre. Dramatic art interests and moves me less than any of the other arts." Sir Max knew the publicity-value of starting off on the wrong foot: a soldier out of step is singled out immediately, while his conforming comrades escape exact attention. But there was more to his ruse than this. His statement was a move towards a less "beglamorised" discussion of the subject. In effect, it served to warn the players that a strong predisposition to things theatrical was not present, in this case, to help obscure or scale down their imperfections. With this critic, there was no relying on a generous "free" start. In addition to this, Sir Max's reference to his interest in "the other arts" implied that he did not look upon the theatre as the "be-all and end-all" of aesthetic creation. It suggested that drama and acting should be judged by standards on a par with those applied to music, painting, and letters; that here was a critic completely unenchanted by the magic isolation of the green-room and the footlights.

From this, one might easily suppose that Sir Max was in favour of "the theatre of the future"; a champion of "intellectual" *avant-garde* drama, with but little attention for the ordinary "straight piece." In fact, his patronage was almost for this latter, for if he extended a blithe poetic welcome to the stage innovations of Mr. Gordon Craig,[13] the general course of his criticism was what "advanced circles" might term "reactionary." For this, there were several reasons. Pre-eminently his judgments were delivered upon the play as a "performance"; not as the text of, or blue-print for, one. In other words, his care was not to know how the play might *read* off the stage: what concerned him was how it *acted*, with one particular cast, on the night in question. This made him a close and keen critic of acting; balanced as it was by a pinch of disdain for the inanities and vanities of performers.

For the "high-brow" notion of drama, he had small liking.[14] "The value of the thing said," he insisted, "depends not on the value of the thing it is said about. . . . Good sense about trivialities is better than nonsense about things that matter."[15]

A third aspect of Sir Max's "traditional" preferences as a critic derive from his instinctive understanding of the relationship between drama and society. This comes out especially in his notices on the music-halls, which contain some of his best dramatic writing. "The mass of people, when it seeks pleasure," he maintained, "does not want to be elevated: it wants to laugh at something beneath its own level."[16] Speaking in favour of "The Older and Better Music Hall," he observes that, "This is one of the advantages of the old music hall over the new: it does reflect, in however grotesque a way, the characters of the class to which it consciously appeals."

To "refine" the music-hall by transforming it into cabaret or musical comedy seemed to Sir Max an anti-social action, fraught with danger to the Constitution.[17]

Great art requires great audiences; but the following of a "fit though few" minority is not the public a dramatist desires. Somehow he must touch and come home to one social stratum or an entire cross-section. And to do this, he must probably combine his innovation and uniqueness with a friendly proportion of the known, as a reassuring bait for the popular mind.[18] This, or something a deal more subtle, is implied in Sir Max's dramatic writing; and is the one chief intuition unifying his theatrical outlook.

Regarding the limits of criticism—his own and that of critics in general—Sir Max was unreservedly clear. "A definite self—that is what one most needs in a critic," he wrote in a review[19] of Arthur Symons' book *Plays, Acting and Music.* "'It takes all kinds to make a world.' . . . Every quality has its defect, and it is only by eclectic reading that we can behold that monster, the perfect critic."

Derek Stanford

His own preferences in critical writing, he expressed with witty succinctness: "I revere the expert in an art: but I prefer the occasional critic. The mischief of being an expert is this: long before you have fairly earned the title, you have exhausted what you had to say; and, moreover, your knowledge of life and of the other arts has been rusting."

Well, Sir Max has earned his title right enough: not a name to be found, for a little space, in the transient directories of specialised knowledge; but a place in the Almanach de Gotha of art—a knighthood possessing the longevity of letters.

[1955]

Notes

1. *The Poets' Corner, Zuleika Dobson, Seven Men and Two Others.*
2. First published in 1924.
3. *And Even Now* (1920).
4. *And Even Now.*
5. Contained in the volume *Yet Again* (1909).
6. François Mauriac's description.
7. "Dandies and Dandies," *The Works.*
8. "Why I ought not to have become a Dramatic Critic," *Around Theatres.*
9. Of all the parodies in *A Christmas Garland*, "P. C., X, 36" is the most unsparing. If this is studied in conjuction with "Kipling's Entire" (a review of the novelist's dramatised story *The Light that Failed*, included in *Around Theatres*) and the caricature entitled "Mr. Rudyard Kipling takes a bloomin' Day aht, on the blasted 'Eath, along with Britannia, 'is Gurl," in *The Poets' Corner* (1904), it would seem that Sir Max "had it in" for his subject. In "Kipling's Entire" he strikes at the cult of Kipling's "manlydom through violence" by suggesting that the author's name may be "the veil of a feminine identity." The "case" is brilliantly developed.

I think this triple assassination, on the part of a writer as kind as he is pert, is to be understood in terms of the parodist's insight into Kipling's literary psychosis— the radical unhealthiness underlying his prepossession with virility and brutality.

10. All quotations in this section of the essay, unless otherwise indicated, are taken from the volume *Around Theatres*. The titles given in these endnotes are the itles of reviews and articles appearing in that volume.

11. *More* (1899).
12. "Why I ought not to have become a Dramatic Critic."

13. "Mr. Craig's Experiment."

14. Shaw, however, escaped with few scars; though much that he wrote irritated Sir Max.

15. "An Inquiry into a Convention."

16. "At the Tivoli."

17. See "At the Gaiety."

18. We have convincing evidence of this in Mr. T. S. Eliot's dramatic development. How much more "popular," in aim and appeal, is *The Confidential Clerk* to *The Cocktail Party*, and *The Cocktail Party* to *The Family Reunion*!

19. "An Aesthetic Book."

Evelyn Waugh

Max Beerbohm: A Lesson in Manners

Because of his early precocity and his open old-fashioned scorn of the new royal circle, of the new, popular writers of the Edwardian era, of Arnold Bennett and of H. G. Wells, because of his antiquated elegance in dress, Max Beerbohm came to be regarded as a man of the 1890s. In fact his full flowering was in the 1920s. He wrote little then, but it is the decade of his best collections of essays, of his most brilliant drawings, exhibited at the Leicester Galleries, of the publication of *A Survey* (1921), *Rossetti and His Circle* (1922), *Things New and Old* (1923), *Observations* (1925).

He lived abroad, and from being a ubiquitous man about town he had become a secluded and exclusive celebrity. On his rare visits to London everyone strove to meet him. I was not one of the young men to whom invitation cards came in great profusion—I was the author of one light novel and a heavy biography—but on one of these later visits I managed to find myself in his company.

To say that I was invited to dine with him by my solicitor gives a wrong impression. I had no solicitor in those happy days. There were no japanned deed cases painted with my name in E. S. P. Haynes's office. He had acted for me, it is true, in a single disagreeable piece of legal business, but he gave me far more in oysters and hock during its transaction than he charged me in fees. He was the most remarkable of solicitors, a man who actually enjoyed the company of literary men of all ages and reputations. A second Watts-Dunton? the reader will ask. Not a second Watts-Dunton.

Evelyn Waugh, "Max Beerbohm: A Lesson in Manners," *The Atlantic Monthly*, 198 (September 1956), 75-76. Reprinted by permission of A. D. Peters and Company.

Haynes did not seek to restrain the pleasures of his clients; however extravagant, he applauded and promoted them.

I kept no diary then. I think it must have been in the spring of 1929 that I received the invitation to dine *en famille* in St. John's Wood to meet Max Beerbohm. I came with joy, for Max Beerbohm was an idol of my adolescence to whom every year had deepened my devotion. It was my first visit to Mrs. Haynes. Hitherto my meetings with Haynes had been in a subterranean bar in Chancery Lane. Now I saw him at home, in a home that might have come straight from the pages of du Maurier's *Punch*; Mr. Vandyke Brown, A. R. A. at home.

As soon as I entered the drawing room I realized why I had been asked: I was by far the youngest man present and I was there to provide a lively partner for the youngest Miss Haynes. Everyone else was illustrious, each an idol of mine. It was my first sight of Hilaire Belloc and of Maurice Baring. Either of these on any other night would have been a prodigious treat, but my eyes and ears were for Max. He was very polite and quiet. I stood far off with the youngest Miss Haynes, who had been dandled on the knees of these resplendent beings and regarded them as jolly old buffers. Preposterous to record, she seemed genuinely more interested in me and my friends than in them.

In the dining room the separation persisted. Max sat far away, and between us hung the barrier of elderly intimacy and allusion. How well everyone talked and how loudly! All save Max. How they laughed and chaffed! What robust vocabularies, what rare knowledge, what exuberant fancies vollied and thundered between me and the object of my devotion! How splendidly lacking they were in any sort of side! What capital good fellows they were! And how Max enjoyed them, and they him! Every now and then with perfect timing, but quite inaudibly to us at the end of the table, the gentle exquisite inserted his contribution. How joyously Belloc and Baring acclaimed him! Admirable wine circulated. I spoke freely to Miss Haynes about Robert Byron and Harold Acton. Then the ladies left us, and chairs were about to be drawn up when there irrupted two or three youngish men who (with their women folk, now in the drawing room) had been "asked in later." Chairs drew apart again. More glasses were brought. The decanter went from hand to hand. It was a memorable evening, but through it all thrilled the faint Panpipe of disappointment. When at length I left I had nothing to remember of Max Beerbohm; a "Good evening" and a "Good night." I returned to the club where I lived, slightly drunk but slightly crestfallen.

It was there that I was vouchsafed a second chance. I found that club a convenient place to sleep, but already my then fast, smart preferences were alienating me from it. It was the genial resort of respectable men of letters, where the spirit of Edmund Gosse still reigned in the morning room and the younger members seemed mostly to be employed by the B. B. C. The truth must be told, I felt rather superior to the place. And there in the hall next day at one o'clock, watch in hand, a host evidently expecting a guest, stood Max Beerbohm. He did not wear the tall hat and tubular coat of the Nicholson portrait; he was military rather than aesthetic in his dandyism. But he was smart as paint.

I sidled forward wondering whether to accost him or not. He observed my movement, smiled and held out his hand. I remarked that the previous evening had been very pleasant. He agreed and added that he greatly looked forward to seeing the portrait on which he understood I was at work. He had heard Tonks speak of it with unusual warmth. In that awful moment his friend arrived. I slipped away broken. No luncheon for me that day; rather the Hamam Baths, which in that happy epoch existed for just this purpose—to soothe the wounded heart.

Under that exotic cupola I sprawled and sweated; I plunged into the raftered hall where the bust of "Sligger's" father gazed down on mobled mankind. I dozed through the afternoon and at sundown had hot buttered toast and whisky and soda. Then, a better man, I returned to the scene of my disaster to dress for the evening.

I was greeted by the porter with a letter addressed—could it be?—in the fine little handwriting which fills the spaces of the famous drawings. How I wish I had kept it! Part of the anarchy which I then professed, was a disdain for personal records. I remember the gist but not the inimitable diction. It was an apology. Max Beerbohm was growing old, he said, and his memory played tricks with him. Once in his own youth he had been mistaken by an elder for someone else and the smart troubled him still. He reminded me that he knew my father well and had seconded him in days before I was born for this very club. He said he had read my novel with pleasure. He was on his way back to Italy. Only that prevented him from seeking a further meeting with me.

It was an enchanting document. More exciting still was the thought that, seeing my distress, he had taken the trouble to identify me and make amends.

Good manners were not much respected in the late twenties; not at any rate in the particular rowdy little set which I mainly frequented. They were regarded as the low tricks of the ingratiating underdog, of the climber. The test of a young man's worth was the insolence which he could carry off without mishap. Social outrages were the substance of our anecdotes. And here from a remote and much better world came the voice of courtesy. The lesson of the master.

[1956]

Sir Sydney Roberts

MAX BEERBOHM

I

If we could all of us follow Mr. H. G. Wells's good example, dismiss the present from our minds, and fix our eyes steadfastly on the future, then we could share his wholesome contempt for the past. But we can't.

So spoke Max in a broadcast of 1936 which he entitled "A Small Boy Seeing Giants". In that, as in other broadcasts, he liked to describe himself as "an interesting link with the past," and it may reasonably be assumed that many of his listeners shared his inability to rise to the futurism of H. G. Wells and preferred to look back. For my own part, if I were asked to name a year which evokes in me a wondering nostalgia, I would select the year 1894.

In that year I was a small boy and had no opportunity of seeing literary giants; but now, as I contemplate them bibliographically, I can recognize their stature. In 1894 Swinburne, standing at the head of living poets, produced his *Astrophel*; in the same year John Davidson's *Ballads and Songs* and William Watson's *Odes* appeared; drama was represented by Pinero's *The Weaker Sex*, Wilde's *A Woman of No Importance*, and Yeats's *Land of Heart's Desire*; amongst the novels were Meredith's *Lord Ormont and his Aminta* and Gissing's *In the Year of Jubilee*; Hardy, too, was still a novelist and produced *Life's Little Ironies*; George Moore's

Sir Sydney Roberts, "Max Beerbohm," in *Essays by Divers Hands: Being the Transactions of the Royal Society of Literature*, NS 30, ed. N. Hardy Wallis (London: Oxford University Press, 1960), pp. 115-129. [The Giff Edmonds Memorial Lecture, read 12 July 1957.] Reprinted by permission of R. J. L. Kingsford.

Esther Waters provoked trouble with the circulating libraries; and for those who liked what George Moore scorned as the "healthy school" of writers there was *Trilby* or *The Prisoner of Zenda* or *The Diary of a Nobody* or *The Memoirs of Sherlock Holmes.* It was a rich and varied harvest and into the middle of it the first number of *The Yellow Book* was plunged.

Max was in his last year at Merton. A meeting with Aubrey Beardsley led to an invitation to contribute an essay to the projected journal and Max's career as a satirist was begun. His "Defence of Cosmetics" was printed in the first number of *The Yellow Book* and he was soon to learn that satire is one of the dangerous trades.

> For behold! [he had written] The Victorian era comes to its end and the day of sancta simplicitas is quite ended. The old signs are here and the portents to warn the seer of life that we are ripe for a new epoch of artifice. Are not men rattling the dice-box and ladies dipping their fingers in the rouge-pot?

But the sedate journals of the period were not amused. *The Times* described the first number of *The Yellow Book* as a "combination of English rowdyism with French lubricity", though later it conceded that the second number was less impudent than the first.

"The first volume," wrote *The Athenaeum*, "evidently aims at novelty and yet it is not unlike in appearance the annual volumes of *Chatterbox* and other periodicals for young people. . . . Mr. Beerbohm's 'Defence of Cosmetics' is silly . . . Mr. Beardsley's portrait of Mrs. Patrick Campbell is libellous." Other critics were more violent, and Max was at pains to explain in the second number of *The Yellow Book* that his essay, "in opinion so flippant, in style so wildly affected", was meant for a burlesque upon the "precious" school. To later numbers he contributed further essays. Among them was a satire on the Aesthetes and the Mashers of 1880 ("Dados arose upon every wall, sunflowers and the feathers of peacocks curved in every corner, tea grew quite cold while the guests were praising the Willow Pattern of its cup"). The period fascinated him, but he concluded that an exhaustive account of it would need a far less brilliant pen than his and accordingly he resigned his claims to Professor Gardiner and the Bishop of Oxford. At the end of 1895 he wrote an essay "Be it Cosiness" for another periodical, *The Pageant.* Surveying the distant past of his undergraduate days, he sought the quietism of a London suburb where he could see the laburnum flowering in the little front garden and be grateful to the retired military man next door for the loan of his copy of *The Times*. In short, he belonged to the Beardsley period and felt himself a trifle outmoded. Younger men, with fresher schemes, had pressed forward and he stood aside with no regret.

It was clearly appropriate that the scattered writings of so distinguished a veteran should be collected. The publisher of *The Yellow Book* was a willing collaborator and *The Works of Max Beerbohm, with a Bibliography by John Lane* appeared in 1896. Thus, compactly, between the scarlet covers of a tiny quarto was the corpus of Max's literary work enshrined. *Finis coronat opus.* In fact, it was but a beginning and, to a less ingenious mind, the definitive character of the *Works* might have raised difficulties in the entitlement of supplementary volumes. But the problem was easily, and economically, solved. A second volume (1899) was, quite accurately, entitled *More;* it was followed, at stately intervals, by *Yet Again* (1909) and by *And Even Now* (1920).

Of course, this is not the whole bibliographical story, but for the moment I wish to dwell upon the later 1890s and upon the Edwardian period which followed.

In the mind of a reader of today the particular qualities of a Beerbohm essay—the gentle irony, the verbal precision, the neologisms, the careful polish, the consistent urbanity—are so firmly established, that he tends to reflect only upon the almost oracular supremacy which Max, in his later years, achieved. It is not always remembered that for fourteen years (from 1896 to 1910) he was a working journalist. In fact, he began earlier. While he was still at Oxford, he was caricaturing club types and Oxford types for the *Strand Magazine* and in the summer of 1894 he interviewed C. B. Fry at Wadham for the *English Illustrated Magazine*. After recalling a conversation with a decadent friend who deplored the athletic movement of the time—"the growing school of young men who wear their hair short, smoke briar pipes, and ride about to football matches on bicycles"—Max describes how he called upon the great all-rounder on a Sunday morning. It was 11 a.m., but Mr. Fry (as Max punctiliously calls him throughout) was for once not in training and had seized the opportunity of making a very late breakfast and of smoking a pipe after it. Max particularly noted that there were pipes all over the room.

For myself (*egomet*, as Max would say) I find a peculiar fascination in the scene—the cheerful *bonhomie* of the athlete and the professional skill with which Max plied his questions. One can almost hear him asking: "Is it good fun, jumping? Do you enjoy it?"

The reply is prompt and convincing: "Rather, it's the best fun in the world. . . . You seem just to give one spring up and then the air rushes past you in a hurricane and there you are again on your feet, safe and sound."

"But sometimes with a broken record?"

Mr. Fry's attitude towards picture-galleries was similar, it appeared, to Miss Zuleika Dobson's view of music: "I am very fond of pictures", he said, "but I don't know anything about them. . . . I don't really know why a picture is good or bad, only just whether I enjoy looking at it or not. I take a great interest in heaps of things that I know nothing about."

"For instance?"

"Well, politics for one, and golf for another—especially golf. . . . I do think it's a fascinating game."

"Have you any idea of taking it up seriously, as a change from cricket and football?"

"Good heavens, no! I only look on golf as a kind of glorified croquet."

Then there is talk about compulsory games in Public Schools and Max concludes: "When I got out into the great quadrangle, I could not but envy the young athlete, with his off-hand ways and transparent happiness, living in this beautiful college. . . . I felt altogether that I should like to be 'Fry of Wadham' myself."

There is, I am convinced, more of wistfulness than of irony in that conclusion and I am tempted to digress for a moment on the subject of cricket. Remote as the game was from Max's interest, its very distance seems to have lent a wondering enchantment to his view. Thus, in the series of "Words for Pictures" which he did for the *Saturday Review* was a comment on a wood-engraving by William Nicholson, entitled "Cricket":

> Observe the batsman! Slogger is legible in every bulging curve of him and the fielders have been scattered beyond the sides of this wood-block. See how fiercely, yet freely, he grips the willow in his fat hands, how ogreishly he smiles between his whiskers at the doomed ball which must even now be flying towards him! The wicket-keeper, humped down on outspread

legs, is more like an arch than a human being . . . We are apt to forget how great a place in the world's economy is filled by this strange pastime.

But when the spirit of this strange pastime threatened to influence the work of the actor, Max scented danger. Commenting on the production of *Henry V* by another Oxford athlete, F. R. Benson, he wrote:

> Alertness, agility, grace, physical strength—all these good attributes are obvious in the mimes who were, last week, playing "Henry the Fifth" at the Lyceum. Every member of the cast seemed in tip-top condition—thoroughly "fit". . . . The fielding was excellent, and so was the batting. Speech after speech was sent spinning across the boundary, and one was constantly inclined to shout "Well *played*, sir! Well played *indeed*!". As a branch of university cricket, the whole performance was, indeed, beyond praise. But, as a form of acting, it was not impressive.

This is from one of the 470 pieces of dramatic criticism written for the *Saturday Review*. The cream of these was skimmed by Max himself in two volumes entitled *Around Theatres* (1924). But was it? When, in May 1898, Max succeeded Bernard Shaw as dramatic critic, he insisted that while he had a genuine love of literature and some knowledge of its technicalities, he took neither emotional nor intellectual interest in the drama. He had, he said, accepted an absurd post which might spoil and exhaust the talent he might otherwise be exercising in literary art. It is, therefore, not surprising that Max interpreted his function in a liberal sense and that among the pieces which have not been reprinted there are enshrined many reflections which throw light on his outlook, not only upon the drama, but on literature and on life.

In the exercise of the literary art he never lowered his standards. He was cursed, he said, with an acute literary conscience and he conceived that one of the duties of a writer was to seem to write with ease and delight.

> What distinguishes literature from jounalism [he wrote] is not vigour and sharpness of expression: it is beauty of expression. To a man who shall create literature language must not indeed be an end in itself: it must be a means, a noble and very dear means. The true artist must love the material in which he

works. . . . If he be a writer, it will not be enough for him to have so expressed his meaning that nobody can miss it or forget it: his meaning must have been so expressed as to waken in himself a pious joy in those harmonies of words and cadences which can be found if they are sought for.

At the same time, he dismissed with scorn the notion of the artist's self-sufficiency:

No artist does write merely for his own pleasure. Man is a gregarious animal and the artist himself is, despite all that has been said to the contrary, more or less human. . . . You may be sure that if you took the most intense and single-hearted artist in literature that ever lived and set him down, with pens, ink and paper on a desert island, he would produce little or nothing unless he had some reason to believe that he would ultimately be rescued; and be sure that if you came to rescue him, and if he had not been idle, he would meet you with his manuscript and would immediately read it to you on the beach.

Written in a decade which is commonly associated with the theory of "Art for Art's sake", how salutary is the sheer common sense of such a paragraph. Furthermore, for all his pious search for harmonies of words and cadences, Max was sensitive to the dangers of the cult of the *mot juste,* and a consideration of the dramatic version of *The Prisoner of Zenda* led him to a comparison of Robert Louis Stevenson and Anthony Hope which is as refreshing as it is unexpected:

[Stevenson] was always whittling and filing, embroidering and confectioning. He was always preoccupied with words . . . Mr. Hope's invention of stories may be inferior to his, but Mr. Hope has this vast advantage: that no reader gives him a moment's thought, and no reader can but be obsessed by Stevenson. . . . For my own part, I am quite happy to sacrifice a story for style. I rate the essayist far higher than the romancer. . . . But I cannot persuade myself to admit that Mr. Hope's romances, as written by him, are not superior to Stevenson's. If this is a heresy, so much the better. It is only through heresies that criticism can progress.

Evidently *The Prisoner of Zenda* had a particular interest for Max, for when it was revived it led him to reflect upon the true criteria of dramatic excellence. Did the play offer a criticism of life as we know it? Did it create illusion in the playgoer? The answer is clear: "Mr. Hope's manner of making his play was not as of a man asking us to believe the story, but as of one inviting us to agree with him how delightful it would be if such things *could* happen. His play was, in the direct sense, a criticism of life. Its great point was in being so frank a fantasy."

This reference to fantasy is peculiarly relevant to one part of Max's own work and to this I shall shortly return. Meanwhile it may be noted that the dramatic illusion he demanded must be one of two kinds: either the play should make him feel that he was listening to men and women whose problems and sufferings and gaieties were a part of actual life; or it should transport him to some realm of fancy in which he could willingly be absorbed while the curtain was up. Only rarely did the playwrights of the period satisfy one or other of these conditions. There were certain plays that he hated and he was not afraid to say so—*The Light that Failed*, for instance, or *The Passing of the Third Floor Back*. Sometimes he was captivated by the constructive skill of the playwright. Thus he wrote of Pinero's *His House in Order:* "I cannot ignore the play's fundamental weaknesses. But do not forget that my inferior self enjoyed the play immensely. . . . Judged on a low plane, *His House in Order* takes very high rank indeed."

Here the acute critical conscience is at work. It was not enough that a play should, in the modern phrase, be just "good theatre".

When Max looked back on his long period of apprenticeship on the *Saturday Review,* he was astonished at his own proliferation: "On and on I went doggedly from the age of 25 to the age of 37. It seems incredible; but it is a fact," and he adds, without false pride or false modesty, that he never scamped his work. Like Samuel Johnson and some others before him, he might find the weekly demand irksome, but that was no excuse for the blunting of the literary conscience. Bernard Shaw once remarked, characteristically, that nothing that is not journalism will live as literature; Max might well have retorted that nothing that is not literature will live as journalism.

II

The *Saturday Review* was not the only journal for which Max wrote. When in 1909 he selected the material for *Yet Again,* he

had no notion, he said, that he had put his eggs into so many
baskets—and by this time there were different kinds of eggs and
different kinds of baskets. His first book of caricatures, *Caricatures
of Twenty-Five Gentlemen* (1896), was followed by *The Poets'
Corner* (1904) and *A Book of Caricatures* (1907). Here I am concerned
with the writings of Max Beerbohm, but I do not forget what Bohun
Lynch wrote in 1921:

> The caricatures and the writings are not manifestations of
> two arts but of one. There are a number of proverbs . . .
> about shoe-makers sticking to their lasts and Jacks-of all-Trades
> being masters of none. But these do not apply to Max Beerbohm
> who has but one trade. He is a satirist.

One of the most natural media of a satirist is that of parody,
and the parodies collected in *A Christmas Garland* (1912) may,
perhaps, provide the closest analogue to the caricatures. Yet the
analogy may not be very close. Open one of the books of caricature,
say, at a representation of Arthur Balfour. The immediate impression may well be one of grotesque absurdity—a prodigiously
tall, slim figure surmounted by a tiny head. Max has seized upon
the long frock-coat which dominated Balfour's appearance and
exaggerated it to the highest point. The caricature of H. G. Wells
in the same volume shows a reverse of the treatment. Wells's figure
was short and undistinguished, with a brain bursting with futurist
ideas; accordingly he is portrayed with a massive head and a stunted,
insignificant body. In his face is all the earnest melancholy of the
Utopian prophet.

From these two portraits one may suitably turn to the parody
of Wells in *A Christmas Garland*. In the opening paragraphs of
chapter xx of "Perkins and Mankind" there is little or no exaggeration. Much of it is so faithful to the original that although there
is much to amuse there is nothing to shock or startle:

> The enormous house was almost full. There must have been
> upwards of fifty people sitting down to every meal. Many of
> these were members of the family. . . . For the rest there were
> the usual lot from the Front Benches and the Embassies.
> Evesham was there, clutching at the lapels of his coat; and
> the Prescotts—he with his massive mask of a face, and she with
> her quick, hawk-like ways, talking about two things at a time;
> old Tommy Strickland, with his monocle and his dropped g's,

103

telling you what he had once said to Mr. Disraeli; Boubou
Seaforth and his American wife; John Pirram, ardent and
elegant, spouting old French lyrics; and a score of others.

That might well be a paragraph taken straight from *The New
Machiavelli*. But the satirist shortly appears—and the subject is
Arthur Balfour:

> True there was Evesham. He had shown an exquisitely open
> mind about the whole thing. He had at once grasped the under-
> lying principles, thrown out some amazingly luminous
> suggestions. Oh yes, Evesham was a statesman, right enough.
> But had even he ever really *believed* in the idea of a Provisional
> Government of England by the Female Foundlings?

It is the same with many of the other pieces in *A Christmas
Garland*. The parody is the work of the same satirist, but the
material requires different treatment. In the portrait the dominating characteristic is conveyed in a flash. As Raven-Hill said: "If
Max sees a little man with nothing particularly strange about him
except a big moustache, he goes for that big moustache." Similarly,
Max goes for Arthur Benson's sentimentality, for Arnold Bennett's
provincialism, or for Chesterton's paradox; but he goes more
quietly, opening with gentle pastiche and only gradually exposing the idiosyncrasies of the writer.

Occasionally he would employ what he called his "habit of
aping" in the spirit of an imaginary conversation, and there is no
better example of his astonishing capacity for imitation and
adaptation than the poem which he entitled "A Luncheon." In
1923 the then Prince of Wales lunched with Thomas Hardy on his
way to visit the estates in his Duchy of Cornwall. It is not difficult
to imagine how the scene would appeal to Max's percipient mimicry. On the one hand was the veteran poet and novelist:

Intensive vision has this Mr. Hardy
With a dark skill in weaving word-patterns . . .

On the other hand was the young prince whose career Max had
followed from the perambulator onwards:

Lift latch, step in, be welcome, Sir,
Albeit to see you I'm unglad
And your face is fraught with a deathly shyness
Bleaching what pink it may have had.
Come in, come in, Your Royal Highness.

Beautiful weather?—Sir, that's true,
Though the farmers are casting rueful looks
At tilth's and pasture's dearth of spryness.—
Yes, Sir, I've written several books.—
A little more chicken, Your Royal Highness?

Lift latch, step out, your car is there,
To bear you hence from this antient vale.
We are both of us aged by our strange brief nighness,
But each of us lives to tell the tale.
Farewell, farewell, Your Royal Highness.[1]

Such a piece, as Johnson said of Gray's "Elegy," it is useless to praise. But I remember with pleasure that when I once told Max how highly I rated this poem, he replied, "Yes, that was a good one." It was the considered verdict of an acute and detached critic.

Some of Max's best known and best loved satire is contained in *Seven Men*. Enoch Soames and "Savonarola" Brown are both ridiculous, but they are both infinitely pathetic. Max wants you to laugh at them, but he also wants you to be sorry for them. It is otherwise with T. Fenning Dodworth; there he is exposing a humbug and the satire is persistent and merciless:

> There was an old-established daily newspaper whose proprietor had just died . . . Dodworth was installed in the editorial chair, gave the keynote to the staff, and wrote every night a leading article with his own incisive pen. . . . To uneducated readers the almost-daily-recurring phrase *Quos deus vult* had no meaning. Half-educated readers thought it meant "The Lord watch between thee and me when we are absent one from another". The circulation fell by leaps and bounds. . . . Within six months . . . that old-established newspaper ceased utterly to be. "This," I thought, "really *is* a set-back for Dodworth." I was far from right. The set-back was rather for myself. I received no payment for three or four of the book-reviews that I had contributed, and I paid two guineas for my share of the dinner offered to Dodworth at the Savoy Hotel. . . .

Irony was inherent in Max's writing, but in the period following the First World War a mellow benevolence replaces the
deliberately impish arrogance of the 1890s. Consider, for instance,
the essay entitled "Hosts and Guests." Light and cheerful in treatment, it is derived from an acute and accurate perception of the
varieties of social experience: "You ask me to dine with you in a
restaurant, I say I shall be delighted, you order the meal, I praise
it, you pay for it, I have the pleasant sensation of not paying for it."
What could be simpler or more fundamental than this candid
dichotomy? And how characteristic is Max's own apologia at the
end of the essay:

> I will not claim to have been a perfect guest. . . . I was a
> good one, but . . . I was rather *too* quiet, and I did sometimes
> contradict. And, though I always liked to be invited anywhere,
> I very often preferred to stay at home. If anyone hereafter shall
> form a collection of the notes written by me in reply to invi-
> tations, I am afraid he will gradually suppose me to have been
> . . . a great invalid, and a great traveller.

By the disruptions of war and the social changes which they
accelerated Max was profoundly saddened, as when, lingering
by the Golden Drugget, he paused "to bathe in the light that is as
the span of our human life, granted between one great darkness
and another". Sadness of a more intimate kind is the theme of
"William and Mary." Except for some light chaff of William in his
undergraduate days, there is no satire; its place is taken by a restrained
but profoundly sympathetic picture of human happiness and
human tragedy—*simplex tristitiis*. Sympathy, of a retrospective
kind, is also the keynote of "'A Clergyman,'" that superb reconstruction of a Boswellian scene in which Max immortalizes a
cleric whose name even Boswell did not trouble to record:

> Fragmentary, pale, momentary; almost nothing; glimpsed
> and gone . . . he forever haunts my memory and solicits
> my weak imagination. Nothing is told of him but that once,
> abruptly, he asked a question, and received an answer.

And having told the story of that question and answer, Max concludes:

"A Clergyman" never held up his head or smiled again after the brief encounter . . . He sank into a rapid decline. Before the next blossoming of Thrale Hall's almond trees he was no more. I like to think that he died forgiving Dr. Johnson.

Coming from a writer of "weak imagination," it is a notable essay. What, in fact, was the quality of Max's imagination? Here I recall his dramatic criteria—either convincing presentation of actuality or convincing transference to a world of fantasy. To the world of fantasy he could be easily drawn; he commended *The Prisoner of Zenda* for being frankly a fantasy, a story which made people feel not that it was credible but "how delightful it would be if such things *could* happen". But is this, in fact, true of the multitude of common readers who have been captivated by Anthony Hope's romance? There is nothing magical or miraculous at the bottom of Rudolf Rassendyll's adventure. The theme, as Anthony Hope said himself, is the ancient one of mistaken identity with royalty and red hair thrown in; and the common reader found no difficulty in believing in the close likeness between two distant kinsmen. But when Max turned from essays and parodies to the creation of a story of his own, he went further. Free of the shackles of credibility, he could wander into fairy-land and, in *The Happy Hypocrite*, could endow Lord George Hell's mask with the power of transforming the insolent and purple face of a Regency buck into that of a virtuous lover. Here, indeed, is a story that is "frankly a fantasy," but it is something very different from *The Prisoner of Zenda*.

For the scene of his most famous fantasy Max wandered not into fairy-land, but into Oxford—which for him, perhaps, was the same thing.

The story was begun while he was still in London, writing for the *Saturday Review*, but laid aside. In a letter to Will Rothenstein in the autumn of 1911 he wrote:

Zuleika will be with you anon. The proofs are flowing in, and the book will be out not later, I hope, than the first week in October. I am really very glad I found it impossible to go on writing the book in London years ago. I have developed since then; and the book wouldn't have had the quality it has now. It really is rather a beautiful piece of work—though it may be a dead failure in point of "sales"—and on the other hand might sell quite well: just a toss up. . . . If the binders and paper-makers don't play me false, the book will *look* nice; not like a beastly *novel,* more like a book of essays, self-respecting and sober and ample.

"More like a book of essays"—one recalls his earlier remark that he rated the essayist far higher than the romancer. Yet the subject demanded something more than a series of orderly essays. "Oxford!" he wrote, "The very sight of the word printed, or sound of it spoken, is fraught for me with most actual magic." So there must be a story (Oh dear, yes, a story, as Mr. Forster would say) and the story must not be trammelled by conventional probabilities; the magic must be allowed to work.

In a note to a new edition of the book in 1946 Max wrote: "I myself had supposed it was just a fantasy; and as such, I think, it should be regarded by others"; and those who enjoy fantasy for its own sake may well be happily carried along by the narrative as the pearls change colour and the Tankerton owls hoot and the Duke parades in the Meadows in his Garter robes and the undergraduates hurl themselves into the river for love of Zuleika. Less imaginative readers may, perhaps, grow a little weary of the ebb and flow of adoration and abuse between Zuleika and the Duke and of the Duke's meditations on the eternal verities; they prefer to re-read the descriptions of the many facets of the character of the heroine—the character, that is, not of Miss Dobson, but of Alma Mater Oxoniensis. What, for instance, is more Oxonian than that line of Roman Emperors who are commemorated in the first chapter of the book?

> Here in Oxford, exposed eternally and inexorably to heat and frost, to the four winds that lash them and the rains that wear them away, they are expiating, in effigy, the abominations of their pride and cruelty and lust. Who were lechers, they are without bodies; who were tyrants, they are crowned never but with crowns of snow; who made themselves even with the gods, they are by American visitors frequently mistaken for the Twelve Apostles.

There follows the brilliant sketch, in three pages, of the history of Judas College and, more intimately, the musings of a Merton man in the meadows:

There lay Oxford far beneath me, like a map in grey and black and silver. All that I had known only as great single things I saw now outspread in apposition and tiny; tiny symbols, as it were, of themselves, greatly symbolising their oneness. There they lay, these multitudinous and disparate quadrangles, all their rivalries merged in the making of a great catholic pattern. . . . But if a man carry his sense of proportion far enough, lo! he is back at the point from which he started. He knows that eternity, as conceived by him, is but an instant in eternity, and infinity but a speck in infinity. How should they belittle the things near to him? . . . Oxford was venerable and magical, after all, and enduring.

Max's criticism of Stevenson as a novelist is surely applicable in some measure to himself, for the reader of *Zuleika Dobson* is obsessed not by Miss Dobson, but by Max. Does not Zuleika confess that the literary flavour of her talk was an unfortunate trick she had caught from a writer, a Mr. Beerbohm, who had once sat next to her at dinner somewhere? In short, we read *Zuleika Dobson* as Johnson read the novels of Samuel Richardson, not for the story, but for the sentiment—and the satire.

This somewhat lukewarm appreciation of the fantasy on my part may indeed seem ungracious, since I owe the friendship which I was fortunate to enjoy with Max for the last twelve years of his life entirely to the last page of *Zuleika Dobson*. For years that final, imperious demand for a special train to Cambridge had worried me. Was the journey accomplished? I was not prepared to accept Mr. Forster's unsupported theory that the train was deflected into a siding at Bletchley. But if it did, in fact, reach its journey's end, into what maze of Cantabrigian fantasy did it lead? To nothing more serious, I conjectured, than to a special meeting of the Proctorial Syndicate. It was a proud and happy moment for me when Max told me that I had convinced him.[2]

III

In a volume of caricatures published in 1923 and entitled *Things New and Old* Max depicted himself drawing at a small desk outside his Villino. He has long white hair and an even longer white beard; he wears a small skull cap and clumsy carpet slippers. Three caricaturists of the younger generation are looking down on him and "wondering how long the veteran exile will go doddering on".

But Max never doddered. It is true that he gave up drawing in his later years because he found himself producing photographic likenesses and in photographic drawing he was not interested.[3] But, at intervals, he continued to write and at the end of 1935, when he was temporarily living in London, some far-sighted genius induced him to come to the microphone. It was the beginning of the Indian summer of an essayist. Lecturing and public speaking had never been among Max's *parerga* and, with the instinctive percipience of the artist, he realized at once that broadcasting did not mean reading an essay aloud; in fact, he was driven to invent a new word for his essays—"Narrowcasts." As he wrote in a prefatory note to a collection of his broadcasts, the pieces were composed for the ears of listeners and he trusted the inflexions of his voice to carry the finer shades of meaning and expression. It was a trust well placed. Thousands who had never heard of *The Yellow Book* or of the Duke of Dorset or of "Savonarola" Brown were enchanted by the precision, the humour, and the intimacy of the voice which told them what London had looked like forty years before; and for his friends it was like listening to him from the other side of the fireplace.

Two more broadcasts were delivered in 1936 and three more during the war years. "Music Halls of My Youth", spoken in his seventieth year, was remarkable in many ways and particularly in the way in which he entered into the spirit of his subject. Who that heard it can forget the beginning: "Ladies and Gentlemen, or—if you prefer that mode of address—G'deevning"? And when he went on to describe the songs of the Great MacDermott, the artist in him compelled him to give the music as well as the words. He couldn't sing, he said, but he gave what he called a croaking suggestion.

Meanwhile, many honours had come to him—knighthood, honorary doctorates, an honorary fellowship of his college. On such things Max had poured plenty of youthful scorn; but, as he wisely said, "After thirty one should quarrel with no man." One of his rare public lectures was given at Cambridge in 1943—the Rede Lecture on Lytton Strachey. It was rehearsed with scrupulous care and beautifully spoken. His sympathetic treatment of Strachey led him to make some characteristic remarks on the art of writing:

110

A true gift for writing . . . is not widely bestowed. Nor is a true gift for painting, or for playing the violin; and of that we are somehow aware. We do not say to a violinist "Just think out clearly what you want to express and then go straight ahead. Never mind how you handle your bow," nor to a painter, "Got your subject and your scheme of colour in your head all right, eh? Then don't bother about how you lay your paints on, dear old boy." Let us not make similar remarks to writers.

And then he returns to his old theme (*tamen usque recurret*) of the verbal preciosity which spoilt Stevenson as a novelist. But perhaps the most sympathetic reference was to Strachey's quotation of Talleyrand's remark that only those who had lived in France before the Revolution had really experienced *la douceur de vivre*. That was precisely what Max felt about pre-1914 England. Nevertheless, when the end of the Second War enabled him to return to Rapallo, life still retained a measure of sweetness for him. From time to time he was heard again on the air recalling memories of George Moore, or H. B. Irving, or William Morris, and presenting to his listeners a quiet but intensely vivid picture of their idiosyncrasies. At luncheon on his eightieth birthday (not in Rapallo, but in a small inn on the top of the mountain behind the town) he received many tributes which pleased and amused him: there was a sheaf of congratulatory telegrams which included Sir Winston Churchill's; there was a Penguin edition of *Zuleika Dobson* published for the occasion; there was a bound volume of tributes from his friends; and there was a gigantic and incongruous sheaf of gladioli (fashionably enclosed in cellophane) presented by the very small son of the innkeeper. In the lovely Italian sunshine Max was smiling and content. Three years later, though physically frail, he was still happy to welcome an old friend at the Villino and to talk about old times and modern trends.

On my last visit to him, about six months before his death, I happened to show him a proof-copy of a volume of memoirs by an old contributor to *The Yellow Book*. As I expected, he was interested in some passages relating to Edward VII. What I did not expect was his quick perception and correction of a serious mistake in dates which had escaped the proof-reader.

Qualis artifex periit—but I prefer to recall his own dying words and to thank him for everything.

[1957]

Sir Sydney Roberts

Notes

1. See *Max in Verse: Rhymes and Parodies by Max Beerbohm*, ed. J. G. Riewald (Brattleboro, Vermont: The Stephen Greene Press, 1963, and London: William Heinemann, 1964), pp. 118, 155.—*Editor's note.*

2. See S. C. Roberts, *Zuleika in Cambridge* (Cambridge: Heffer, 1941).—*Editor's note.*

3. But the abandonment was not complete. His last drawing (of George Moore) was done in January 1956, four months before his death. [*Editor's note:* the drawing is dated "1955" in Rupert Hart-Davis, comp., *A Catalogue of the Caricatures of Max Beerbohm* (London: Macmillan, and Cambridge, Mass.: Harvard University Press, 1972), No. 1057.]

Roy Huss

The Aesthete as Realist

I

The first real inkling of Beerbohm's thought about form in theatrical realism and its relation to impressionism and naturalism comes in his review of a book of criticism by Arthur Symons, Pater's devoted disciple. Against Pater's and Symons's view that life itself is one of the arts,[1] Beerbohm contended that since "life has no formal curves and harmonies, . . . it is not an art," and therefore Symons's idea "that it is, if you can but see it rightly," was an obvious mistake.[2] Of course for impressionists like Pater and Symons, to see life "rightly" meant to transform it by Pater's "imaginative reason." Likewise Zola, the naturalist, saw life as an art "if you can but see it rightly." But to see it rightly in this case was to see it as a demonstration of the natural laws already deduced about it by science. Significant form of some kind seems to be a necessity in both impressionistic and naturalistic art, but for the impressionist it is structure in the mind of the perceiver, whereas for the naturalist it is structure already inherent in the selected material.

Nevertheless, Beerbohm's aesthetics for realistic art is really closer to impressionism. This becomes clear when we recall his admission that most human affairs, even those of an entire era, could be seen as beautiful if viewed in the perspective of time.

From Roy Huss, "Max Beerbohm: Critic of the Edwardian Theatre," Diss. University of Chicago, Ill. 1959, pp. 25-36. Title of selection supplied by Author. Reprinted, with minor corrections and changes, by permission of Roy Huss.

Perhaps the candid "snap-shot" reveals too many extraneous details distorting the "formal curves and harmonies" of life, whereas the telescope of time not only passes over irrelevancies but insures the artist's emotional detachment—something akin to Wordsworth's "emotion recollected in tranquillity."[3] But an interval of time is in this way more important to the impressionistic artist, for its function is to allow him to create an original form or adapt a traditional one to convey his intended effect.

That both creative and conventional form are essential in Beerbohm's aesthetics for realism is shown by his dictum that in all the arts the artist's acute awareness of, and respect for, traditional form often prevents him from being a "duffer," although it seldom guarantees his being a genius. Mediocre artists have achieved success, he tells us, because they "worked arduously through established disciplines of conventional forms and techniques," whereas the genius is one who simply superimposes his genius on the conventions. Among contemporary artists, especially painters and actors, Beerbohm found that a freedom of choice of form and an attempt to be different marked many as "duffers" because of their lack of a guiding discipline in a formal tradition.[4] Only the genius could afford to "trust in the inspiration of the moment," but even such a person as this would be "in his wild career" creating "a rough but sufficing form."[5]

Beerbohm's continual quarrels with the naturalists for their artless lack of form show that he saw no virtues in naturalism. This is most vividly illustrated, perhaps, in his disparaging remarks on Maxim Gorki's *The Lower Depths*—a play which by its stark portrayal of poverty through sharp characterizations had won critical acclaim as a successful demonstration of Zola's creed.[6] The hostile remarks that Beerbohm leveled against the play revolve almost entirely about the question of dramatic form:

> . . . looseness of form is one thing [he wrote], formlessness is another. . . . There must be a story, though it need not be stuck to like grim death; or there must be, with similar reservation, an idea. Gorki has neither asset. At any rate he does nothing with either asset. . . . "The Lower Depths" . . . is chunks, hunks, shreds and gobbets [of life], clawed off anyhow, chucked at us anyhow. . . . This lack of any underlying idea would not matter if there were any narrative unity. An artist has the right to tell a story without any criticism of its meaning. The story itself produces that artistic

unity which, if there is no story, can be produced only by an underlying idea. . . . Gorki's work is to dramaturgy as snapshot photographs are to the art of painting.[7]

Since a continuum of true-to-life irrelevancies is no more than a series of "snap-shot photographs," one should not "put them together into a large gilt frame" that one uses "only for a large single painting."[8] Gorki's naturalism within the framework of a play therefore seemed to be completely artless.

The value of Beerbohm's attack upon Gorki for writing formless naturalistic plays is that it articulates the essence of his concept of dramatic structure. This is his requirement that a play have either a "narrative unity,"[9] based on rules of probability, climaxes, denouements, reversals, etc., or an "intellectual unity," made by the arrangement of ideas into an implicit theme or explicit argument. Order of this type is what makes form in art more significant than the accidental form or symmetry in nature.

One of the tests of Beerbohm's prescription for "narrative unity" and "intellectual unity" in realism was the vogue of the "inconclusive ending" in the dramas of the "slice of life" naturalists. In the play *Joy* by John Galsworthy—a playwright then rapidly becoming known as a master "representationalist" in the theatre— Beerbohm found the unfinished action to be artistically unsatisfactory. "Life is often very inconclusive, no doubt," he reminded his readers, "but art is not life, any more than painting is photography; and an artist must so use his materials that some significance is forthcoming for us; he must, implicitly, interpret as well as portray."[10] Conclusiveness of some sort was therefore a necessity for artistic unity. Detail must be arranged in such a way that even if the play did not have a logical terminus in action, the ending could be surmised.

To judge a play inconclusive solely on the basis of its incomplete "narration," however, might be a serious mistake. The apparently irrelevant incident upon which the curtain is brought down might in reality underline an idea or prevailing tone and thus give an "intellectual unity" to the play. Heijermans seemed to Beerbohm to offer this acceptable kind of ending in *A Case of Arson* when he made his last scene "fraught with that kind of relevant irrelevance of which Shakespeare knew so well the value—an inconclusive ending, and therefore a right ending, in that it leaves our imagination free and so holds our memory when all is over."[11]

Clearly Beerbohm's feeling that narrative unity marked the superiority of realism over slice-of-life naturalism in the theatre makes his conception of realistic art non-naturalistic. Moreover, his recognition of a second value in realism, that of intellectual unity, or theme,[12] is also alien to the naturalist's worship of the *a posteriori* idea "discovered" in experience.

II

As soon as Beerbohm insisted that the realist impose a structural unity upon his observations of life, he was in effect demanding that theatrical realism be responsible both to the beauty of form and the truth of actuality. In spite of his original pairing of these two as contraries, this was his ultimate wish. A double responsibility of this sort would force the playwright to imitate life in such a way as to foster a convincing illusion of actuality, and, at the same time, produce an aesthetic harmony of plot, character, and theme.

At first thought, the artifices in imaginative form might seem to jeopardize an illusion of life, since life itself is mostly formless. But Beerbohm had discovered that, far from being a threat to "realistic" illusion, "imitating" life in this way was actually essential to it. Any serious artist—whether sculptor, painter, or dramatist— who tried to mirror life more faithfully by attempting to overcome the limitations inherent in his medium or by ignoring certain traditions in execution committed the fatal error of destroying a sense of reality. In

> a serious form of art [Beerbohm wrote], . . . the aim is so to imitate life as to produce in the spectator an illusion of life. . . . *For its power to illude, an art depends on its limitations.* Art never can be life, but it may seem to be so if it do but keep far enough away from life. A statue may seem to live. A painting may seem to live. That is because each is so far away from life that you do not apply the test of life to it. A statue is of bronze or marble, than either of which nothing could be less flesh-like. A painting is a thing in two dimensions, whereas man is in three. If a sculptor or painter tried to dodge these conventions, his labour would be undone. If a painter swelled his canvas out and in according to the con-

vexities and concavities of his model, or if a sculptor over-laid his material with authentic flesh-tints, then you would demand that the painted or sculptured figure should blink, or stroke its chin, or kick its foot in the air. That it could do none of these things would rob it of all power to illude you. *An art that challenges life at close quarters is defeated through the simple fact that it is not life.*[13]

Once again Beerbohm was obliged to Pater for a significant precept in his aesthetics of realism. In an early essay on Madame Tussaud's wax-works museum, written before he became a dra-matic critic, he acknowledged a debt to Pater for showing him that art can come close to life only through conventions:

> . . . statuary, as Pater pointed out, in a pregnant (if rather uncouth) sentence, moves us to emotion, "not by accumu-lation of detail, but by abstracting from it." I think that wax-works fail, because they are not made within any of those "exquisite limitations" of colour, texture, proportion, to which all visual arts must be subjected. Life, save only through conventions, is inimitable. The more closely it be aped, the more futile and unreal its copy. . . . Good painting and good sculpture inspire us with some illusion, thus compensating us for what were otherwise the fatigue of gazing at them.[14]

Arthur Symons had echoed these same sentiments when he com-mented that "all art is a compromise, in which the choice of what is to be foregone must be left somewhat to the discretion of nature," that is, to the nature of the art-medium. This "kind of necessity in things" is what is being honored, Symons argued, "when the sculptor foregoes colour, when the painter foregoes relief, when the poet foregoes the music which soars beyond words and the musician that precise meaning which lies in words alone. . . ."[15] In a sense, Aristotle anticipated in his *Poetics* this same admonition against destroying the conventions of art by over-documentation when he drew a careful distinction between the object or action that art imitated and the *manner* and *means* of its imitation.[16]

An illustration of how Beerbohm's dramatic criticism reflects the principle that the intelligent use of conventional form serves both "truth" and "beauty" in realistic drama is shown in his de-fense of the anti-climax. In answer to the pedestrian view of some of his colleagues that an anti-climax blunts a play's emotional effect, he argued that the diminuendo of an anti-climax was needed both to give symmetry to the piece's crescendo beginning and to simulate the "well-rounded life of a human creature."[17] Another of its purposes was to transpose the audience gradually back to the real world from the play's illusory one; in short, it brought the audience's empathy into a balanced "relation with the mimic world. . . : Hamlet is dead, but he was only one of many men in that world. . . ."[18] Finally, Beerbohm justified the anti-climax on the basis of its service to narrative unity. It became important to the "unraveling" or final exposition,

> where the highest point in a play is not a death, but some great situation, portending great consequences [which] you must know. . . . In most of the serious modern plays the highest point is a situation of this kind—a catastrophe to be made the best of. And this scene comes usually at the end of the third act. Thus the fourth act must be one long anti-climax.[19]

When we re-examine Beerbohm's three rationalizations of the anti-climax, we see that as a formal element it offers both beauty and truth. First, as a link between the play's illusion and the audience's reality it is artistry; second, as an explanation of subsequent dramatic action it is logical necessity; and finally, as an imitation of a "well-rounded life," symmetrical by nature, it is both grace and precision. All three of these defenses amply demonstrate Beerbohm's idea that traditional form in drama may foster both beauty and truth simultaneously.

Even the most basic component of a play—the style of its diction—could be made to fulfill this double allegiance. One of the most obvious aims of dialogue in realistic drama is to achieve an impression of ordinary conversation. Naturally the playwright cannot directly reveal his own individual style and tone in speech because the objectivity of the dramatic method precludes the obtrusion of his personality. An unconscious attempt to transcend this limitation of the play-form was the reason Beerbohm felt Henry James to be a failure in the theatre, for James's over-refinement of dialogue was really the highly individualized style of the essayist. Although the personal style that came into James's novels was only "a trifle disconcerting," in a play it reduced the language spoken by actors to "mere gibberish."[20]

As far as the aim of dramatic dialogue is to suggest colloquial speech, there is no problem. Since the image of the spoken word for the stage is the spoken word itself (unlike the novel which must use the written phrase to suggest oral speech) the Beerbohm-Pater rule for imitation has no relevance. That is, drama does not have to depend on conventions to approach the intonations of real speech. But if diction is to be a part of the formal beauty, as well as of the representational truth of a play, style had to accomplish this. Of what can dramatic style be constituted, since it is to be neither an unrealistic over-refinement nor an unattractive literal transcription?

Skillful compression of actual speech was the only means Beerbohm could suggest to the realistic dramatist for creating dialogue that is both natural and pleasurable. "Dialogue spoken on the stage must be composed in a natural and un-literary manner," he wrote in his article " 'Style' and the Stage," and added, "Style, in dialogue, is thus a matter of compression from real life, of translation never."[21] What Beerbohm really meant by this compression became clear later in 1909 when he scrutinized the dialogue in the dramas of three of the most prominent English playwrights of the time—Alfred Sutro, Henry Arthur Jones, and George Bernard Shaw. Since diction is the most elemental aspect of literary structure, Beerbohm had made stylistic analysis one of his ultimate tests for determining a dramatist's success as a realist. He said of Sutro, Jones, and Shaw:

> Human speech, for dramatic purposes, must be abridged and sharpened, all the time; and yet we must be kept unaware of the process. In the art of writing seemingly natural and actually telling dialogue Mr. Sutro is, with Mr. Henry Arthur Jones, foremost among our playwrights. Mr. Shaw has an ear for the rhythm of human speech; his characters never talk like books; but there is always something noticeably metallic about the concision of their utterance. Except when Mr. Shaw determines to show us that he can achieve beauty with the best of 'em—as in the long speech made by the mystic priest at the close of "John Bull's Other Island"—there is no charm of rhythm in his dialogue. Mr. Sutro never sets out to display beauty of word and cadence. But he is a constant purveyor of it.[22]

Unfortunately, Sir Arthur Wing Pinero, often thought to be the best playwright of the period, employed a kind of dialogue which seemed to Beerbohm (as well as to the critics A. B. Walkley and Arthur Symons[23]) to be so stilted and pseudo-literary as to contribute neither to beauty nor truth. In a review of *Letty* Beerbohm burlesqued the verbosity of Pinero's "literary" style, describing it as "nothing but the lowest and most piteous kind of journalese.[24]

Surprisingly enough, Beerbohm found that the playwright who surpassed most of the veteran dramatists in creating charming rhythmic diction, while at the same time preserving the quality of actual speech, was Mrs. Humphry Ward. Although a tyro in the theatre, she seemed to be "one of the few persons who have solved the secret of what dialogue ought to be." Her advantage "over the ordinary playwright [is] that she gives to her dialogue a careful beauty of phrase and cadence." On the other hand, her triumph "over the extraordinary playwright—the literary amateur [is] that her dialogue sounds (though it is not) like the ordinary language of real human beings."[25] Although in the perspective of literary history it is hard to regard Mrs. Humphry Ward as a significant contributor to English drama, Beerbohm was able to distill from her work the essential ingredients of style for theatrical realism: the simple communication that conveys the logic of both plot and theme, the unembellished naturalness that maintains an illusion of life, and, finally, the graceful rhythm (achieved by compression) that satisfies the artistic demand for formal beauty.

[1959]

Notes

1. Evidence for Pater's concept of life as occasionally achieving the perfect form of art can be found in numerous places, but chiefly in his Conclusion to *The Renaissance* (New York: The Modern Library, n. d.), pp. 196-7. Arthur Symons seconds this view: ". . . Life too is a form of art, and the visible world the chief storehouse of beauty. . . . ," Preface to *Plays, Acting and Music* (London: Duckworth and Co., 1903), p. i.

2. "An Aesthetic Book," *Around Theatres* (London: Rupert Hart-Davis, 1953), p. 275.

3. Beerbohm had, in fact, endorsed Wordsworth's theory that art, as well as

criticism, should be the result of "emotion remembered in tranquillity." See *Around Theatres*, ed. cit., p. 472.

4. "Comfort for the Academic," *Last Theatres: 1904-1910* (London: Rupert Hart-Davis, 1970), pp. 266-269.

5. *Lytton Strachey* (Cambridge: The University Press, 1943), p. 15.

6. See "Naturalism," *The Oxford Companion to the Theatre*, ed. Phyllis Hart-noll (London: Oxford University Press, 1951) pp. 564-65.

7. " 'The Lower Depths,' " *Around Theatres*, ed. cit., pp. 303-305.

8. Ibid., p. 305. As we know, Gorki's play makes some pretense at intellectual unity by introducing the character Luka as mouthpiece for Gorki's own philosophy that life ought to be based on mutual respect between men and that belief in something, whether true or not, is essential. But Beerbohm, as well as successive critics like Martin Lamm (see his *Modern Drama*, trans. Karin Elliott, Oxford: Basil Blackwell, 1952, p. 218), have realized the all too obvious fact that what Beerbohm calls the "vague sentimental optimism" of Luka is superimposed. In fact the persons of the play remain totally unaffected by the temporary intrusion of this fragment of sentimental rationalizing. Such a philosophy is not only irrelevant to, but weakens, the apparent aim of naturalism—to show the characters as victims of a "mechanistic," but faulty, social determinism.

9. Strictly speaking drama does not, of course, use the narrative method, but in Beerbohm's sense "narrative unity" refers to the organization of the story which the author "wants to tell" into a plot, and therefore applies equally to drama and fiction.

10. "At the Savoy Theatre," *Last Theatres*, p. 326.

11. "Mr. De Vries's Performance," *Last Theatres*, p. 147

12. For a discussion of Beerbohm's views on intellectual unity in theatrical realism, particularly in relation to the plays of George Bernard Shaw, see my article "Max the 'Incomparable' on G. B. S. the 'Irrepressible'," *The Shaw Review*, 5 (January 1962), 10-20.

13. " 'The Ragged Regiment,' " *Yet Again* (New York: Alfred Knopf, 1928), pp. 229-230. (Italics mine.) Edwin Muir in his *The Structure of the Novel* (London: The Hogarth Press, 1954), pp. 62-87, carries this concept one step further. He speaks of novelists like Emily Bronte, purposely and effectively sacrificing the customary detailed account of the passage of time, in order to give the reader a sense of the "dimension" of eternity.

14. "Madame Tussaud's," *More* (London: John Lane, The Bodley Head, 1899), p. 42.

Failure to observe this principle was also Beerbohm's explanation for why modern prose was not capturing the sense of the colloquial it was struggling to achieve: "Modern prose style," he wrote, "is further removed from colloquialism than was the prose style of the eighteenth century, for this paradoxical reason: that colloquialism is [now] its model." What this meant, Beerbohm explained, was that since in print the gestures and tone of speech or a personal calligraphy are absent, a literary style, to seem colloquial, must substitute devices far removed from speech. Thus artificial conventions are more effective than exact documentation.— " 'Style' and the Stage," *More Theatres: 1898-1903* (London: Rupert Hart-Davis, 1969), p. 307.

15. *Plays, Acting and Music*, p. 18.

16. *Poetics* 1447a-1447b.

17. "Last Acts," *Around Theatres*, ed. cit., p. 102.

18. Ibid., pp. 102-103.

19. Ibid., pp. 103-104.

20. " 'Style' and the Stage," *More Theatres*, p. 307. In determining style to be the basis of the failure of *Guy Domville*, Beerbohm differs from Shaw, who placed the blame on the audience's inability to appreciate James's delineation of characters as persons whose "passion is subordinate to intellect and to fastidious artistic taste." (Shaw, *Dramatic Opinions*, New York: Brentano's, 1907, I, p. 8).

21. *More Theatres*, pp. 307-308.

22. " 'The Making of a Gentleman,' " *Last Theatres*, p. 488.

23. See A. B. Walkley, *Drama and Life* (New York: Brentano's, 1908), pp. 182-184, and Arthur Symons, *Plays, Acting and Music*, p. 54.

24. "Mr. Pinero's Literary Style," *Around Theatres*, pp. 286, 289.

25. "Mrs. Humphry Ward's Play," *More Theatres*, p. 505.

S. N. Behrman

THE SILVER THREAD OF LUNACY

After we had listened to the Caine record, Max talked a bit about
what is a perennial literary phenomenon—the vast discrepancy between writers who attain popular success and are anathema to the
cognoscenti and those who are approved by the cognoscenti and
have no public at all. In his youth, Max said, the great popular
successes were Marie Corelli, "Ouida," Mrs. Humphry Ward, and
Hall Caine. At the parties he used to go to, he said, you could get a
laugh just by *saying* "Hall Caine."

Max then went on to discuss other members of the Rossetti Circle.
It was characteristic of Max that in speaking of the Rossetti Circle
he should tell me he admired Dante Gabriel's sensible brother William Michael and, of the ladies—that is, the models employed by
the Pre-Raphaelites—preferred the healthy Fanny Cornforth to
the doomed Elizabeth Siddal. It must have been hard work for the
Pre-Raphaelites to be constantly ethereal, and Miss Cornforth was
bosomy and earthy. She afforded the Pre-Raphaelites a nice change
from Pre-Raphaelitism; she was Rubensy. In the mid-thirties,
Max had received from Sydney Cockerell several photographs of
the Rossetti brothers, Swinburne, and Miss Cornforth. Cockerell
had at that time just bought three drawings of Max's for the Fitzwilliam Museum, which he directed, and Max wrote, in acknowledgment of both benefactions:

From S. N. Behrman, *Portrait of Max: An Intimate Memoir of Sir Max Beerbohm*
(New York: Random House, 1960), pp. 275-284. Originally published in *The New
Yorker*, 6 February-19 March 1960. Published in England under the title *Conversation
with Max* (London: Hamish Hamilton, 1960). Title of selection supplied by Editor.
Copyright ©1960 by S. N. Behrman. Reprinted by permission of Random House, Inc.

S. N. Behrman

DEAR MR. COCKERELL,
It is a grand thing to be represented in the Fitzwilliam; and I
am so glad that this honour is to befall me, and glad that I have
been deemed worthy of it by you. . . .
Meanwhile I return, with very many thanks for the joy they
have given me, those wondrous little photographs. Miss Cornforth is incredible. Credo accordingly—and indeed am but confirmed in a belief I already had—that she must have been just
like that and almost like what (reading between the lines of
D. G. R.'s presentments of her) I had made of her in one of those
cartoons of which you were speaking in such kind terms the
other day. William Michael is decidedly the most distinguished
in aspect of the figures in that group of four. You and I were
arguing, in Nicholson's studio, that William Michael had
been underrated because he happened to be the one (super-
ficially) dull man in a bevy of brilliant ones. Perhaps a time will
come when he will be *over*rated, as having been the one sane
man among lunatics!—for there was, wasn't there? a silver
thread of lunacy in the rich golden fabric of 16 Cheyne Walk.

In a drawing of Hall Caine in *Rossetti and His Circle,* Max rep-
resents the time when Caine was living with Rossetti. Theodore
Watts-Dunton, the chronic caretaker of genius, is admonishing
Caine, who is truculent. They are in the studio at 16 Cheyne Walk,
Caine red-headed, red-mustached, red-goateed, and with a fanatical
gleam in his eye—the gleam of a man who knows that he carries
greatness in each hand, in the shape of two manuscripts of his own,
which he is determined to read to Rossetti. He is, plainly, not going
to take the advice that Watts-Dunton is offering him. Frederick
Shields, a painter friend of Rossetti's, is standing near Watts-Dunton,
backing him up. In the background, lying-sitting on a sofa, is
Rossetti, corpulent, brooding, hearing the argument that concerns
him but not listening. The caricature is called "Quis Custodiet
Ipsum Custodem?" and Max's caption reads:

THEODORE WATTS [-DUNTON]: "Mr. Caine, a word with you!
Shields and I have been talking matters over, and we are agreed
that to-night and henceforth you *must* not and *shall* not read any
more of your literary efforts to our friend. They are too—what
shall I say?—too luridly arresting, and are the allies of insomnia."

In another caricature in *Rossetti and His Circle,* Max shows Rossetti embarked on an exciting project for a set of murals in the Oxford

Union—"The Quest for the Holy Grail." Rossetti, in brown smock and trousers, has one foot on a ladder, on his way to put the finishing touch on a symbolic Miss Siddal, who, with outstretched arms, is ready, presumably, to receive the find. Benjamin Jowett, a little man in a flat hat, is standing at the foot of the ladder. Max's caption is:

THE SOLE REMARK LIKELY TO HAVE BEEN MADE BY BENJAMIN JOWETT ABOUT THE MURAL PAINTINGS AT THE OXFORD UNION.
"And what were they going to do with the Grail when they found it, Mr. Rossetti?"

It was in the winter of 1917 that Max, re-creating a vanished milieu that he had never known first-hand, drew the caricatures for *Rossetti and His Circle*, while staying in a rented cottage at Far Oakridge, in Gloucestershire, near the home of William Rothenstein. The Beerbohms took their meals with the Rothensteins. To Rothenstein, who worshipped Giotto, Max once sent a sketch he had made of the Rothenstein family. He apologizes for what his sketch may make various members of the family suffer. "But," he goes on to say, "there is in the whole design a sense of a *family*, I think—something spiritually real, though not up to the mark or our old friend Giotto—(I say *our* old friend, because I regard any friend of yours as a friend of mine)." Sir William describes in his memoirs how Max, wearing gloves and with a cane over one arm, used to walk over the snow carrying the Rossetti drawings carefully protected in a portfolio. "No wonder Max was nervous of leaving his Rossetti caricatures in an empty cottage," he writes, "for they are now regarded as classics. What a remarkable reconstruction of a period! So intuitively truthful, that one of William Michael's daughters wrote that no person living within their circle had given so accurate a picture of its physical and spiritual composition. Max, with his air of delicate sprightliness, is the profoundest critic of men I have known."

As Max saw things, the silver thread of lunacy that wound through 16 Cheyne Walk also wound through the lives of many of his friends and acquaintances. From the Rossetti Circle, we went on to talk about D. H. Lawrence. Max leaned forward a bit in his chair. "Oh,

Lawrence," he said. *"Poor* D. H. Lawrence!" The adjective was not uttered in condescension but in true sympathy for the afflicted. "Poor D. H. Lawrence. He never realized, don't you know—he never suspected that to be stark, staring mad is somewhat of a handicap to a writer."

I told Max that I had been tremendously moved by *Sons and Lovers* when I first read it, and that I had tried two later novels, which I couldn't read.

"Oh, of course," Max said. *"Sons and Lovers!* Although his prose style was slovenly, he was a man of unquestionable genius. But then he became afflicted with Messiahdom, don't you know. Now, what equipment had poor D. H. Lawrence for Messiahdom? He was, in so many ways, a foolish man. He was not fastidious in his friendships. Anyone who took him for a great man he would welcome. He did not stop to question, don't you know, what other qualifications a person had. Anyone who would commune with him on Destiny"—Max capitalized the word with his voice—"he would welcome. As a result, he was always involved with quite inferior people. He was one of those unfortunate men who think that merely because they have done something, it is at once first-rate. Simply because *they* have done it. He had a glowing gift for nature, a real feeling for nature, and in this he was at his best. But through his landscapes cantered hallucinations."

About the other Lawrence, T. E., the Arabian one, Max said he couldn't talk much, because in that Lawrence the mixture of genius and insanity was too heady for him to do more than sample it. Lawrence had translated the *Odyssey* and then denounced it, as "pastiche and face powder." "He confused the *Odyssey*, you know, with his translation of it," Max said to me. About Lawrence's translation of the *Odyssey*, Max once wrote Rothenstein:

> What a strange thing, to be a super-eminent genius and hero, as Lawrence was, plus such streaks of sheer silliness. . . . I have read various extracts from that translation—read them with gasps. And I would rather not have been that translator than have driven the Turks out of Arabia.

Tracing the silver thread led Max to Ezra Pound. Pound had lived for a time in Rapallo, and Max used to see him. He laughed in recollection of one of those meetings. "Ezra idolized his parents, you know, and they idolized him," Max said. "They thought the sun rose and set in him. They came from Idaho. He brought them here, and very nice, simple, unaffected people they were, too. Anyway, one afternoon we were all sitting down there on the terrace of one of the cafés"—Max waved a hand toward downtown Rapallo and the sea front—"and Ezra was talking away. Very entertaining! He was fond of making extravagant statements to amuse his friends, which, of course, he didn't expect them to take seriously. He was in one of those moods. His parents were staring at him, rapt, while he made these utterances. Ezra said, 'The greatest master of French literature was Louis the Eighteenth.' Ezra's father, who was sitting next to me, nudged me and beamed at me. 'That kid,' he said, 'knows *everything!*' "

I told Max that I had been shown an anti-Semitic poem written by Pound against him. In it the spelling of Max's name was distorted. Max was interested, and not at all surprised. "I am not Jewish," he said. "I cannot claim that. But then, you know, he is crazy. He greatly admired Mussolini. All that Fascist business! He did have one trait, though, that I didn't much care for." Evidently, Max expected crazy people, outside of their craziness, to live up to some code of gentlemanliness. "He would start out to rave about some friend, and you thought you were in for a paean of praise. And then the qualifications would creep in. And then you realized that he had begun with the paean in order to conclude with the denigration. The treacle of admiration, don't you know, was always strongly tinctured with the vinegar of envy."

Max distinguished between people he considered all-out cranks and lunatics and those who were simply idiosyncratic. In his introduction to *Rossetti and His Circle*, he wrote:

> Byron, Disraeli, and Rossetti—these seem to me the three most interesting men that England had in the nineteenth century. England had plenty of greater men. Shelley, for example, was a far finer poet than Byron. But he was not in himself interesting: he was just a crystal-clear crank. To be interesting, a man must be complex and elusive.

On this ground, Max found neither Pound nor D. H. Lawrence interesting. Two complex men·Max greatly admired as writers and liked as friends were G. K. Chesterton and Hilaire Belloc. "They had blind spots," he said, "but they were delightful men. Such enormous gusto, you know, such gaiety, and feeling for life." Max was merely amused by people who had blind spots. Sometimes, when he mentioned a blind spot in conversation, he would tap his forehead to indicate it. Max conveyed the idea that Chesterton and Belloc were men whose minds were vast and hospitable houses, with little dark closets in the attic into which—there were so many other rooms, gay and sunny—you didn't have to go. Robert Speaight, in a biography of Belloc, quotes Max as saying to his hero, "When you really get talking, Hilary, you're like a great Bellocking ram, or like a Roman river full of baskets and dead cats." Speaight also repeats a dry observation of Max's when he was told that Belloc had been to a cricket match: "I suppose he would have said that the only good wicket-keeper in the history of the game was a Frenchman and a Roman Catholic." Max told me he felt that Belloc was, on occasion, a victim of monomania. "He had the conviction that there was only a single lane to Heaven," Max said. "It suited him, for example, to believe that Dreyfus was guilty. Ergo"—Max tapped his forehead—"Dreyfus *was* guilty."

Somerset Maugham, in a series of articles on ten great novelists he wrote some years ago for the London *Sunday Times,* made the flat statement that Balzac was the only one of them to whom he would without hesitation ascribe genius. Commenting on this, Max told me that he thought it was absurd to single out Balzac. "Tolstoy and Dostoevski had great genius," he said, "and Dickens had it, too, in spite of his dreadful faults." Nevertheless, except for Turgenev and, at times, Tolstoy, Max had serious doubts about the Russian novelists. He felt that too much of what they wrote was also touched by lunacy. He knew that Dostoevski was terrifying, and even majestic, but then so was Mont Blanc, and Max wouldn't have liked to live on Mont Blanc. In 1913, Max wrote an essay, "Kolniyatsch," in which he lampooned the vogue for the Russian novelists among the British intelligentsia. Kolniyatsch (the word is a Russification of Colney Hatch, which was once London's most famous lunatic asylum) is a Russian writer— a composite of Dostoevski and Gorki. Kolniyatsch, says Max, developed slowly: "It was not before his eighteenth birthday that he murdered his grandmother and was sent to that asylum in which he wrote the poems and plays belonging to what we now call his earlier manner." Was Kolniyatsch an optimist or a pessimist? Max analyzes:

By more than one critic he has been called a pessimist, and it is true that a part of his achievement may be gauged by the lengths to which he carried pessimism—railing and raging, not, in the manner of his tame forerunners, merely at things in general, or at women, or at himself, but lavishing an equally fierce scorn and hatred on children, on trees and flowers and the moon, and indeed on everything that the sentimentalists have endeavoured to force into favour. On the other hand, his burning faith in a personal Devil, his frank delight in earthquakes and pestilences, and his belief that every one but himself will be brought back to life in time to be frozen to death in the next glacial epoch, seem rather to stamp him as an optimist.

Max's great enthusiasms in literature were for Jane Austen, Trollope, Turgenev, George Meredith, Charles Lamb, Henry James, E. M. Forster. He adored Meredith's early manner—*The Adventures of Harry Richmond* particularly—and Henry James's later. *The Golden Bowl* and *The Wings of the Dove* were, Max thought, James's greatest achievements. These writers had no chalets on Mont Blanc, but they took him into realms where he did want to live. Max was on especially good terms with Trollope. "He reminds us," said Max, "that sanity need not be Philistine." Max told me he thought *The Warden* a perfect novel, and the cello-playing Mr. Harding was one of his favorite musicians, especially when he was playing a cello he didn't have with him. The literature of epilepsy, of cosmic soul-searching, of uncontrollable violence simply had no appeal for him. About the Elizabethans he felt something of what he felt about the Russians. In a Rede Lecture he gave at Cambridge, in which he paid tribute to Lytton Strachey, the only reservation he made was about Strachey's *Elizabeth and Essex*. He said that it was a "brave" thing for Strachey to have tried but that, at best, it was only "guesswork." To Max, that far-off world, where murders, sudden decapitations, rushings off to the Tower were part of the climate, as natural as April showers, was incomprehensible and unseizable, and he felt that it must have been so to Strachey also, who was a master of style, and hence of form. He said, "A very robustious, slapdash writer might convince me that he was in close touch with the souls of those beings whose actions and motives are to me as mysterious as those of wild animals in an impenetrable jungle. You rightly infer that I am *not* a Sixteenth Century man. And I make so bold as to say 'Neither was Lytton Strachey.' "

Max shied away from lunacy not only in its violent forms but also in its milder forms, one of these being utopianism. "Good sense about trivialities is better than nonsense about things that matter," he once said. He had a horror of utopians, a suspicion of "big" ideas. Some of Shaw's writings bored him because they were impressments into what he called "the strait jacket of panacea." The effort to force men into this strait jacket had caused untold misery and suffering to the human race, he thought. Rothenstein once said of Max that he was always amiable except when his sense of sanity was outraged. For Max, even to take oneself entirely seriously was a form of insanity. Listening to Max on the subject, I came to see that what for him constituted sanity was a recognition of one's own limitations. He had—without ever formulating it—a Theory of Limits. Max countered Browning's "Ah, but a man's reach should exceed his grasp, Or what's a heaven for?" with the statement that many of his friends had gone to hell in just that way. Max liked the attainable, the tangible, the comprehensible, the small in scale.

[1960]

Katherine Lyon Mix

MAX ON SHAW

Of all the men with whom Sir Max Beerbohm was associated during his eighty-five years, no one more persistently occupied his mind than his predecessor on the *Saturday Review*, Bernard Shaw.[1] When Shaw relinquished his post as dramatic critic to the "incomparable Max," thereby bestowing an epithet from which Max never escaped, he became inextricably enmeshed in Beerbohm's consciousness. "What's that man doing now?" was his perpetual, if unspoken query. He answered it publicly in the *Saturday* when he criticized the playwright and author, but privately in conversations and letters, as he passed judgment on the man.

He used Shaw more frequently in caricatures than anyone else and a collection of these drawings would present a recognizable record of Shaw's career. One however would not be available for exhibit, as Mrs. Shaw had destroyed it. "Max once did a thing of me in which I looked slightly tipsy," Shaw told Hesketh Pearson. "She bought it at the exhibition and tore it up in front of his face."

Another projected drawing Max apparently never carried out. When Sir Charles Holmes was Director of the National Gallery in 1909, Max came to see him seeking likenesses of the trustees. He planned to show them, as after Shaw's death they examined stack after stack of portraits in every conceivable pose and medium, trying to choose the one to be hung in the Gallery.[2] Shaw's amiability in sitting for photographs or posing for portraits or busts, Max interpreted as egotism and vanity. When he learned in 1914 that Shaw

---

Katherine Lyon Mix, "Max on Shaw," *The Shaw Review*, 6 (September 1963), 100-104. Reprinted by permission of Katherine Lyon Mix and the Editor of *The Shaw Review*.

131

had allowed an effigy of himself to be placed in Madame Tussaud's, he was appalled, and when Shaw explained that it would have seemed snobbish to refuse, Max sensed his secret pride. Max once gave his inventive pencil full play over many of the Shaw portraits, when he altered and amended a copy of the 1911 edition of Henderson's *Shaw* for the benefit of William Archer. This unique volume may now be seen in the Berg Collection of the New York Public Library.

A sentence in Max's first article as dramatic critic of the *Saturday Review* indicated what was to be his perpetual attitude toward Shaw. "With all his faults, grave though they are and not to be counted on the fingers of one hand—he is I think, by far the most brilliant and remarkable journalist in London."[3] This paradoxical pattern varied little over the years; praise mingled with censure, or disapproval veiled in commendation. On Shaw's ninetieth birthday he wrote that "my admiration for his genius has during fifty years and more been marred for me by dissent from almost any view that he holds about anything."[4] Max admitted that his "vicissitudes in the matter of G. B. S. were lamentable."[5] Small wonder Shaw complained that all Max's blessings were "thinly disguised curses."[6]

This ambivalent point of view is nowhere better demonstrated than in a "Note" Max wrote on Shaw for Rothenstein's *English Portraits*. Rothenstein explained that since he had asked his subjects to sit for him, he could not subject them to unflattering criticism nor sugary praise, and therefore he had to reject some contributed comments.[7] Max on Shaw was one of them. He had said:

> Dramatic-musical-literary-art critic, orator-lecturer, pamphleteer, Fabian-Saturday Reviewer, vegetarian-Hibernian, cyclist-anti-tobacconist, abstainer-aesthete, atheist-churchgoer and vestryman-dramatist, Mr. Shaw is a jewel of many facets. He is, indeed, rather too complex to be taken seriously by the public (for which, being a good Socialist, he has a profound contempt) and he is likely to remain as he has ever been, a mystery-man with a big drum, and an egoist who might himself be puzzled to say exactly where his sterling affections end and his frivolous convictions begin. It is in dramatic criticism that he has loomed largest, hitherto. As Henri Rochefort to the ministers of France, so is "G. B. S." to the London managers. But for all his pugnacity and *intransigeance*, his brogue keeps him from being disliked in private, and his keen humour from being a bore

in public. [Interposed:] He contradicts and jibes at no one more than himself, and if his judgments are often scatterbrained, he has, at any rate, brains to scatter.[8]

Riewald has suggested that Max found in Shaw qualities which were lacking in himself.[9] But whatever lay behind his summing-up of Shaw's character, the debits and credits are clear. He disliked Shaw's vegetarianism, his abstinence, his Socialism, his didacticism, his vanity, his rationalizations, and his lack of sensitivity. Conversely he admired his integrity and fairness, his generosity to lesser colleagues, and his intellect, or as Max put it, "that exquisite machine, his brain."[10]

Max considered Shaw's treatment of Mark Twain on one occasion as evidence of this lack of sensitivity. Both Alan Dent[11] and S. N. Behrman[12] have recorded this incident. In 1907, according to Professor Archibald Henderson, the Shaws were entertaining at luncheon for the American humorist, who had been introduced to them by Henderson. Max was among the guests. As soon as the meal was over, Shaw hurried away to keep a dental appointment. Mr. Clemens's displeasure must have been evident, for Henderson, though not mentioning Shaw's departure, says Clemens paced up and down like a caged lion, waiting for his cab.[13] Max was much distressed by the lack of reverence for a renowned visitor. Perhaps a shade of Clemens's discomfort is evident in the cartoon Max made of him and presented to Shaw, who in turn gave it to his secretary, Miss Patch.[14]

Max was frequently entertained at the Shaws' and he was genuinely fond of Mrs. Shaw. After his marriage and his departure for Italy, he wrote Mrs. Shaw that as soon as they again visited London, "I will write to warn you and Mr. Shaw that we stand waiting hand in hand for an invitation to lunch with you."[15]

Shaw's attitude about the First World War was as distasteful to Max as it was to many other members of the Dramatists' Club. The playwright Henry Arthur Jones was particularly enraged at Shaw's pacificism and he kept up an unremitting attack on his one-time friend. Later Max tried to make peace between them, asking Jones to "shake hands with the Demon," but though Shaw, yielding to Max's importuning, wrote to Jones, there was no reply. "It's very queer," Max told Jones in 1926, "that a man should be so gifted as he is (in his own particular way nobody has been so gifted I think, since Voltaire) and so liable to make a fool of himself. I have never read anything of his without wishing he had never been born *and* hoping he will live to a very ripe old age. One of the reasons is that he . . . is entirely free from any kind of malice. That is one of his great points."[16]

Three years later, when John Galsworthy received the O. M., Max commented to Will Rothenstein that it was exactly right, for "neither Shaw nor Wells, the only other two men worthy would have been suitable. Wells is a Republican and wouldn't have accepted the gaud. Shaw is really too irresponsible in his public utterances and seems to grow more and more so. I dare say he would have accepted, on some principle of his own. But he would certainly have made a point of guying the whole thing to the first interviewer who came along."[17]

Max was well aware of Shaw's kindness to some of their less successful literary colleagues, of his generosity to John Davidson and his assistance to the discredited Frank Harris. Once, however, when Max tried to appreciate Shaw's altruism, the result was unfortunate. At a dinner party at the Nicholsons shortly after the First World War, someone raised the matter of an attack on Shaw by one of the younger writers. W. H. Davies, Poet and Super-Tramp, defended Shaw, saying the man should not have written so about a person much greater than he and old enough to be his father. Max, who had not read the article, asserted that age should make no difference in criticism. When the meal was over, he approached Davies, asking, "How long is it since Shaw discovered you?" Davies felt something derogatory in the question, but answered as calmly as he could that it had been thirteen or fourteen years. "Shaw," began Max, hesitating and stammering—"Shaw at once saw that you were—a real poet; and of course—he being a decent fellow—like a good many more—just lent a hand—the same as most people— would have done—and—helped a lame dog over the stile."[18] This Davies took as a blow beneath the belt, for he was physically lame. Years later Max learned of his disastrous choice of metaphors; he had not known of Davies's lameness, he said, and he apologized in the *Times*.[19]

Shaw's membership in the Fabians and his personal concern for money, Max considered anomalous. In 1932 the theatre critic James Agate, preparing an anthology of dramatic criticism, told Max he would like to reprint two of his *Saturday Review* articles. He also planned to include something from Shaw. Max gave his permission, but wrote, "I can imagine that G. B. S. has been very thorough with his homemade contracts etc. Such things are to him as her dolls to a little girl. But the fact remains that he is an old man and ought to be making his soul. I am making mine; but as no publisher can step in to do business in this instance, I suppose I better say . . . that a fee of £5 would keep me quiet and happy." Then it transpired that Shaw insisted all contributors should fall in line with him and donate any profit to the Society of Authors. To this Max retorted, "I flatly refuse to let G. B. S. meddle in my private affairs, illustrious and well meaning though he is," but on second thought, Max feared he had been grasping; "hence the cancellisation (lovely word) of my demand." Now he asked to be paid as the rest, or rather to be credited with the same sum. "Do you please, intercept the actual cash and go with it straight out into the street and give it to the first man or woman or child (1) whom you like the look of and (2) whom you think hard up and likely to be pleased and grateful. And say to him or her or it, 'This comes to you from a non-Fabian being.' " If Agate wouldn't do this and report the transaction to Shaw, he couldn't have Max's review. Max added in a postscript that Shaw would be shocked and that was just what he wanted. Agate demurred that he couldn't do this until he had Shaw's article. For the moment he would let sleeping dogs lie. Max agreed. "Or rather, as I would more specifically and diagnostically put it, let the pointer with insomnia be for the moment kept in the dark."

He advised Agate to write an introduction to the book—"You must string the pearls.—But what is the word 'must'? I am beginning to talk like G. B. S. . . . Talking of G. B. S. I wonder what articles of his you have selected. I admire him *as dramatic critic* beyond all other men. I never tire of his two volumes. He was at the top of his genius when he wrote them."[20] (They had appeared when Shaw was forty-two; he was now seventy-six.) That ended the discussion over the anthology, but not Max's concern with Shaw. Shortly he inquired of Agate, "Did you hear that G. B. S. has gone to the Wall of China by aeroplane?"[21]

In an interview Max once gave, which appeared in the *Saturday Review,* he described Shaw as a "marvellous piece of construction—efficient, rigid, unassailable, like steel girders."[22] This inflexibility, this unyielding determination, seemed the trait which the amiable Max most deplored in Shaw. Variations on this theme are apparent in a series of memoranda which Max jotted down for a projected article on Shaw. A sheet of foolscap paper in the Berg Collection of the New York Public Library contains these random notes, done in no particular order, but summarizing Max's impressions. Some of the fragmentary phrases must be clues to Max's private memories, defying identification, but most are readily linked with known experiences. Shaw, said the introductory statement, had a "temperance beverage face," but he was soon acknowledged to possess "the best brain in England." He was, however, "inhuman, uncomfortable, never playing with dog or child or talking about the weather or nonsense." He had "no pity for the poor . . . no feeling for father, country, woman;" such things he considered "absurd." Max agreed with Mrs. Shaw that her husband was a "reformer, not an artist," with "no love of beauty." Though Shaw was a musician and had once claimed that he wrote "operatic dialogue," Max disagreed, saying Shaw's music was that of a "carpenter, who nails [a] board."[23]

Thus, Max on Shaw. And what about Shaw on Max? The name occurs infrequently in the dramatist's correspondence, though there are evidences that he read Max's reviews. Once Shaw took issue with him in the *Saturday,* but it was about *The Power of Darkness,* not a play of his own. He seemed unaware of Max's preoccupation. On the occasion of Shaw's ninetieth birthday, Max wrote a letter to be included in Stephen Winsten's memorial volume. On being invited to Max's seventieth birthday celebration, G. B. S. declined, with thanks.

[1963]

Notes

1. Manuscript material in this article is quoted with the kind permission of Mrs. Eva Reichman of London, the Houghton Library at Harvard, and the Henry W. and Albert A. Berg Collection of the New York Public Library.

Max on Shaw

2. C. J. Holmes, *Self and Partners* (London, 1934), p. 303.
3. *Saturday Review* (London), May 21, 1895, p. 883.
4. S. N. Behrman, *Portrait of Max* (New York, 1960), p. 22.
5. Max Beerbohm, *Around Theatres* (London, 1953), p. ix.
6. Stephen Winsten, *Jesting Apostle* (London, 1956), p. 129.
7. William Rothenstein, *Men and Memories* (London, 1931), I, p. 295.
8. Manuscript for *English Portraits*, Houghton Library, Harvard.
9. J. G. Riewald, *Sir Max Beerbohm* (The Hague, 1953), p. 161.
10. *Saturday Review* (London), July 1, 1905, p. 14.
11. Alan Dent, *Saturday Review of Literature*, August 30, 1952, p. 20.
12. Behrman, op. cit., p. 23.
13. Archibald Henderson, *G. B. S.: Man of the Century* (New York, 1956), p. 790.
14. Blanche Patch, *Thirty Years With G. B. S.* (New York, 1951), p. 38.
15. Ibid., p. 137.
16. Doris Arthur Jones, *Taking the Curtain Call* (New York, 1930), p. 367.
17. William Rothenstein, *Since Fifty* (London, 1939), pp. 29-30.
18. W. H. Davies, *Later Days* (New York, 1926), pp. 195-200.
19. *Times Literary Supplement* (London), November 26, 1925, p. 812.
20. James Agate, *Ego II* (London, 1935), pp. 220-228.
21. Ibid., p. 271.
22. A. S. Frere-Reeves, *Saturday Review*, December 25, 1926, p. 799.
23. Manuscript in the Berg Collection, New York Public Library.

Edmund Wilson

A MISCELLANY OF MAX BEERBOHM

On the afternoons of March 15 and 16, 1954, I was taken to call on
Max Beerbohm by S. N. Behrman, the New York dramatist, who
was then writing a book about him. Max was living in his villa at
Rapallo, taken care of by Miss Elisabeth Jungmann, who for years
had been the secretary of Gerhart Hauptmann. Miss Jungmann was
intelligent and highly educated and, though German, she spoke
and read English perfectly. She had specialized in men of genius
and had been a godsend for Hauptmann and Max Beerbohm, who
had known her when Hauptmann lived at Rapallo. I was told by
Sam Behrman that Max had once said to her that if his wife should
die, he did not know what would become of him. She had answered
—Hauptmann died in 1946—that she would come to him wherever
he was, and gave him an address that would reach her. He had
put it in a book and forgotten about it and, after his wife's death,
had not been able to find it; but she heard about him and immediately came to him. She was devoted to him and now took care of
him, running the villa with one maid.

The Villino Chiaro was pleasant and simple. It hung high above
the blue water and had a terrace from which one looked down on
the sea and a tower room that Max used for a library and studio.
We came in through a hallway, on the wall of which one recog-

Edmund Wilson, "A Miscellany of Max Beerbohm." From Edmund Wilson, *The
Bit Between My Teeth: A Literary Chronicle of 1950-1965* (New York: Farrar, Straus
& Giroux, 1965), pp. 41-58. Originally published under the title "Meetings with Max
Beerbohm," *Encounter*, 21 (December 1963), 16-22. Copyright © 1939, 1940, 1947,
1950, 1951, 1952, 1953, 1956, 1957, 1958, 1959, 1960, 1961, 1962, 1963, 1965 by Edmund
Wilson. Reprinted by permission of Farrar, Straus & Giroux, Inc.

nized the harlequin inn sign which is described in the "Words for Pictures" section of *Yet Again*. At the feet of the harlequin, who looked rather like Max, lay a mask on a tambourine, which so much resembled a bearded face that one took it at first for a decapitated head like that of John the Baptist in *Salomé*. (We were later shown a harlequin dressing-gown sewn together like a patchwork quilt from bits of material of different colors.) On the walls of a sort of anteroom hung a miniature of Max's father—who had been known, Sam Behrman told me, in his youth in Paris, on account of the magnificence of his style of living, as—a pun on his name—*"Super-be-homme."* On the same wall as the miniature were portraits of Max's grandparents on the continental side—both with a half-smiling look, the grandmother *"l'oeil espiègle."* They had a recognizable resemblance to Max, but seemed so much like the idealized characters of an eighteenth-century opera that I almost suspected Max, with his inveterate love of hoaxes, of having invented these grandparents himself; but when I met him the moment after, I felt that he must indeed have behind him a tradition of wit and elegance.

He had just had an attack of flu and received us sitting in a chair in front of a little fire. He was eighty-two—it was two years before his death—and he was suffering from an inflammation which had encircled his round blue eyes with red rings. But his appearance surprised me by a kind of impressiveness which I had not expected to find. He always liked to represent himself in his caricatures with an almost cherubic head and a frail and wispy figure, the extremities also diminishing; but he was actually rather taller than he looks in these, and his head was larger and stronger than I had imagined even from his photographs. There was something rather Germanic about his nose and jaw and his blond mustache. He struck me as both very Edwardian and as rather continental than English. He was a good deal more positive, also, than his writing would have led me to believe, even a little contentious—though it may be that I stimulated this tendency. His hands were quite astonishing—they seemed unlike any others I had ever seen. Instead of being slender with tapering fingers, the fingers were long and of uniform thickness, almost like the legs of a spider crab, and they were sharpened at the ends like pencils. It was as if they were very large engraver's

139

tools, the instruments of a formidable craftsman. He wore one ring with a green scarab.

I talked about the book on him, very scholarly but rather boring, written in English by a Dutchman, J. G. Riewald, and he was polite about it but obviously not much excited.[1] He had not read "the parts he remembered," but there were many things he found he had forgotten. I asked about certain points in his caricatures which I had never understood. His memory of his drawings was perfect, and he was able to answer at once, in a way that showed how very carefully every detail of these had been planned. Who were the people in the procession of hump-nosed monsters who appeared in his *Fifty Caricatures*, with the simple caption, "Are we as welcome as ever?" Those, he said, were "the friends of Edward VII," and he went on to explain rather slyly that the occasion for this caricature had been the accession of George V. The friends were Sir Ernest Cassel, two Rothschilds, Lord Burnham and Baron de Hirsch. He added, after a second, referring to the new king: "Didn't need to borrow money so often, don't you know?" He said nothing about these friends being Jewish. He was not, as has been sometimes said, Jewish himself, and I think that it was probably his delicacy which had restrained him from making the caption more explicit. He went on, as if apologetically, to describe how, having started the picture, he had found that his hand went on drawing without his thinking about it—as if he wanted to represent this caricature as having been executed involuntarily. I asked him whether the Polish of the question that the young Conrad puts to the old Conrad, in the series called "The Old and the Young Self," were not a language that Max had invented. He said it was and repeated verbatim this imaginary exclamation in Polish.

Why, I asked, weren't his drawings collected? Oh, he answered, it would be impossible to dig them all up. He had had periodical exhibitions, and the pictures had been bought by Tom, Dick and Harry—he had been very glad to sell them!—but Tom had given his away, and Dick had left his somewhere, and Harry didn't know what had become of his. I inquired about Walter Sickert, the only one of Max's subjects who looks different in almost every drawing— "He was Protean," Miss Jungmann put in—and Max gave me an account of Sickert. At first, he had been completely Whistlerian, his painting was all black and blue; but he was always having new ideas and deliberately changing his manner, and he would also transform his appearance. At one point, he had his hair cropped short; at another, he had had made for himself an enormous top hat—"he must have found an ancient block"—and wore trousers striped black and white in some curious way. He was a great linguist, his French was perfect, and he was able in a few weeks to pick up the patois of Venice. It was only after the First World War that his father became Danish, not German. I mentioned Max's drawing of Sickert "explaining away the Piazza San Marco." Why was he explaining it away? He was always explaining, said Max. Sickert theorized too much; he would perhaps have made a good critic. The painter should be "an impassioned eye that sets down what he sees, or thinks he sees." (But he later went on to complain about painters who set down things "as nobody would see them.") The idea that Walter Sickert was the best English painter of his time was, Max declared, perfectly ridiculous. A question from Behrman brought out that Max thought Wilson Steer was immensely superior.

I found that he much enjoyed having his own jokes fed back to him. When I told Sam Behrman in his presence about his drawings or *bon mots*, he would chuckle without self-deprecation. I spoke of the little hoaxes, intended to upset the scholarly, that he used to let drop in his dramatic articles. "What are you thinking of?" "Well, your statement that Lady Macbeth was originally played by Shakespeare himself." He had forgotten about this and laughed. I told the story I had heard from Isaiah Berlin of his meeting Max somewhere in London and hearing a young lady say that she had just seen Lady—. "How is she?" "Just the same as ever." "I'm very sorry to hear it." He smiled: "Oh, did I say that?" Lady—had a loud voice and came from Chicago, and had married a conventional Englishman, who loathed her, and this was always apparent at their parties. One was accustomed to the situation of the wife's not liking the husband, but the case was somehow different when the husband didn't like the wife.

I said something about his last album of caricatures: Noel Coward and the actors in *Bitter Sweet*. He explained that in this and a series that he had undertaken for the *Spectator*, he found that he was simply doing very careful likenesses that really expressed pity for their subjects—and then he had decided to stop. Pathos (pronounced with a short *a*) was no quality for a caricaturist. I could see that this had been true: the drawing of Noel Coward had brought out a certain weakness but had also made him appealing. He went on to say that something similar had happened in the case of Pelle-grini ("Ape"): he had begun, after a certain age, making excellent likenesses which were no longer caricatures. So many of the drawings nowadays were ugly. (He meant artistically ugly. He had made clear in a foreword to a book by Ronald Searle that he regarded Searle's goblins and witches as distinguished exceptions to this.) Now, his own things—"though I am perhaps not the one to say it, and I had nearly left it unsaid"—were very pretty drawings. "I venture to say that even the Milner [which I had told him of having seen in the common room of one of the Oxford colleges] is not disagree-able to have around." At one point, he brought out and showed us a little pink-and-blue watercolor of Edward VII, which I believe he had recently done, and said something like, "Now, that's a pretty little drawing."

I asked about the additional passage for his parody of Henry James, "The Mote in the Middle Distance," which he had sent to Edmund Gosse and which Gosse had written him of pasting in his copy of the *Christmas Garland*. That, he said, was a new and better ending that he had thought of after the book was published— a more emotional ending, like those of *The Golden Bowl* and *The Wings of the Dove*. He recited a part of the latter: " 'Well she stretched out her wings, and it was to *that* they reached. They cover us.' . . . But she turned to the door, and her headshake was now the end. 'We shall never be again as we were!' " This had not im-pressed me much when I read it, but Max Beerbohm thought it beautiful, and he made it sound beautiful. I quoted the first line of the sextet of the very funny sonnet that he and Gosse, doing al-ternate lines, had written about Henry James: "How different from Sir Arthur Conan Doyle"—and he went on to recite the rest, making it, too, sound quite beautiful:

> You stand, marmoreal darling of the Few,
> Lord of the troubled speech and single Eye.[2]

His sensitivity to language reminded me of the way my old teacher, Alfred Rolfe, used to read, at school "morning exercises," his fastidiously chosen passages of prose or verse. I reflected, in con-nection with this afterwards, that that kind of fine appreciation of literature was something that had largely disappeared. Such con-noisseurs as Max Beerbohm and Rolfe experienced the words in an intimate way and seemed to caress the cadences. Max made a remark that puzzled me in connection with something I had written about *The Wings of the Dove*, and I asked him what he thought of the theory that the governess in *The Turn of the Screw* was intended to be a neurotic case, suffering from hallucinations. This aroused him: he denounced this theory, starting out with a sentence which began, "Some morbid pedant, prig and fool . . ." I explained that this objectionable person was me, and we argued about the subject a little. We argued, also, about the new alphabet advocated by Bernard Shaw, which Max thought was an absurd and outrageous idea. I pointed out that the abolition of five of the characters of the old Russian alphabet and certain other spelling reforms had encountered a similar opposition but had made the language easier and clearer. "When England and America are communized [he would have spelt it with an *s*]," he answered, "they will doubtless have a phonetic alphabet." He was under the erroneous impression that Shaw had invented an alphabet and wanted it imposed by law.

It was evident that he personally disliked Bernard Shaw, as it was plain that he loved Henry James. He said that Shaw had "queered his chances" of being buried in Westminster Abbey by making some démarche to that end. He had insisted on getting the Webbs buried there, which was entirely "inappropriate." Then in his will he had left instructions hat his ashes should be sprinkled in his garden— "a dreadful idea, you know, with dogs and cats about!" I said that I did think it was rather absurd for Shaw to have left as a national shrine his apparently rather commonplace house; but I tried to soften the picture—Shaw has always been a hero of mine—by suggesting that egoism like Shaw's was a disability like any disability—which you had to carry with you all your life. When he was young, it had been amusing, he had carried it off with panache; but it had become disagreeable in his later years, and one saw then that it was compulsive, incurable.

Max described to us in great detail how Shaw had looked when he had first known him in London. He had had smallpox (I do not know whether this is true), which had left his complexion absolutely white, and he had whiskers so straggling that, as someone said, they looked like seaweed on a rock. His eyes were very pale, too pale. Later, his eyebrows grew shaggy and shaded them, which somewhat improved the impression. Shaw perhaps hadn't liked

Max's caricatures, but for him any kind of attention paid him was better than none at all. I said that Max had brought out in his caricatures that Shaw had had well-shaped hands. "Yes: he had beautiful hands—the hands of a woman rather than a man." "He had an erect carriage," I said. "Yes, and he moved well. He made a good impression in this way—unless one saw him from the back: the back of his head came straight down and made a line with his neck. At first nights in his early days, he wasn't true to his principles: he wore evening clothes to the theater, but an old suit so shiny that, if you were behind him, you could see your face in it like a mirror. Later he became quite well-dressed. I was rather sorry. I think people ought to dress according to their . . ." He left it in the air. He had heard Shaw speak once at a meeting, at which, after his speech, he had answered questions and hecklers, with perfect readiness, without notes. "In a way it was better than what he wrote, you know. He was a wonderful debater—as [slyly] you see in his plays."

Max's animus against Shaw appeared, further, in the laborious pains he had taken to disfigure Archibald Henderson's biography. Miss Jungmann brought out this volume—it had been given to William Archer, then returned after Archer's death—but I did not think it really very funny, because it showed too much a jeering hatred that Max usually kept in leash in his drawings. One felt that it was not merely a question of kidding the awe-stricken biographer, but that Max could not stand the idea that Bernard Shaw had become a great man. He himself had perhaps a little always felt on the margin of things, and he was likely to betray irritation in dealing with great men who took themselves seriously and became public institutions: see his attitude toward Goethe in "Quia Imperfectum." He had, in any case, by a cunning use of ink, turned the photographs of such people as William Morris and Granville Barker into horrible prognathous gorillas. One felt that he really wanted to degrade Bernard Shaw and everyone connected with him. The only thing I can remember in his published work that at all approaches these monsters is his drawing1 of the Warden of Merton in his earliest album of caricatures. The bad little schoolboy in Max Beerbohm was also in evidence in the doctored books which we were taken to his study to see. Some of his "misleading title pages" are reproduced in the Sotheby catalogue for the sale of his papers and books: a picture of a seasick Victorian couple in Belloc's *The Cruise of the "Nona,"* a grinning and winking cockney in Meredith's *Essay on Comedy,* and a villainous-looking Irishman with a gun in an early volume of Yeats's poems. There was also Housman's *Last Poems,* with a drawing of the cast of a Wagner opera, and the title page of a volume of Chesterton's essays was covered with an expanding caricature, in which Chesterton displayed in his open mouth the printed words "thirteenth edition." I found these a little shocking, and when I came down, I told Max that my nerves had been shaken by them. He had operated on such an extensive scale in desecrating the books of his friends that it was as if he did not want them approached without their first having been put in a comic light. Going back to his work after visiting him, I came to recognize that the feelings behind it were somewhat harsher than I had suspected. Henry James had been treated with relative tenderness. On the title page of one of his books, Max had done a little drawing of him, leaning forward and gesturing with his hands, in a paroxysm of "getting wound up," as Sam Behrman said, to express some complex impression. I have heard that he was in the habit of pasting unexpected and scandalous words into the volumes of such Georgian poets as John Drinkwater, breaking the books at those places and leaving them for his guests on the bedside table, and I was sorry to hear that none of these turned up for the Sotheby sale.

I was surprised to discover that Max did not care for Virginia Woolf's novels. He had a good word only for her criticism, and he did not seem enthusiastic about that.[3] He had just been reading her diary, which he said showed low vitality and was "pettifogging," overanxious about things that concerned herself and not considerate about anyone else. I had somewhat shared this last impression. Leonard Woolf, he said, must have taken very good care of her, and I said that he must have needed patience to talk her over her reviews. "Poor soul!" he added. I said that she had evidently been a peculiar kind of snob—a snob without really belonging to a social group with whom to be snobbish. She had been so extraordinary about Thomas Hardy. It is plain that when she went to see him, she expected to find something like the old gaffers in his novels, and she expressed surprise at his *savoir faire* in offering her husband a whisky and soda. Apropos of Mrs. Woolf's novels, he spoke contemptuously and pettishly about the "stream of consciousness" in general. Everybody had thoughts that went through his head, but it was absurd to try to make a novel of them. He liked to read a *story,* to have characters and see what they did. I stood up for

Between the Acts, which he had not read, but I did not attempt to argue with him about the stream of consciousness. I was rather dismayed to discover that by the time Virginia Woolf had appeared, Max Beerbohm had got to a point where he was unable to appreciate new excellence in an art he had practiced and loved. I should have thought that for the author of the *Christmas Garland,* with his exquisite sense of style, Mrs. Woolf would have been the writer of the Bloomsbury set in whom he would have felt most interest. But he never seemed to have got beyond Lytton Strachey. He had lost the pleasant world of his youth, the world to which he had belonged. The cities were no longer attractive. People in London, he said, were always in a crisis about something—about going somewhere or catching a bus. The old leisurely days were gone. Lytton Strachey had still lived in this world; Virginia Woolf somehow not.

They invited us to tea the next day, and we came at 4:30 instead of 3:30 and did not stay so long. Today he sat up at the table and presided over the tea. His head was sunk between his shoulders, and the hair at the back of his bald domed head was uncut and hung over his collar. He would look up at us as he chuckled in a way that seemed a little deprecatory. We had tea and sherry and an aperitif, with cakes and hors d'oeuvres. Max drank a single glass of something from a bottle without a label. While Miss Jungmann was out of the room, he sneaked an extra cigarette, and when she came back and saw it, she commented, "When the Devil . . . !"

He said that he had never been able to caricature Somerset Maugham, had tried it several times, then given it up; but he implied that Sutherland, in his portrait of Maugham, had made up for Max's failure—he had, he said, "carried caricature as far as it would go." After painting Somerset Maugham, Sutherland had written to Max asking him to sit for his portrait, and Max had replied that though he had in his time "made monsters of people" himself, "the bully was always a coward," and that, knowing the portrait of Maugham, he had decided to decline this offer. "Now that I'm old and afflicted-looking, I shouldn't want to be painted anyway, but even in my prime, I don't think I should have wanted to be painted by Sutherland."

I asked him about Sem, the French caricaturist, whose work I greatly admired. Max had caricatured Sem and had known him.

He said that Sem had been able to do things that he couldn't do. He was able to make sketches on the spot, which Max never did—sometimes just drawing parts of people: an ear and an arm, etc.—and then would put them together, and there would be a perfect likeness. Sem was extremely good at doing the types at the races and Monte Carlo: *"Tout Paris."* He came to England and drew people at Ascot, and then would ask who they were, and one could always tell him because the likenesses were unmistakable. Max himself could not caricature people unless he had seen quite a lot of them—had heard their voices, caught the tone of their minds. I spoke of the animated album, in which Sem has *Tout Paris* doing the Charleston and the Black Bottom—so wonderful in its imagining of the movements of different bodies and different personalities. Sem's people were always in movement. The loyal Miss Jungmann, at this, produced the recently published volume of R. C. Trevelyan's *Selected Poems*, with its frontispiece by Max of Trevelyan slogging along with a knapsack on one of his long walks. Max had lunched once with Sem at Dieppe, and they had known that people were thinking, "Two caricaturists lunching together: they must be up to something!" Sem was a good mimic, and he had imitated Coquelin, who was also there: *"Je ne parle jamais de moi. Pourquoi? Parce-que . . ."* and there would follow a long explanation of why it was characteristic that he should never speak of himself. They decided to send Coquelin a note, saying that they had arranged for a window from which to watch the fireworks that night and inviting him to share it with them. He had not answered. "I think he must have been insulted," Max added with a certain complacency. Sem could caricature women, which Max had never been able to do. I said that he had done well with Zuleika Dobson in his frontispiece to the new edition of the novel. "Oh, that was just a caricature of a pretty girl." I thought the point was—since he had caricatured the women of the Rossetti circle and occasionally imaginary women—that he was too much of an old-fashioned gentleman to be willing to make real living ones ridiculous.

I had said to Sam Behrman that I thought Max's head rather resembled Bismarck's, and Sam now repeated this to him. It was not, it turned out, the first time that this comparison had been made, and he got out a little drawing that he had done of himself as Bismarck—wearing an iron cross which contrasted with his mild dreamy gaze. Bismarck had had, he said, an astonishingly high voice, like a woman's. Hilaire Belloc, also, with his square jaw, his thickset figure and his head set down between his shoulders, surprised one by his high voice. He used to sing French hunting songs in a sweet and exquisite way—"It was rather like a very large nightingale."

I asked him what he thought of P. G. Wodehouse—the enthusiasm for whom of some people I have never been able to understand—and he replied that he could never read more than fifty pages of any of Wodehouse's books. At first he would be entertained by Wodehouse's handling of language—"almost like Cinquevalli" (the great juggler of the last century, of whom Max had once written), but he lost interest after that. It was difficult for him now to read novels: he couldn't believe any longer in the things that were supposed to happen in them. Apropos of George Moore, he said that Dr. Johnson had declared that there were two kinds of talkers: those who talked from a stream, of whom Burke was the example, and those who talked from a tank. Moore talked from a stream, like so many Irishmen. When I mentioned Compton Mackenzie, he said. "Ah, there's a man who writes from a stream!" *Sinister Street*, he thought, would last. It was wonderful how Mackenzie, in writing of Oxford, had caught with such delicate precision the nuances of the seasons and their moods: Eights Week, St. Mark's Eve, Lent term, Easter holidays, etc. I said that I had just been in Oxford and told him that the traffic there now, on account of the Nuffield works, was as bad as in any big city. Yes, he said, and they could perfectly well have prevented it. Nuffield had kept a bicycle shop when Max had been an undergraduate. Almost nobody rode a bicycle then: it was "the earmark of vulgarity."

I tried to draw him out about the suicides of the nineties and the early years of the present century: Hubert Crackanthorpe, St. John Hankin, John Davidson. I had always wondered about them. Did they lack conviction of their talent? Or did they and the other writers and artists who died relatively young at that time really feel that the *fin de siècle* implied that their world must come to an end? Max did not throw much light on this—whether from discretion in discussing the private lives of men he had known or from a distaste for dwelling on tragedy or from simple lack of interest, I could not tell. Hubert Crackanthorpe he had known a little. His father had been a successful barrister, and Max had sometimes gone to his parents' house. He had "thrown himself into the Seine and couldn't swim—some sudden fit of insanity, I suppose." His short stories had shown talent, but "*le mot juste*" had a way of coming between the lady and gentleman that the story was about." Hankin he had known quite well. He had not been surprised when *he* committed suicide—he was rather a sad man. He was supposed to be unhappily married. Of John Davidson, he said, too, strangely, that he had "thrown himself into the water and couldn't swim." I said something favorable about Davidson's poetry, and Max responded warmly that he was the best English poet of that period. Davidson had been a dominie in Scotland, and had thrown it up and come to London. Once, in the Café Royal, he had set out to sing to Max a translation of the Psalms into Scots and had been told by the headwaiter that he was annoying the other guests. I tried to probe further by asking whether Davidson had been poor and desperate. "Yes," he replied rather vaguely, "but he had enough for himself and his family to live on."

He talked always with natural style—quietly and unemphatically, the words well and easily chosen, always trying to express what he thought, and except for an occasional quaint phrase, with no effort to talk for effect. There is, fortunately, a recording made by Angel of his reading of two of his essays—"The Crime" and "London Revisited"—which preserves the sound of his voice, so casual and conversational even in rendering these carefully-written pieces.

When we left, I told Max that I was going to send him Angus Wilson's *For Whom the Cloche Tolls* and my essay on *The Turn of the Screw*, in a simplified phonetic alphabet, but provided with a key.

In the entrance hall and in one of the rooms, he had painted some murals of his favorite subjects: Chamberlain and Churchill and Balfour, Chesterton and George Moore and Henry James, old friends like Will Rothenstein and Reginald Turner, who had now become rather obscure. He had taken his creations with him, his whole vision of the London world, into the long retirement of his exile. To his villa on the Gulf of Genoa, they still flocked to keep him company. I have spoken of his new watercolor of Edward VII, and I learn that the last caricature he drew was still another of George Moore. And seeing them there made me recognize as I had not quite done before the excitement and variety of this vision. Has there ever been anything like it in the realm of caricature? Gillray has his recurrent characters and a grotesque world in which they move, but he is brutal and crude beside Beerbohm. Sem is perhaps the nearest thing; but he does not have Max's historical sense or his intellectual insight. Though Max makes all his subjects absurd, though no one is ever idealized except in a comic way, there is a hierarchy of values here: men he despises and men he admires, men that he rejoices in and men that he likes to make ugly. His work as a caricaturist is in general on a higher imaginative level than his stories, his essays and his parodies. Virginia Woolf in her *Diary* quotes him as saying to her: "About his own writing, dear Lytton Strachey said to me: 'First I write one sentence; then I write another.' That's how I write. And so I go on. But I have a feeling writing ought to be like running through a field. That's your way. Now, how do you go down to your room after breakfast—what do you feel? I used to look at the clock and say, 'Oh, dear me, it's time I began my article. . . . No, I'll read the paper first.' I never wanted to write. But I used to come home from a dinner party and take my brush and draw caricature after caricature. They seemed to bubble up from here . . . [he pressed his stomach]. That was a kind of inspiration, I suppose. What you said in your beautiful essay about me and Charles Lamb was quite true. He was crazy; he had the gift: genius. I'm too like Jack Horner. I pull out my thumb. It's too rounded, too perfect."

Yet I read and reread Max Beerbohm as I do not do any other British prose writer of the period in which I grew up, with the exception of Bernard Shaw. It seems to me queer when I find Max Beerbohm speaking, as he does in some essay, of G. K. Chesterton as "a genius" whose brilliance quite put Max in the shade. The paradoxical epigrams of Chesterton, which became so mechanical and monotonous, are mostly unreadable today. But Max Beerbohm's prose has endured. Since it never asserts itself—except in the comic exuberance of his *Yellow Book* preciosity—one can always forget it and find it fresh.

[1963]

Notes

1. The reference is to J. G. Riewald, *Sir Max Beerbohm, Man and Writer: A Critical Analysis with a Brief Life and a Bibliography* (The Hague: Martinus Nijhoff, 1953, and Brattleboro, Vermont: The Stephen Greene Press, 1961).—*Editor's note.*

2. The complete text of the sonnet is now published in *Max in Verse: Rhymes and Parodies by Max Beerbohm*, ed. J. G. Riewald (Brattleboro, Vermont: The Stephen Greene Press, 1963, and London: William Heinemann, 1964), p. 19.—*Editor's note.*

3. Since this memoir was published in *Encounter*, Mr. Leonard Woolf has written to the editors to put on record a letter from Max to Virginia Woolf:

"Dear Virginia Woolf—I can't help this familiarity: I seem to know you so well, from *The Common Reader*, a book which I have read twice, and have often dipped into since, and rate above any modern book of criticism (rating it thus quite soberly, all unconfused by your habit of going out of your way to be nice about my essays!)...."

Any report of a conversation is likely to be somewhat unreliable, since the reported may give way to a mood and the reporter may misinterpret.

151

John Updike

Rhyming Max

Max in Verse: Rhymes and Parodies by Max Beerbohm. 167 pp. The Stephen Greene Press, 1963.[1]

Into the present twilight of light verse an oblique ray has entered from the unexpected direction of Vermont, where the Stephen Greene Press, a Brattleboro outfit, has published (handsomely) *Max in Verse*, a collection, painstakingly scavenged from widely scattered sources, of everything from the pen of Max Beerbohm that can be construed, however remotely, as a poem. The construing and scavenging, along with much annotating, have been performed by Professor J. G. Riewald, Beerbohm's bibliographer. His labors have been heroic—in fact, considering the fragility of his subject's claim to the title of poet, mock-heroic. The literary oddments of Shakespeare, were some to turn up, could not be more reverently handled. Eighty-four items by Beerbohm, many of them tiny, are buttressed fore and aft by (1) acknowledgments to forty-eight institutions and individuals for their help; (2) a foreword by S. N. Behrman, one of America's leading "Maximilians," to use a term that apparently has the same relation to Beerbohm that "Mohammedans" does to Mohammed; (3) a preface by Professor Riewald; (4) thirty pages, in eight-point Baskerville, of sources and annotations; (5) an index of titles and first lines; and (6) another index, of "Persons," ranging from

---

John Updike, "Rhyming Max." From John Updike, *Assorted Prose* (New York: Alfred A. Knopf, 1965), pp. 256-263. Originally published in *The New Yorker*, 7 March 1964, pp. 176-181. Copyright © 1964 by John Updike. Reprinted by permission of Alfred A. Knopf, Inc.

Of the four-score-and-four poems so elaborately enshrined in print, twenty or so were jotted by Max on the flyleaves or in the margins of books, two were scribbled in letters to friends, and one was found in his top hat. Five are in Latin; seven are sonnets of which Beerbohm, playing a game with Edmund Gosse or the William Rothensteins, wrote only alternate or third lines; one is a collection of spurious country saws (e.g., "It isn't the singing kettle that scalds the cook's hand" and "He that hath no teeth hath no toothache" and "A dumb woman sees more things than a blind man hears"); and another is a four-line epitaph for Bernard Shaw recited to two professors at St. Elizabeth's Hospital, in Washington, D. C., by an inmate, Mr. Ezra Pound, who had learned the quatrain at Max's knee when they were neighbors in Rapallo—a remarkable modern instance of the oral poetic tradition, employing none but the most distinguished personnel. The longest items in *Max in Verse* are the pseudo-Shakespearean burlesque "Savonarola," already available in the book *Seven Men*, and "A Sequelula to *The Dynasts,*" a blank-verse parody of Hardy that is woven into *A Christmas Garland*. Professor Riewald not only superfluously reprints these staples of Maxiana (as the Maximilians say), he snips from their familiar contexts several parodic snatches of Belloc and Kipling, the decadent poems of the fictional Enoch Soames, and two three-line fragments composed (in Latin and the Oxfordshire dialect) by Zuleika Dobson's unhappy admirer the Duke of Dorset. This accounting leaves to mention a number of elegantly turned ballades, rondeaux, and triolets; some limericks no better than most; a few infallibly deft takeoffs on Kipling, Yeats, and Tom Moore;

two relatively heavy and personal ballads; and, here and there, redeemed from quaint corners, delicate as fossils, epigrams marking the flitting imprint of Max's daintily waspish temper.

One might suppose that a collection so curious, a portentously served potpourri of private jokes and *déjà vu*, would add up to a worthless book. But *Max in Verse* is precious in both senses; it is both overrefined and valuable. Its value, which is felt in terms of delight, can perhaps be understood through some consideration of light verse.

Modern light verse, as it was created by Calverley, calls into question the standards of triviality that would judge it. When we open Calverley's *Fly Leaves* to the first page, and read

> 'Tis the hour when white-horsed Day
> Chases Night her mares away;
> When the Gates of Dawn (they say)
>   Phoebus opes:
> And I gather that the Queen
> May be uniformly seen,
> Should the weather be serene,
>   On the slopes,

a universe of importance is pulled down. The conceits and figures by which men have agreed to swear and live are tripped up by metrics, flattened by the simple inopportuneness of rhyme.

Language is finite and formal; reality is infinite and formless. Order is comic; chaos is tragic.[2] By rhyming, language calls attention to its own mechanical nature and relieves the represented reality of seriousness. In this sense, rhyme and allied regularities like alliteration and assonance assert a magical control over things and constitute a spell. When children, in speaking, accidentally rhyme, they laugh, and add, "I'm a poet/And don't know it," as if to avert the consequences of a stumble into the supernatural. The position of rhyme in Western literature is more precarious than is popularly supposed. The Greeks and Romans were innocent of it, and it appears in Latin poetry as an adjunct of the Mass, probably as an aid to the memory of the worshippers. Rhymed sacred poetry, of which classical examples are the "Stabat Mater" and the "Dies Irae," dates from the fourth century; for a thousand years rather pell-mell rhyme and alliteration dominated verse. As the sea of faith ebbed and consciousness of chaos broke in again upon civilization, rhymelessness returned—in England, as both the deliberate revival of quantitive measure sponsored by Gabriel Harvey and the spontaneous ascendance of the pentameter blank verse invented by Surrey and developed by Marlowe and Shakespeare. The bulk of great English poetry, from Shakespeare to Milton, from Wordsworth to Wallace Stevens, is unrhymed. And those poets of the first rank, like Pope, who habitually rhyme do so unobtrusively—that is, Pope's couplets turn on unspectacular monosyllables; there is no glorying in rhyme, as there is in a medieval poet like John Skelton or a modern light-verse writer like Ogden Nash. The last considerable poets who preferred to rhyme are Emily Dickinson, Yeats, and Housman. Emily Dickinson's rhyming is often off-rhyme, Yeats was a magician in pose, and Housman's verse verges on being light. When all the minority reports are in, the trend of our times is overwhelmingly against formal regularity of even the most modest sort; in the *Cantos*, Pound has passed beyond free verse into a poetry totally arhythmic. Our mode is realism, "realistic" is synonymous with "prosaic," and the prose writer's duty is to suppress not only rhyme but any verbal accident that would mar the textural correspondence to the massive, onflowing impersonality that has supplanted the chiming heavens of the saints. In this situation, light verse, an isolated acolyte, tends the thin flame of formal magic and tempers the inhuman darkness of reality with the comedy of human artifice. Light verse precisely lightens; it lessens the gravity of its subject.

Weigh, for example, the opening lines of Swift's "Verses on the Death of Dr. Swift":

> The time is not remote, when I
> Must by the course of nature die;
> When I foresee my special friends,
> Will try to find their private ends:
> Though it is hardly understood,
> Which way my death can do them good . . .

When the same expressions are recast in prose, with the rhymes suppressed, the pert effect turns sombre:

> The time is not remote when I must, by the course of nature, die. Then, I foresee, my special friends will try to find their private advantages, though it is hardly understood which way my death can benefit them . . .

The melancholy of the passage survives transposition into blank verse:

155

> The time is not remote, when by the course
> Of nature I must die: when, I foresee,
> My special friends will seek their private gain,
> Though it is hardly understood which way
> My death can do them good . . .

And even pentameter couplets permit, in their length and variability, a certain speaking seriousness of tone:

> The time, I fear, is not remote when by
> The foreseen course of nature I must die:
> When those that I considered special friends
> Will try to comprehend their private ends;
> Although as yet 'tis hardly understood
> Which way my sorry death can do them good . . .

Pentameter is the natural speaking line in English; hexameter loses track of itself, and tetrameter chops up thoughts comically. Tetrameter is the natural light-verse line.

> So this is Utopia, is it? Well,
> I beg your pardon, I thought it was Hell.

This couplet was written by Beerbohm in a copy of More's *Utopia*, and most of the poems in *Max in Verse* are footnotes, of some sort, to serious literature:

> Milton, my help, my prop, my stay,
> My well of English undefiled,
> It struck me suddenly today
> *You* must have been *an awful* child.

On the verso of the title page of a copy of *The Picture of Dorian Gray*, Max, while still at Oxford, wrote a "Ballade de la Vie Joyeuse," beginning:

> Why do men feast upon wormwood and gall
> When there are roses for every day?
> Let us not leave them to fade on the wall,
> Knowing of naught but 'la vie limitée.'
> Is there a heaven? Be that as it may
> Conduct's an image of priest-eaten wood.
> We are but bits of elaborate clay.
> Let us be happy without being good.

Thus the neo-hedonism of the nineties is wickedly satirized merely by being too neatly put. *Max in Verse* is an enchanted island of a book, and its Ariel is a hovering, invisible, luminous insistence on the comedy (above and beyond the wit of the precious little that is being said) *of versification itself.* Beerbohm, following the lead of his master Calverley, whose parody of Browning abounds in tormented lines, repeatedly frames lines whose scansion is an absurd triumph of pedantry:

> Automata these animalcula
> Are—puppets, pitiable jackaclocks.

> Savonarola will not tempted be
> By face of woman e'en tho' 't be, tho' 'tis,
> Surpassing fair. All hope abandon therefore.
> I charge thee: Vade retro, Satanas!

> Tho' love be sweet, revenge is sweeter far.
> To the Piazza! Ha, ha, ha, ha, har!

Examples abound: one final one. On the copyright page of his first book, *The Works of Max Beerbohm*, Max found the imprint

> London: John Lane, *The Bodley Head*
> New York: Charles Scribner's Sons.

Beneath it, he wrote in pen:

> This plain announcement, nicely read,
> Iambically runs.

The effortless a-b-a-b rhyming, the balance of "plain" and "nicely," the need for nicety in pronouncing "Iambically" to scan—this is quintessential light verse, a twitting of the starkest prose into perfect form, a marriage of earth with light, and quite magical. Indeed, were I a high priest of literature, I would have this quatrain made into an amulet and wear it about my neck, for luck.

[1964]

John Updike

Notes

1. After this review appeared, I received a letter from a very old lady who said she had been a personal friend of Beerbohm's and that he had detested being called "Max." I meant no offense; I was misled into impudence by the jaunty title of the collection itself, and by its cozy tone.

2. Perhaps this sibylline sentence should be expanded. I think I meant that order is comic in the sense that it is deathless. The essence of a machine is its *idea*; though every part is replaced, the machine persists, as the (successful) embodiment of certain abstract notions. There is a something Platonic about machines; we speak, for example, of *the* 1937 Chevrolet as of a reality distinct from all the Chevrolets built in 1937. Likewise, a poem is a verbal machine infinitely reproducible, whose existence cannot be said to lie anywhere or to depend upon any set of atoms. Even a poem buried in a dead language can, with scholarship, be dug up and made to "work" again. Whereas that which is organic is specific and mortal. Its essence lies in its unique and irreplaceable animation. One says "He is gone" of a man whose body lies perfectly intact on the deathbed. Natural beauty is essentially temporary and sad; hence the impression of obscene mockery which artificial flowers give us, and our aversion—unlike the ages of faith—from duplicatory realism in painting. Chaos is tragic because it includes one's individual death, which is to say the waste and loss of everything.

W. H. Auden

One of the Family

I never enjoy having to find fault with a book, and when the author is someone I have met and like, I hate it. Lord David Cecil possesses all the qualifications for writing a first-class biography of Max Beerbohm—an understanding love of his hero, the industry and scholarship to insure that the facts are both correct and complete— but his *Max* is not nearly so good a book as it could have been. What he has published should, I feel, have been his first draft, which he should then have spent another six months condensing to at least half its present volume. As it is, he has given us a ponderous, repetitious Victorian tome of four hundred and ninety-six densely printed pages. So expansive a commemoration is singularly unsuited to the man who once counseled a prospective biographer thus:

> My gifts are small. I've used them very well and discreetly, never straining them; and the result is that I've made a charming little reputation. But this reputation is a frail plant. Don't over-attend to it, gardener Lynch! Don't drench it and deluge it! The contents of a quite *small* watering-can will be quite enough. This I take to be superfluous counsel. I find much reassurance and comfort in your phrase, "a *little* book." Oh, keep it little!—in due proportion to its theme.

With my other objection, I have learned, I can expect very few

From W. H. Auden, *Forewords and Afterwords*. Selected by Edward Mendelson (New York: Random House, 1973), pp. 367-383. Originally published in *The New Yorker*, 23 October 1965, pp. 227-244. Copyright © 1965 by W. H. Auden. Reprinted by permission of Random House, Inc.

people in this age to agree, but I must state it, however eccentric it may seem. I consider the publication of long extracts from Max's letters to Florence a violation of personal privacy for which I can see no justification whatever. Max seems to have destroyed all her letters to him—an indication, surely, that he wished their correspondence to remain private. There may be some excuse for disregarding the wishes of a dead man—though I do not myself consider it valid—if the contents of his private papers reveal important aspects of his life and character, hitherto unsuspected, but Max's letters to Florence tell us nothing we could not learn from public sources. Furthermore, to a detached reader, nearly all love letters are either boring or embarrassing. Letters between friends who share the same interests and jokes can be most entertaining, as are Max's letters to Reggie Turner, superbly edited by Mr. Rupert Hart-Davis, and published, incidentally, with Max's consent on condition that certain excisions be made. But the noises of erotic devotion, however musical they may sound in the ears of the couple concerned, can seldom stir a third party's. As one would expect, there is nothing scandalous or shameful about Max the lover, only a certain kittenishness, harmless enough—but to me, at any rate, shy-making.

One more criticism, or, rather, suggestion. When I read biographies, I find myself constantly having to turn back and hunt for the date of the event I am reading about. I wish that when they print a biography publishers would make it their practice to set at the top of each page at least the year with which it is concerned.

Mr. S. N. Behrman's *Portrait of Max*, published some five years ago, in three hundred and four pages of widely spaced print, is a better book than Lord David Cecil's, but since he confined himself to describing his encounters with Beerbohm and made no attempt at a full biography, his task was of course a very much easier one. I am astonished to find both Mr. Behrman and Lord David Cecil talking of Max as a man who deliberately adopted and cultivated a mask. To say that a man wears a mask is to say that the person as he appears to be to others, perhaps even to himself, differs from the person he really is. He may wear one for various reasons. He may simply be a crook, like the man who professes love to lonely spinsters in order to swindle them out of their savings. He may be someone who is afraid or ashamed of certain aspects of his nature, which he therefore tries to hide from others and himself.

Young people, who are still uncertain of their identity, often try on a succession of masks in the hope of finding the one which suits them—the one, in fact, which is not a mask. Another possibility is described in Beerbohm's story "The Happy Hypocrite": in order to win the heart of a nice girl, a rake assumes a mask of virtue, but ends up by becoming in reality what at first he had only pretended to be. Lastly, among artists of all kinds—though here the use of the word "mask" is questionable—it is not uncommon for their artistic *persona* to express but a limited area of their total experience.

Max Beerbohm falls into none of these categories. He was certainly no crook. At an astonishingly early age he knew exactly the sort of person he was, and he never showed the slightest desire to be anyone else. Lucky enough to be equally gifted in two artistic media, and without any ambition to transcend his limitations, he made his caricatures and his writings between them say everything that was in him to say. The behavior and conversation of most people vary a little according to the company they happen to be in, but Max's were the same wherever he was. Indeed, if there does seem something not quite human about him, something elfish, it is because, as an adult, he retained the transparency of a child. Intentionally or unintentionally, Oscar Wilde's wisecrack about him is acute: "Tell me, when you are alone with Max, does he take off his face and reveal his mask?"

Late in his life, Max told a journalist that he had been lucky once—when he was born. And one cannot read about his family without agreeing with him. His father, a corn merchant from Memel, who took up the study of Anglo-Saxon when he was over sixty, married Constantia Draper, an absent-minded lady with literary interests, by whom he had three sons and a daughter. On her death, he married her sister, efficient but affectionate and humorous, and begot three daughters and one more son, Max. Max was four years younger than his next sister and twenty-two years younger than his eldest half brother. Eccentricity and charm ran in both families. Ernest became a sheep farmer in the colonies and married a colored lady, Herbert became the famous actor-manager Herbert Tree, Julius turned into a passionate dandy and compulsive gambler whose hopes of making his fortune were never dimmed by his repeated failures to do so. Constance helped her stepmother run the house and came out with such remarks as:

161

Mr. X tells me he has a wonderful parrot. It can judge the
year of wine vintages. I want to write an article about it for
the papers.

(Actually, Mr. X had said "palate.") Agnes, a beauty, was "always
very gay," even after her marriage went on the rocks. Dora, the
person to whom Max felt closest all his life, became a nun and wrote
a music-hall song:

> Left, right, left, right.
> The girl that I left
> Is the girl that is right.

And Max became Max.

This seems a good point at which to dispose of the ladies. Since
his half brothers were already out in the world, Max grew up in
a mainly feminine society, the adored baby boy. Such a situation
encourages imaginative precocity and an unconscious selfishness, which takes it for granted that one will always be loved and
looked after. The assumption, oddly, is usually justified, and at no
time in his life was Max without some woman—his mother, Florence,
his secretary Miss Jungmann—who was delighted to look after him.
As he himself admitted:

> I can only stand life when it is made pleasant for me.
> Usually it *is* made pleasant for me. I have really been rather
> pampered than otherwise. So I have been all right, on the whole.
> But I do not like life when it does not offer me something
> nice every day. And if it ever offered me something *not* nice I
> should feel myself very aggrieved.

One can very well understand why he was pampered, for few
people can have been by nature so adapted to a life of cozy domes-
ticity. He was charming, affectionate, intensely loyal, good-tempered; and none of the common threats to a happy home life, like
promiscuity, the bottle, or the race track, seem ever to have tempted
him.

His first two attempts to find an exogamous substitute for his
sister Dora ended in failure. In the case of Grace Conover—Kilseen,
as he called her—the fault was his: he was evidently more fascinated by the idea of being in love than interested in her, and she
was perhaps the only person in his life whom he could be accused

of having treated badly. In the case of Constance Collier, the fault was mostly hers: she needed the kind of hot-blooded passion which she must have known it was not in Max to provide. When his friends learned of his engagement to Florence Kahn, they must have felt great misgivings. He, one of the most popular men-about-town, a wit, a caricaturist and writer with an established reputation; she, socially gauche, without any sense of humor, an actress who had not quite made it: how could such a union be expected to last? Had they set up house in London, it probably wouldn't have lasted, and it seems that Max himself realized this, for he did not propose until he had decided, six years after they became acquainted, to leave England and make his home abroad.

To Reggie Turner he wrote:

> . . . we *may* live in Italy. One thing is certain: we shan't live in *London*, but somewhere that is uncomplicated and pleasant and easy and un-fussy and lets one be oneself. . . . Of all my charming and un-charming acquaintances I want to get rid: they are a charming or un-charming nuisance, taking up one's time—clogs and drags. Henceforth I am going to be as exclusive as the Duchess of Buccleuch. There will be no one but Florence, and my people, and *you*—one or two others *perhaps*, such as the Nicholsons, but I am not sure.

One part of him had dreamed of such a life for a long time. As early as 1893, when he was only twenty-one, he had written:

> I would make myself master of some small area of physical life, a life of quiet, monotonous simplicity, exempt from all outer disturbance.

Edwardian High Society had amused him and given him copy, but at the same time living in it exhausted him:

> If I were naturally a brilliant and copious talker, I suppose that to stay in another's house would be no strain on me. I should be able to impose myself on my host and hostess and their guests without any effort, and at the end of the day retire quite unfatigued, pleasantly flushed with the effect of my own magnetism. Alas, there is no question of my imposing myself. I can repay hospitality only by strict attention to the humble, arduous process of making myself agreeable. When I go up to dress for dinner, I have always a strong impulse to go to bed

and sleep off my fatigue; and it is only by exerting all my will-
power that I can array myself for the final labours. . . . It's
a dog's life.

Again, although at no time in his life well off, he never envied
the rich their style of living:

> The great English country houses are built for gods; an
> exaggerated conception of the human being led to their scale.
> It is nightmarish to think of living in those terribly big rooms.

His natural taste was for a family kind of social life, intimate and
on a small scale. And his imaginative life was not of the kind that
needs constant outside stimulus or even an audience. He retained the
child's capacity to be happily absorbed, playing games by itself or
with one other. And so, though his friends sometimes found
Florence difficult, the marriage was a success. He was happy and,
for him, productive:

> It is no news merely to say that I am consciously happy
> during sixteen hours out of the daily twenty-four, and un-
> consciously happy during the other eight; and yet that is the
> only news I have. . . . Absolutely nothing "happens."
> Florence and I "see" nobody. . . . The sun shines, and the
> sea shines under it, and I eat a good deal twice a day, and the
> camellias are just beginning to bloom, and the oranges and
> lemons are ripe, and I do a great deal of work.

If one says that the ladies—and the men, too—were not very important in Max's life, one means that neither his character nor his
art was decisively affected by his relationships with them. The decisive events in his life had already occurred at home, long before
he ever met them. Important as our childhood years are to all of us,
most of us cannot become ourselves without in one way or another
reacting against them. Not only did Max never rebel against the
values and habits of his family; he lived happily with them until
the age of thirty-eight.

By the time he was eight, the adult Max begins to be visible:

> Somehow, mysteriously, when I was eight years old or so,
> the soldiery was eclipsed for me by the constabulary. Some-
> how the scarlet and the bearskins began to thrill me less than

164

the austere costume and calling of the Metropolitan Police. . . .
It was not the daffodils that marked for me the coming of the
season of Spring. It was the fact that policemen suddenly wore
short tunics with steel buttons. It was not the fall of the leaf
nor the swallows' flight that signalled Autumn to me. It was
the fact that policemen were wearing long thick frock-coats
with buttons of copper. . . . By the time I was eleven years old
I despised the Force. I was interested only in politicians—in
Statesmen, as they were called at that time.

From this interest in the clothes of others, Max soon developed,
stimulated by the example of his half brother Julius, a fastidiousness about his own. He never seems to have passed through an inky-
schoolboy stage (a Max with pimples is unimaginable), and by the
time he was fifteen he was already a dandy:

My new black trousers are beautifully stripey and well made,
perhaps a little loose about the knee but *very* nice. . . . I am
still wearing my flower which has lasted wonderfully.

So at fifteen. At twenty-four, we find him dressed for Sunday in
"flannel coat, white waistcoat, purple tie with turquoise pin, duck
trousers and straw hat" and possessing "a smoking suit of purple
silk with dark red facings," and at eighty, when Mr. Behrman first
met him:

He wore a double-breasted suit of gray flannel with a prim-
rose sheen, and a low-cut vest that had wide, soft lapels. On
his head was a stiff straw hat set at a rakish angle. . . . Also,
he was wearing neat, well-fitting patent-leather pumps and
white socks.

Being one of those persons who generally look like an unmade
bed, I have always felt a certain resentment when confronted by an
impeccable turnout. I am therefore as delighted as I am surprised
to learn that Max's was not always faultless. According to a fellow-
dandy, William Nicholson, "The perfection of his toilet was occasionally marred by a missing button or a split glove."

Growing up in the society of siblings so much older than himself,
his imaginative fantasies were directed very early toward grown-up
life:

165

I disbelieved in fairies, was not sure about knight errants, was glad to hear that the sea had been cleared of pirates and that Indians were dying out. . . . After dark, I was simply a man-of-the-world. . . . I dined at my club on chicken and cherry-tart and went to a party. . . . I cannot imagine what happened at the party except that I stayed late and was the guest of someone I had heard of in grown-up conversation.

A boy who on the football field wishes he were playing hunt-the-slipper and at the swimming pool looks forward to returning to the latest novel by Miss Braddon might be expected to have a hard time at his boarding school. But it was not so for Max at Charterhouse. Adolescent boys are conformists and inclined to persecute the odd individual, but only if the latter, as he usually does, shows fear; the fearlessly peculiar they leave alone and even respect. Having always at home been encouraged to be himself, Max the schoolboy had a self-confidence which made him invulnerable. He continued to draw caricatures and began also to write. In his last year at Charterhouse, he printed his first literary effort—a parody of the footnotes of Classical Scholarship of which any adult humorist could be proud.[1] As an undergraduate, he first displayed his talent for hoaxes when he succeeded in sending no less august a personage than Professor Furnivall, the Shakespeare scholar, trotting off to the British Museum to trace down an Elizabethan heraldic device invented by Max himself. Professor Furnivall was not to be his last victim. Bernard Shaw, to mention only one, was to be bewildered:

Max discovered a volume of photographs of Shaw in youth. Carefully he altered each for the worse; in one amplifying the nose, in another diverting the eyes into a squint. He then had these new versions rephotographed and sent them to various friends in England accompanied by a request to post them back to Shaw along with a letter from some imaginary admirer stating that he had found the enclosed photograph of Mr. Shaw and would so much like him to sign and return it. The friends obeyed. Max was delighted to learn that as one monstrous likeness after another arrived by post, Shaw grew steadily more baffled.

Though his character and tastes were fully formed by the time he was twenty-one, it naturally took Max a little longer to find the style, visual and verbal, in which to express them. But not much longer. His first exercises in wit are modeled on Oscar Wilde's. For example:

> What is your favourite day? Tuesdays make me feel very gentlemanly, Wednesdays bring out my cleverness. . . . On Saturdays I am common, have you noticed that?

This was written in 1893, but four years later, in a review of a volume of verses by a Mr. Clement Scott, he has already found his own voice. After quoting a stanza by that unfortunate gentleman containing the lines "You meet me with your beauty unimpaired" and "You sit and laugh at men who loved your hair," Max gets down to work:

> It is possible that a careless reader would imagine that the lines were really addressed to some lady. We prefer to think,—indeed, we are sure—that they were addressed to some seaside resort, whose identity is cunningly veiled under the pseudonym of "Violet," lest Cromer or another should wax jealous. Surely it would be rather prosaic to speak of a lady's beauty as being "unimpaired." On the other hand, if we take it that, say, Broadstairs is apostrophized, then "not built over" would be the meaning, and the phrase would be felicitous and pretty. Surely, again, no lady, worthy of the name, would sit down on a chair and guffaw at men who had loved her hair, even though their proceeding had seemed ridiculous. We are sure that the *h* in "hair" is a conversational sort of *h*, dropped in to hide a sly reference to ozone. A popular seaside resort, moreover, can afford to "laugh" at the defection of a few visitors more or less.

Similarly, while his first published caricatures show the influence of Pellegrini, the "Edwardyssey" series of 1899 could have been drawn by nobody else.

To Max, caricature was an objective art:

> When I draw a man, I am concerned simply and solely with the physical aspect of him. I don't bother for one moment about his soul. . . . I see all his salient points exaggerated (points of face, figure, port, gesture and vesture), and all his insignificant points proportionately diminished. . . . In the salient points a man's soul does reveal itself, more or less faintly. . . . Thus if one underline these points, and let the others vanish, one is bound to lay bare the soul.

W. H. Auden

In literature, on the other hand, his ideal was a subjective one:

> True style is essentially a personal matter . . . in fact, not a mere spy-hole to things in general, but a spy-hole to things as they are reflected in the soul of the writer. . . . To express through printed words all the little side-lights of thought and fine shades of meaning that are in him is the task of the modern stylist; and the tricks and formalities which must be gone through in accomplishing that task carry him further and further away from his ordinary manner in colloquy. . . . Modern prose style is further removed from colloquialism than was the prose style of the eighteenth century, for this paradoxical reason: that colloquialism is its model.

This difference between his conceptions of the two arts, together with the fact that he began drawing as a child and started to write only in adolescence, may account for the curious contrast between his working methods in each. For caricatures he had to be in the mood, but when the mood came he drew with great rapidity and ease, almost as if in a trance. Writing, on the other hand, he always found a slow and difficult business, not only when he was faced with a journalistic chore but even when he was writing *con amore*. The initial conception of *Zuleika Dobson*, for example, came to him many years before he succeeded in realizing it.

To mature so early, to be certain of one's identity, tastes, and talents at an age when most people are still floundering around, confers many blessings—a happy, contented life is practically guaranteed—but a price has to be paid for them. Biologists tell us that much of the achievement of our species may be put down to the fact that in comparison with other animals we are so slow in reaching physical maturity, and it would appear that in most fields of human activity—music and mathematics are exceptions—the greatest achievements are attained by those who, emotionally and intellectually, are late developers. The price which Max paid was that after about the year 1910 he became incapable of responding imaginatively to anything happening about him, whether in society or the arts. That he should have felt a nostalgia for the "good old days" is not unusual; anyone who has had the luck to have been born into a home where there existed love and good things to eat feels the same. And Max the man, though a Tory and at times a frightened one, was too intelligent and too just to become a Colonel Blimp:

168

Where are all the gentlefolk of the world gone to? Not a sign of them in London (barring in the private houses one went to). Not a sign of them in the train or on the boat or anywhere. Only this rabble of dreadful creatures—who aren't of course dreadful at all, except from the standpoint of a carefully-brought-up person who remembers the days when enjoyment of life was a thing reserved for a few other carefully-brought-up persons.

What is peculiar is that in his thirties Max should as an artist have ceased to be able to transmute his current experiences into art. Another kind of caricaturist might have agreed with him that the notables of the nineties and early nineteen-hundreds were easier to draw:

They walked, and they walked slowly, so you could observe them. There wore whiskers without mustaches and mustaches without whiskers . . . Men wore beards of different shapes and different cuts; they wore their hair in varied styles; and they took much more care about their dress, and there were so many ways of dressing.

But another kind of artist would have felt the clean-shaven, uniform, and informal figures of the younger generation as a challenge, and studied them until he had learned how to bring out their comic points.

For many of us, some of our most important "new" experiences are discoveries about the hitherto unknown past. Max's favorite authors in his youth were Thackeray, the early George Meredith, the later Henry James. That he should have found few younger authors to add to his list is less strange than his apparent inability to add any older ones. More seriously, he never learned to see the experiences which did matter to him in any light but that in which he had first seen them. Consequently, if one compares two drawings or two books of his, it is almost impossible, on the evidence of the works themselves, to date them. Despite this lack of development, his work doesn't "date," as one would expect, and as the work of so many of his contemporaries does. If one asks why this should be so, the answer is, I believe, that in him the aesthetic sensibility was never divorced, as it was in many of his colleagues, from the moral feelings. Fashions in what is considered beautiful or interesting are always changing, but the difference between a man of honor

169

and a scoundrel is eternal. Reggie Turner introduced Max into one of his novels under the fictional name Hans Branders, of whom he says:

> There was a strain of cruelty in him, not harshness nor brutality, but cruelty simple and isolated. But there was no malice in him, no pettiness, and he had the kindest of hearts.

What Turner means, I think, is that an artist whose eye immediately detects moral failings in his subjects and whose hand instinctively reveals them is bound to seem cruel. It was not personal animosity which made the drawings of Oscar Wilde and the Prince of Wales so deadly (Wilde, indeed, was his friend); he simply could not help revealing the moral truth about them both—that Wilde was a man "whose soul had swooned in sin and revived vulgar" and that the First Gentleman of Europe was an ineffable bounder. It is this immediate clarity of insight, free from all malice or prejudice, which makes Max superior to most caricaturists, even to Daumier. Even his most devastating portraits never strike one as unjust; one never feels that for personal or ideological reasons he had decided to uglify his victim before he looked at him.

While we are on the subject, I wish either Mr. Behrman or Lord David Cecil had taken advantage of our morally permissive culture and included among his illustrations a cartoon of Frank Harris which few persons can have seen but many must be dying to see:

> During a moment of silence Harris's voice was heard booming out. "Unnatural vice!" he was saying, "I know nothing of the joys of unnatural vice. You must ask my friend Oscar about them. But," he went on, with a reverential change of tone, "had Shakespeare asked me, I should have had to submit!" Max went home and drew a cartoon of Harris, stark naked and with his moustache bristling, looking coyly over his shoulder at Shakespeare who shrinks back at the alarming prospect. Underneath was written, "Had Shakespeare asked me . . ."[2]

As in his caricatures, so in his literary judgments. His adverse criticisms of other writers, whether in table talk or parody, are directed against their moral defects—the sadism in Kipling, the caddishness in Wells, Shaw's indifference to individual human lives —and when he tries to explain his admiration for Henry James, it is of James as a moralist that he speaks:

Greater than all my aesthetic delight in the books is my moral regard for the author. . . . Despite his resolute self-suppression for his "form's" sake, Mr. Henry James, through his books, stands out as clearly to me as any preacher I have ever seen perched up in a pulpit. And I do not happen to have heard any preacher in whom was a moral fervour, or one whose outlook on the world seemed to me so fine and touching and inspiring, so full of reverence for noble things and horror of things ignoble.

Though Max was certainly underestimating his appeal when he said that he had an audience of fifteen hundred, much that he wrote is unlikely now to be widely read. His drama reviews will be read in bulk only by historians of the drama. For the ordinary reader, the only journalism which remains readable after the occasion which caused it has been forgotten is a piece of comic attack. Jerome K. Jerome's play *The Passing of the Third Floor Back* has sunk without trace, but Max's review of it remains afloat; Duse is now a mere name to all but a few elderly fogies, but Max's comment on her acting is remembered by many: "Age cannot wither her nor custom stale her endless uniformity."

A good deal that he wrote took the form of the "pure" essay, written, as Lord David Cecil says, "not to instruct or edify but only to produce aesthetic satisfaction." I do not know why it should be so, but today the "pure" essay is a literary genre to which no reader under sixty can bring himself to attend. We expect an essay to instruct or edify; for aesthetic satisfaction we turn to poetry or fiction.

As a literary critic, Max was wise to confine himself for the most part to literary parodies of the few writers he knew well. Of poetry, as of music, he had no understanding—Henley's "Invictus" was one of his favorite pieces—and both his taste and his reading in fiction were too limited to make him a critic of note. His table-talk criticism is sound enough as far as it goes: he is never mean—though he should have spotted the difference between Virginia Woolf's handling of "the stream of consciousness" and Joyce's—and even in writers whom he finds antipathetic he is always ready to admit their virtues. If his admiration for "Eminent Victorians" now seems excessive, one can understand it: he recognized that Strachey's literary ideal was akin to his own. In noting the authors whom he singles out for praise, I am puzzled by one thing. Had I been Max, there would have been two persons, both living, of whom I should

171

have felt wildly envious—Ronald Firbank and James Thurber. I have searched through the Turner *Letters, Max,* and *Portrait of Max* and have found but one slight reference to Thurber and none to Firbank. Can it have been that he was?

As a parodist, he is probably the finest in English. His only rivals are James and Horace Smith, the authors of *Rejected Addresses.* Unfortunately, literary parodies can never appeal to more than a limited and highly sophisticated public, for they can be appreciated only by a reader who is intimately acquainted with the authors parodied. Caricature, or visual parody, is much more accessible, since to "get" a caricature it is not necessary to have seen the subject oneself. Thus, while Max's caricatures should delight almost everybody, the only writings of his which are likely to reach a wide public are the stories—*Zuleika Dobson, Seven Men, A Variety of Things.*

Greatly as I admire both the man and his work, I consider Max Beerbohm a dangerous influence—just how dangerous one must perhaps have been brought up in England to know. His attitude both to life and to art, charming enough in him, when taken up by others as a general cultural ideal becomes something deadly, especially for the English, an intelligent but very lazy people, far too easily bored, and persuaded beyond argument that they are the *Herrenvolk.* One may be amused—though not very—that after living in Italy for forty-five years Max still could not speak Italian, but such insularity is not to be imitated. "Good sense about trivialities," he once wrote, "is better than nonsense about things that matter." True enough, but how easily this can lead to the conclusion that anyone who attempts to deal with things that matter must be a bore, that rather than run the risk of talking nonsense one should play it safe and stick to charming trifles.

> How many charming talents have been spoiled by the instilled desire to do "important" work! Some people are born to lift heavy weights. Some are born to juggle with golden balls.

True enough again, one thinks at a first reading; at a second, one notices the insidiousness of the metaphor. In the circus, the juggler is superior to the weight lifter, for juggling is an art and lifting heavy weights primarily a matter of brute strength. Had Max written that some are jugglers, some (shall we say?) lion-tamers, the comparison might have been just. As it is, he slyly suggests that minor artists may look down their noses at major ones and that "important" work may be left to persons of an inferior kennel, like the Russians, the Germans, the Americans, who, poor dears, know no better. The great cultural danger for the English is, to my mind, their tendency to judge the arts by the values appropriate to the conduct of family life. Among brothers and sisters it is becoming to entertain each other with witty remarks, hoaxes, family games and jokes, unbecoming to be solemn, to monopolize the conversation, to talk shop, to create emotional scenes. But no art, major or minor, can be governed by the rules of social amenity. The English have a greater talent than any other people for creating an agreeable family life; that is why it is such a threat to their artistic and intellectual life. If the atmosphere were not so charming, it would be less of a temptation. In postwar Britain, the clothes, accents, and diction of the siblings may have changed, but, so far as I can judge, the suffocating insular coziness is just the same. Suffocating for nine artists out of ten; it so happened that Max was the exceptional tenth man, whose talents were fostered by family life and exactly tailored to its tastes.

Twice in his life—in 1894, with an essay in the first number of *The Yellow Book*, entitled "A Defence of Cosmetics," which caused *Punch* to call him a popinjay, and in 1923, when his cartoons of the Royal Family caused one newspaper to conclude that their author must be "either a shameless bounder or a stealthy Bolshevist"—he succeeded in shocking Philistia. (Characteristically, when he heard the cartoons had caused offense, he withdrew them from exhibition.) But in literary and artistic circles, from the start of his career until his death, he was a sacred cow. Never once, so far as I know, was he attacked by any critic worth listening to, and this is not a healthy sign. The only person who seems to have realized the danger was Reggie Turner, who wrote to Max in 1911:

> A caricaturist such as you, a satirist of the first and purest water, is not properly treated when people say that "his work can never give offence." "Amiability" is not your most outstanding quality in your work, any more than "gentleness" was in Napoleon's. And I see signs now that "the old country" is waking up to the danger of having you about. I rejoice, I rejoice, I rejoice.

Turner's rejoicing proved premature, and the man who had poured scorn on John Bull, mocked at Queen Victoria's prose, savaged Edward VII, and written a double ballade about George V and Queen Mary with its alternating refrain:

King   Queen

The   is duller than the

Queen   King[3]

ended up with a knighthood and a grave in St. Paul's Cathedral. Of course, Max was not, or only a teensy bit, to blame for this. His charm was, and still is, irresistible, and, which is unlike many charmers, there was nothing phony about him, because, as Chesterton perceived, he did not "indulge in the base idolatry of believing in himself." He had three ambitions in life: "to make good use of such little talent as I had, to lead a pleasant life, to pass muster." He achieved them all. How many of us will be able to say as much?

[1965]

Editor's notes

1. The reference is to "Carmen Becceriense," published in *Max in Verse: Rhymes and Parodies by Max Beerbohm*, ed. J. G. Riewald (Brattleboro, Vermont: The Stephen Greene Press, 1963, and London: William Heinemann, 1964), pp. 1-3.

2. The drawing is now reproduced in Rupert Hart-Davis, comp., *A Catalogue of the Caricatures of Max Beerbohm* (London: Macmillan, and Cambridge, Mass.: Harvard University Press, 1972), Plate 51.

3. The full text of Beerbohm's "Ballade Tragique à Double Refrain" is published in *Max in Verse*, pp. 48-49.

F. W. Dupee

MAX BEERBOHM AND THE RIGORS OF FANTASY

Zuleika (pronounced Zuleeka) *Dobson* was first published in London in 1911. Other editions followed in Britain and America. The book entered the Modern Library early, when the volumes making up that series were still few, and smelled of frivolity, sin, and oilcloth —or whatever those simulated limp leather covers were made of. Like *South Wind*, *Zuleika Dobson* was obligatory reading for those literary initiates of the Twenties whose program included, on principle, an appreciation alike of the trifler and the titan: Douglas with Dreiser and Dostoevsky, Beerbohm with Proust and Joyce. In *Aspects of the Novel* (1927), E. M. Forster called *Zuleika Dobson* "the most consistent achievement of fantasy in our time." "Our time" meant, presumably, the Teens and Twenties. When the Twenties ended, Beerbohm rather faded from one's consciousness.

After his death, in 1956, came the modest resurrection. Beerbohm lived again in Ellen Moers's *The Dandy*, in S. N. Behrman's *Portrait of Max*, and, more recently and completely, in David Cecil's *Max, A Biography*.[1] If he was "easy to forget but delightful to remember," as I wrote some years ago, he has since proved to be ever harder to forget and more delightful to remember. Re-reading Beerbohm one gets caught up in the intricate singularity of his mind, all of a piece yet full of surprises, as one does in Boswell's Johnson. In *Zuleika Dobson* his mind is in full flower, a tropical bloom, lurid and elaborate, prickly but not poisonous, except to the foolish.

F. W. Dupee, "Afterword." From the Signet Classics edition of *Zuleika Dobson* (New York: The New American Library, 1966), pp. 237-255. Originally published in *The New York Review of Books*, 9 June 1966, pp. 12-17, under the title "Beerbohm: The Rigors of Fantasy." The text of the essay has been slightly changed and enlarged for this edition. Title supplied by Author. Reprinted by permission of F. W. Dupee.

That his drawings and parodies should survive is no cause for wonder. One look at them, or into them, and his old reputation is immediately re-established: that whim of iron, that cleverness amounting to genius. What *is* odd is that his stories and essays should turn out to be equally durable. The mandarin of mandarins, Beerbohm wrote with a kind of conscious elegance that has since become generally suspect. This *nouveau riche* English has for us the fault of shamelessly advertising to the world the lush abundance of its verbal resources. The plain declarative sentence is apt to be set off by a dazzle of rhetorical questions and apostrophes to the reader. Ostentatious connectives, from "indeed" to "however that may be," are *de rigueur*. No word is repeated if a synonym can possibly be found. The attack on the mandarin style, carried out variously by such writers as Mencken, Eliot, and Gertrude Stein, made of repetition a virtue. Into the wastebasket went the book of synonyms. The young Yeats had anticipated the new taste for verbal economy when he criticized a sentence about Hamlet in Oscar Wilde's *The Decay of Lying:* "The world has become sad because a puppet was once melancholy." Yeats asked Wilde why he had changed "sad" to "melancholy." "He replied that he wanted a full sound at the close of his sentence, and I thought it no excuse and an example of the vague impressiveness that spoilt his writing for me."

Beerbohm's mandarinism tended to mock itself, subtly or bluntly. Starting a sentence with "indeed" he went on to apologize in parentheses for the "otiose" word. He avoided not only the vaguely impressive but the crudely *ex*pressive. A friend wrote to him praising the sentence about the lightning in *Zuleika Dobson:* "A sudden white vertical streak slid down the sky". Beerbohm replied: "The word 'slid' was in the first draft 'slithered' which, though more accurate really, looked rather *cherché* and so was jettisoned." Thus he profited from the mandarin abundance while generally avoiding or deriding its excesses.

One now reads Beerbohm with recognitions beyond the powers of those of us who were literary neophytes in the Twenties. The elegant trifler contributed more than one had supposed to literary history. Beerbohm played an essential if deliberately minor role in the famous "revolution of taste" that took place between, roughly, 1910 and 1922. True, he was never a "modernist" in his own tastes, preferring the poetry of Swinburne and the novels of Trollope, Meredith, and James to *Ulysses* and *The Waste Land*. Nevertheless,

he discovered before Pound and Eliot did (and independently of La-
forgue) the futility and pathos of the dandy and his lady. As a verbal
caricature of the London literary life, *Seven Men* parallels at several
points Pound's treatment of the same subject in *Hugh Selwyn
Mauberley*. *Mauberley* includes a verse portrait of Beerbohm under
the name of Brennbaum. The portrait is, appropriately, a verse
caricature of Beerbohm as dandy:

> The sky-like limpid eyes,
>   The circular infant's face,
> The stiffness from spats to collar
>   Never relaxing into grace . . .

Naturally, the famous revolution in taste "went too far." In doing
so, it has given work to critics and biographers ever since. Rehabili-
tating the major Victorians and in some cases the Edwardians has
long been a reputable occupation. Tennyson, Kipling, and Queen
Victoria herself have recovered from the clawings of Beerbohm's
velvet glove.

Yet how exhilarating those clawings were at the time. I mean not
only such celebrated caricatures as the one of Queen Victoria attend-
ing with majestic patience to a shrunken Tennyson reading *In
Memoriam*. More devastating were the drawings that caricatured the
political or the literary life in general. There was the bitter series
called "The Second Childhood of John Bull," chiefly inspired by
Beerbohm's disgust with the Boer War. There was the series called
"The Old and the Young Self," in which eighteen well-known
Edwardians were confronted in the fullness of their age and fame
by the specters, gloating or reproachful, of their youthful selves. A
real *terribilità* plays about the latter series. It could scarcely fail to
impress the literary initiates of any period, from the Twenties to
the present.

With the foolish in mind, Max Beerbohm added to the 1947 edition
of *Zuleika Dobson* a warning against interpretation. Inevitably his
remarks recall Mark Twain's admonitory address to the readers of
Huckleberry Finn. Critics have generally disregarded Mark Twain's
threats, sometimes with deplorable results. Taking our chances, we
may dismiss Beerbohm's warning, too. It is only part of the "act,"
the very stagey act that *Zuleika Dobson* is throughout. If first-rate

humorists are never to be taken too seriously, they are to be taken least seriously when they are most at pains to warn us against taking them seriously at all.

Beerbohm maintains that his book is "just a fantasy." No satirical or other serious comment is intended. But this is impossible in the nature of his genre as he names it here. "Fantasy" must have something which to fantasticate, and what can that something be except "reality" or some aspect of it? "Fantasy" is the rather jejune term for a kind of narrative that was uncommon in Western Europe before the eighteenth century. Nobody, I suppose, would call *The Divine Comedy, The Faerie Queene* and *The Pilgrim's Progress* "fantasies." They are allegories in which the events and characters, however implausible themselves, correspond to principles of morality or religious dogma which had a real existence for their authors. The rise of modern fantasy seems to have had a complicated relation, first to the decline of faith in the reality or efficacy of those principles, and second to the advance of "realism" as a literary mode. Fantasy brings into comic question the nature of belief itself. There was the case of the Irish bishop who is alleged to have remarked of *Gulliver's Travels* on its first appearance, "This book is full of improbable lies, and for my part I hardly believe a word of it."

The great fantasies extend from *Gulliver's Travels* to the *Alice* books to the serio-comic writings of Franz Kafka. The great fantasies embrace not only certain aspects of reality but just about all of it, even in some instances God and the gods. The authors make it their business to fantasticate the realities so thoroughly that, presto!, the realities come to look fantastic themselves.

Their business? Good fantasists are the most businesslike of writers. They go about their creative operations as methodically and with as straight a face as the Lilliputians go about taking inventory of Gulliver's pockets. Nor does Gulliver feel surprise, least of all amusement, at their efforts. This exemplary Englishman is only annoyed by the invasion of his privacy. As with Gulliver so with the other protagonists of comic fantasy. They are themselves quite humorless. A grin from Gulliver would spoil the show. A wink from Candide or Alice or Joseph K. or Zuleika Dobson would bring down in rubble the cunningly constructed worlds of unreal reality they inhabit. A total sobriety of tone is the law of laws for fantastic comedy.

For some twelve years (1898-1910) Max Beerbohm wrote a weekly theater article for the *Saturday Review* of London. He was thus exposed to a good deal of trashy fantasy in dramatic as well as narrative form. Even the ballet came to bore him. Much of what he saw or read in this vein seems to have been delinquent in essentially the same way that much of what is today called "black humor" is delinquent. It broke the law of laws: it failed to take itself seriously enough. What he saw or read was not willfully wacky as the worst black humor is at present. For the Kafkan revolution in fantasy, of which black humor is the sometimes depressing offspring—depressing in its merely mechanical frenzies—belonged to the far future. Thus the action of fantasy was not as yet freely generated in the disturbed psyche, where anything goes, as the action of fantasy was as a rule to be for Kafka and his followers. Nor had history itself as yet reached the extremity of mad inventiveness which today leaves the average fantasist far behind and breathing hard.

It was not willful wackiness but mere waggishness that afflicted fantasy during Beerbohm's London years. An air of holiday high jinks, of forced festivity, hung about it. Pre-eminent of its kind and in its time was *Peter Pan, or the Boy Who Wouldn't Grow Up.* Barrie's play was beloved by many and derided by a few, doubtless for the same reason: it gave the frankest possible expression to the prevailing vogue for halfhearted escapism. Reviewing *Peter Pan* on its first appearance, in 1905, Beerbohm noted that Barrie had always incarnated the prevailing "child-worship" of the period but that in *Peter Pan* he had outdone himself. Barrie was there seen "in his quiddity undiluted—the child in a state of nature, unabashed—the child, as it were, in its bath, splashing, and crowing as it splashes." Puck's doings in *Midsummer Night's Dream* were "credible and orderly" compared to "the riot of inconsequence and of exquisite futility" that made up Peter Pan's doings.

Nor was Beerbohm himself an infallible master of fantasy. An early example, *The Happy Hypocrite* (1897), has the interest for us of commemorating a significant moment in his development. As J. G. Riewald has shown, the youthful author of *The Happy Hypocrite* was imitating *The Picture of Dorian Gray* while at the same time trying to free himself from Wilde's influence.[2] *The Happy Hypocrite*, in which a devilish dandy is transformed—not without irony on the author's part—into a loving husband, shows Beerbohm asserting his will to innocence and survival against Wilde's presumed will to the opposite fate. An amalgam of the parable and the fairy tale, *The Happy Hypocrite* is nevertheless a strained performance. So is a much later story, *The Dreadful Dragon of Hay Hill* (1928). This

seems to have been written to order by "The Incomparable Max"—
the title early bestowed, or perhaps foisted, on Beerbohm by a rival
wit, Shaw—rather than by Beerbohm himself. By "Beerbohm himself" I mean the Beerbohm in whom the public and the private
man, the insider and the outsider, the precocious child and the pre-
ternaturally youthful ancient oddly combined to form what I have
called his intricate singularity of mind.

This was the Max Beerbohm who did his best writing *(Zuleika
Dobson, A Christmas Garland, Seven Men, And Even Now)* between
about 1910 and about 1920—years during which he lived for the most
part away from England. *Zuleika Dobson* had been begun and
dropped as early as 1898. S. N. Behrman, who has examined the
early manuscript, notes that it is "scraggly, written in random
columns and riddled with doodles"—that is, sketches for caricatures. Here, Behrman says, "you may watch the struggle between
Max's dual careers. Often the graphic seems to gain the upper
hand." *Zuleika Dobson* was largely written and was brought to
completion in 1910-1911 in a charge of energy released by his resignation from the *Saturday Review,* his marriage to Florence Kahn,
an American actress whom he had long kept on the string, and
their removal to Italy.

In fantastic comedy, many a familiar jest, proverbial saying, or
fashionable phrase comes literally true and many a flower of poesy
is born to blush for its presumption. One sometimes says of an
unfortunate friend, or despairingly of oneself, that he, or one, is
subhuman, a rat, a worm, an insect. In Kafka's well-known story,
a certain self-despising salesman wakes up one morning to find
that he *is* an insect, complete with many wiggly little legs. Not surprisingly, his remarkable feat of self-realization goes unappreciated
by the members of his family, and he presently dies of cruelty and
neglect at their hands. The death of Kafka's salesman is paralleled,
in a purely comic vein, by the fate of Enoch Soames, one of Beerbohm's creations in *Seven Men.* Soames is the harmless author of
a small book of verse called *Fungoids* and a small book of essays
called *Negations.* He is nevertheless an avowed poet of the Diabolist
school, out of Baudelaire by way of Lionel Johnson, and has written such verses as

Round and round the shutter'd Square
I stroll'd with the Devil's arm in mine.

Eventually, and much to Soames's surprise, the Devil appears in person and makes off with Soames.

In that story, a single victim is claimed by the process I have been trying to describe—let us call it the process of comic literalization. In *Zuleika Dobson* the same mechanism is flagrantly at work and the victims are many. The casual wish is father to the dreadful deed on an unprecedented scale. The cliché bears watching lest it come true with a vengeance. Oxford dons, one learns, have often remarked that Oxford would be a splendid place if it were not for the undergraduates; Oxford undergraduates have expressed identical thoughts concerning the dons. The dons win in *Zuleika Dobson*. One evening, following the final race of Eights Week, they learn that the undergraduates have drowned themselves en masse in the Isis, as the stretch of the Thames at Oxford is known. "And always the patient river bears its awful burden towards Iffley," Beerbohm writes. This flower of poesy begins like a line from "Lycidas" and ends like something in small print in a guide to Oxfordshire. Iffley is the grubby-sounding place where the locks are that make boating possible at Oxford.

Meanwhile, the crew of Judas College has won the present series of races. Its shell has "bumped" the shell of proud Magdalen. At Judas the dons have celebrated the traditional Bump Supper in splendid calm owing to the scarcely noted absence of the Judas undergraduates. Only Mr. Pedby's illiterate reading of the traditional Latin grace has disturbed the occasion. But this mishap is forgiven when it is realized that memories of the ill-read grace will provide chuckles for generations of dons to come. Mr. Pedby has contributed his hilarious mite to the vast cocoon of Oxford history—bloody, scandalous or hilarious—which Oxford is forever weaving for itself.

In all of Judas College, only Zuleika Dobson is at this moment unhappy and restless. She is the young woman, a conjurer by profession, for love of whom, ostensibly, the students have drowned themselves—all but the cad Noaks, who has chosen a belated and grimmer death. Zuleika has made more Oxford history, one would think, than Mr. Pedby has. Yet as an outsider, and a woman at that, she is ignored by the dons and obliged to spy on the Bump Supper proceedings from a balcony.

In Zuleika's career the literalizing principle is written large. She is a *femme fatale* whose brief stay at Oxford has been actually fatal to hundreds. Surely she has set a new high in the records of *femme* fatality, exceeding the combined tolls of Keats's Belle Dame, Swin-

burne's Dolores, and Wilde's Salomé. One might expect her to be
beaten to death with oars as Salomé is with soldiers' shields. She
isn't, nor is she herself visited by any feeling except a resentful lone-
liness, like that of a popular actress who has made one curtain call
too many and is suddenly confronted by an empty house. Whither
Zuleika? Zuleika asks herself. After such triumphs, what expectations? True, she has had a gratifying talk with her grandfather.
The stiff old Warden of Judas has confessed that he was in his
youth an *homme fatal* with many female victims to his credit. What
has occurred between the two is unmistakably a "recognition
scene." It recalls—probably not accidentally—the scene in *Major
Barbara* in which the Salvation Army commander and the ruthless
old tycoon slyly discover that each is possessed by the Will to Power
and that they are therefore father and daughter after all. Zuleika is
somewhat cheered by her encounter with the Warden and presently
she finds the answer to her Whither. Consulting her bejeweled copy
of Bradshaw she orders a special train for—Cambridge. Nothing
can stop a fatal woman so long as she believes that somewhere
there are more males eager to be fatalized.

Whether she found Cambridge as compliant as Oxford is not
known. Beerbohm never composed sequels, except to other men's
works (see his "Sequelula to *The Dynasts*" in *A Christmas Garland*). In 1941, however, Sydney Roberts produced a sequel of his
own, called *Zuleika in Cambridge*.[3] I have not read the book but
gather from Riewald's account of it that her visit to the other university disappointed her. Firmly resistant to her attractions was
serious Cambridge, the Cambridge of Milton, Wordsworth, and
Dr. Leavis. No lovelorn corpses cluttered the patient Cam. Beerbohm did, nevertheless, reveal snatches of her later history by way
of a letter signed Zuleika Kitchener and addressed to George Gershwin, who once thought of making a highbrow musical out of her
book. In the letter she berated Beerbohm for misrepresenting her in
the book and added a postscript saying: "I was married secretly to
Lord Kitchener, early in 1915. Being so worried by his great responsibilities at that time, he no longer had the grit to cope with my
importunities, poor fellow."

Nothing came of Gershwin's project. Nor did *Zuleika* ever reach
the New York stage in the form contemplated, and long worked at, by
Wolcott Gibbs and others. They eventually discovered, what might
seem obvious from the start to any but the most obdurate of Broad-

way adapters, that *Zuleika Dobson* would be nothing without the crystalline surface of unreality wrought by the author for the characters and settings of the book. Release these flies from their amber and they would be just dead flies.[4]

"In reading *Zuleika Dobson* as a description of life at Oxford we should be well-advised to allow for ironic intention," Northrop Frye observes in his *Anatomy of Criticism*. Not every reader has been able to make that allowance. The outrageousness of the story has made it a problem to some of its interpreters. To Edmund Wilson the part about the mass suicide of the undergraduates is "completely unreal."[5]

What parts of the book *does* Wilson find "real"? What words of *Gulliver did* the bishop believe? Where fantasy is concerned, there is no accounting for people's credulities.

But Wilson is not alone in his objection to *Zuleika Dobson,* and Beerbohm's dehumanizing of his characters does perhaps ask for a bit of explaining. For me, there is only one moment in the book when it is possible to "feel with" any of them. The Duke of Dorset is watching Zuleika's clumsy performance by moonlight and listening to her arch patter ("Well, this is rather queer"). He is so horribly embarrassed for her that he looks with rage on the other young men to whom his beloved is so recklessly exposing herself ("Damn them, they were sorry for her," he thinks). At this point, one guesses, Beerbohm could not help drawing on his own intimate experience as a friend and lover of actresses, ultimately the husband of an indifferent one whose Pre-Raphaelite ecstasies and graces he found laughable, though lovable, even off-stage. For the rest, the author kept his distance from the goings-on in *Zuleika.* So much so that he was surprised when his oldest friend, Reginald Turner, wrote him that— to quote David Cecil's paraphrase of the letter—"he found the characters almost painfully real; he believed in Katie the serving maid too much . . . to take her sufferings in the spirit of comedy." To this Beerbohm replied that he "certainly hadn't realized that Katie and those others were at all real," adding that if "really dramatic scenes . . . without humanity" were possible in the theater, he "never would have admitted this in the *Saturday.*"
· The reference to the *Saturday Review* seems conclusive. Much of the "ironic intention" of *Zuleika Dobson,* including the dehumanized characters, stemmed from Beerbohm's experiences as a theater reviewer for that periodical. *Zuleika* is not only about "life

at Oxford"; it is about literature, above all the literature of the contemporary London stage, to which Beerbohm had been for so many years "enslaved" (his word) through his connection with the *Saturday*. His reviews show him to have been often sickened by the theater's hackneyed themes, stock characters, trumped-up motivations, transparent mechanics, and false diction. They violated his common sense, they told on his nerves. So did the conduct, professional and private, of certain leading performers: clumsy "conjurers" and would-be *femmes* (or *hommes) fatales. Zuleika Dobson* is life at Oxford seen through the eyes of an inveterate "play-goer," some ideally demoralized veteran of the stalls. Beerbohm, it should be recalled, places the action of his story "in the middle of the Edwardian Age," a time when the theater, bad though much of it was, bulked larger as an institution than it ever has since in Anglo-American culture. Our theater today seems hardly important enough to merit satire, as distinct from kidding, at its expense.

A reading of *Around Theatres,* Beerbohm's collected reviews, is, then, more germane to an understanding of *Zuleika Dobson* than is a short history of Oxford, with maps. The Oxford setting creates itself as one reads, especially the Oxford setting in its legendary or sentimental aspects. Here Matthew Arnold's too memorable paragraph (concluding the preface to his *Essays in Criticism: First Series)* about the "home of lost causes . . . and impossible loyalties" does continual comic service. The parodying of Arnold starts with Beerbohm's first paragraph, where it is Oxford's railroad station and not her Gothic towers that "whisper to the tourist the last enchantments of the Middle Age." We soon learn that these enchantments still prevail elsewhere in the University. The Oxford of *Zuleika Dobson* remains "medieval" in its charm as well as in other, less lovable, ways; and it is still chivalrous, to the point of suicide.

Yes, there have been many Oxfords. There was the Oxford of the various religious revivals, with their Ridleys and Latimers, their Newmans and Puseys. There was the neo-pagan Oxford of Jowett and Pater, when bands of undergraduates are reputed to have marched around chanting the choruses of Swinburne's *Atalanta in Calydon.* There was the eighteenth-century Oxford which to the young Gibbon was wholly barbarous. There was the Victorian Oxford which to Walter Bagehot consisted of colleges that were merely "hotels with bells"—refuges for sporting upper-class youths. There is the Oxford of the present, swamped by the Morris motor plant, made democratic and serious beyond Bagehot's dreams, but still beautiful to look at, still whispering its enchantments and sounding its bells amid the tumult of traffic.

The Oxford Beerbohm knew as an undergraduate in the Nineties was, or seemed to him, lushly end-of-century. It made him, he later said, "insufferable," meaning idle, mocking, snobbish, an adherent of Oscar Wilde's cult and that of past dandies, D'Orsay and Disraeli. He claimed that he had read little at the University except Wilde's *Intentions* and Thackeray's *The Four Georges*. The eating clubs he frequented were exclusive, although not quite so exclusive as the fictional Junta, of which it is said in *Zuleika Dobson* that the Duke of Dorset was for a while the sole member. To the young Beerbohm, abstaining from the more wholesome undergraduate pursuits was an agreeable duty. Once when he was out for a stroll he encountered a fellow student with an oar across his shoulder. "Bound for the river?" the student cheerily asked. "What river?" Beerbohm replied.

His reminiscences of his Oxford life are the caricature of a caricature, the original having been himself. To his role as an undergraduate he brought an amused self-consciousness. He made histrionic capital of his short stature, his large head, his prominent eyes, and the scrutinizing stare of which they were capable. His whole earlier history predisposed him to amuse himself and others, and generally to do what he liked at the University. The belated child of adoring parents, the youngest by far of an animated circle of siblings and half-siblings, he had been early initiated into the Great World by his half-brother, Herbert Beerbohm Tree, already a celebrated actor when young Max was still at Oxford.

There, as elsewhere later on, he was the outsider-insider, capable of mocking things he also cherished, including his own personality. So if he loved Oxford and mocked it only affectionately in *Zuleika Dobson*, as Oxonians tend to say, he loved it on his own terms. These involved much skepticism, enough to set flowing the tricky currents of satire in *Zuleika Dobson*. Here faddishness is seen to flourish in proportion as Oxford believed itself to be supremely privileged, proudly possessed of its own history and legality, grotesquely celibate (if that is the word), and capable of extending to its dons the privilege of indifferentism toward the undergraduates, toward everything but the dons' own studies and society.

185

From Christ Church meadow a mist is described as continually rising and permeating the whole place. A prime characteristic of Oxford, the mist is lovingly evoked by Beerbohm. The passage has become a famous set-piece, but unlike Arnold's set-piece it is full of *double-entendres*. The mist is seen to enclose Oxford in a circle of glamor, like a soft-focus photograph. It also shelters the place from "reality," like a smoke screen. Zuleika penetrates and scatters this mist—for the reader. Her presence at the University shows us that its precious faddishness, its cherished weakness for lost causes and impossible loyalties, exist plentifully in the world at large, where they are known, less flatteringly, as the "herd instinct" or "conformity." Zuleika's triumph at Oxford is only a specialized form of the triumphs she has enjoyed everywhere, from Paris to "final Frisco." The great dandy, Dorset, adores her, but so did George Abimelech Post, "the best-groomed man in New York." Self-destruction threatens the herd wherever it exists, although the herd may elect to die in more dignified ways than do the swine in the parable. This Beerbohm saw as early as 1911, with an instinct born of his own highly cultivated idiosyncrasy.

It is not because she is "real" herself that Zuleika disperses the mist for us. On the contrary, it is because she is that most potent of forces, a figment of the mass mind. As a conjurer her skill is nil. Nor is she "strictly beautiful," Beerbohm states in a passage that has been analyzed into its multiple equivocations by William Empson in *Seven Types of Ambiguity* (Beerbohm's type in this passage is Empson's sixth).

It is true that Zuleika has, or acts as if she had, a devouring passion. She wants to love—love, that is, a man self-sufficient enough to scorn her love. Naturally, the man eludes her. Nobody will let her play Patient Grizzel. The Duke of Dorset matches her in his own lovelessness and in the impossible demands he makes on women. But all these passions are as phantasmal as the two characters themselves are. The passions are "motivations" of the kind forcibly applied to the personages of inferior drama to make their actions plausible. Complaints against the arbitrariness in this respect of Pinero, who finds his motives in the stock room, or of Shaw, who sometimes supplies them from his intellectual laboratory, recur in Beerbohm's theater reviews. So too with those reversals or, as Beerbohm with his mock pedantry calls them, "peripeties," which keep the moral advantage zooming back and forth throughout the long scenes between Zuleika and Dorset. So tangible does this advantage become in its relentless to and fro that it almost materializes as a ball or a brick.

Dorset is more interesting than Zuleika. He is "motivated" by more than his need to love—by his obligations as a great nobleman and dandy. The Duke is no fraud in these particulars as Zuleika is in her conjurer's role. He is just what he claims to be: the sum of all those titles, residences, servants, decorations, accomplishments, and clothes. Among his accouterments are the pair of owls that have always announced the coming deaths of Dukes of Dorset. The owls really appear on the battlements of Tankerton; they hoot *this* Duke of Dorset to his doom, even in the age of pre-paid telegrams. For the other undergraduates he sets the styles of dressing, of loving, and of dying. As a stage duke, Dorset is complete.

The Noakses and Batches are also complete, as stage plebeians. Noaks is a "foil" to the over-privileged Duke. As such he may briefly arouse our democratic sympathies. But his sentiments are soon discovered to be as heavy as his boots and the iron ring he wears to charm away rheumatism. The plebeian creations of Shaw, the great humanitarian, often surprise us by turning out to know their place: the clownish place traditionally reserved for members of the lower orders, from Dogberry to Doolittle. Nor, one suspects, are Zuleika's French maid, Mélisande, and the American Rhodes scholar, Abimelech V. Oover, "strictly" caricatures; they are, again, caricatures of caricatures: the stage French maid and the stage American.

To what in the story itself apart from the mass suicide does Edmund Wilson's cry of "unreal" *fail* to apply? To nothing, I fear. Our demoralized playgoer has "seen everything," the London theater's entire "offering." Not for the world would he have missed the fashionable performances of Greek tragedy in Gilbert Murray's florid English, complete with inverted syntax and doubled negatives, with messengers, *dei ex machina*, and choruses. The busts of the Roman emperors outside the Sheldonian Theater afford *Zuleika* a peculiarly original chorus, helpless, solicitous, whimpering with pity, sweating with fear.

Not that the patent unreality of the story doesn't occasionally pall. Beerbohm's achievement in the art of fantasy is here possibly *too* consistent. The lengthy speechifying, the tireless parodying of motivations and peripeties, make certain scenes tedious. For the wary reader, however, the tedium is continually relieved by all sorts of "tricks" on the author's part—puns, *double-entendres,* dissonances, parodies within parodies, lyrical set-pieces in the descriptive or historical mode, intrusions of the supernatural, brief realistic "shots," so to speak, as of Zuleika applauding at the concert with her hands high above her head like the thorough professional she is. The ironic vision is, moreover, apt to shift its objects abruptly from one type of stage convention to another. Our playgoer gets his Maeterlinck mixed up with his Wycherley. Romance envelops the moonlight walk of Zuleika and Dorset to her quarters in Judas after the concert and her own impromptu performance, the latter a great scene. But crude farce breaks in when, from her bedroom window, she dumps on the Duke's waiting figure the contents of a water pitcher (read chamberpot).

Romance is a recurring attraction in *Zuleika.* The moonlight, the floating mist, the nodding lilacs and laburnums, the weedy bottom of the Isis—all are summoned on stage from the greenwood of English pastoral tradition. They remain lovely, though invariably touched with mockery—the mockery of the purple patch, of eloquence itself. Eloquence itself, high or low, is another motif. There are speaking parts for all: the flowers, the bells, the stony Emperors, together with the more or less human beings. And oh, the things people *say!* Nothing in *Zuleika Dobson,* I find, stays in the memory better than the things people say in it. "She doesn't *look* like an orphan" (the wife of the Oriel don referring to Zuleika). "By God, this College [Judas] is well-named!" (Sir Harry Esson, betrayed by a former Warden, as he is stabbed and dies). "Death cancels all engagements" (The Duke of Dorset). "What harm has unrequited love ever done?" (Zuleika). "I say he was not a white man" (Oover of a legendary Oxford libertine). "I don't know anything about music, but I know what I like" (Zuleika). *"Je me promets un beau plaisir en faisant la connaissance de ce jeune homme"* (George Sand's ghost). "For people who like that kind of thing, that is the kind of thing they like" (Pallas Athene, of *The Decline and Fall of the Roman Empire*). "I, John, Albert, Edward, Claude, Orde, Angus, Tankerton, Tanville-Tankerton, fourteenth Duke of Dorset, Marquis of Dorset, Earl of Grove, Earl of Chastermaine, Viscount Brewsby, Baron Grove, Baron Petstrap, and Baron Wolock, in the Peerage of England, offer you my hand. Do not interrupt me" (The Duke of Dorset to Zuleika).

The verbal tricks, the shifts of focus, the imagery of romance, the things people say—all these go to make up the marvelous surface of

Zuleika Dobson. Indeed, one's pleasure in the book is largely in following the contours of this surface. *It* is real, however cunningly strewn with surprises. It assumes a reader who is capable of responding to it and who is therefore real, too. The author, above all, is real. He is never more so than when he writes, "You cannot make a man by standing a sheep on its hind legs. But by standing a flock of sheep in that position you can make a crowd of men. If man were not a gregarious animal, the world might have achieved, by this time, some real progress towards civilisation. Segregate him, and he is no fool. But let him loose among his fellows, and he is lost— he becomes just an unit in unreason."

Unlike its heroine, *Zuleika Dobson* is not an exacting mistress. It is not a book for everyone, the children included. One can enjoy it without claiming too much for it. Whether *Zuleika* is Beerbohm's "masterpiece" is itself open to question. What is almost any writer's masterpiece except a token award for critics to quarrel about? *Seven Men* is as lively and pertinent as *Zuleika* is and has a less taxing consistency of ironic intention. In none of his writings is Beerbohm the fantasist in the same class with Swift or Gogol or Kafka. He was too reasonable to indulge, like the half-mad Swift, in prodigies of invention called forth in the name of Reason. *Zuleika Dobson* is a comic criticism not so much of passion itself as of the fashion for passion, the same phenomenon that Mario Praz was seriously to illustrate and analyze in *The Romantic Agony.* If we can judge by what we know of his love affairs, Beerbohm was not himself susceptible to the grand passions. His early history—to intrude that once more—probably predisposed him to feel affection rather than passion for others, possibly to feel affection more strongly because the exclusive ardors of sexual passion were foreign to him. It need hardly be said that popular Freudianism has perpetuated the romantic agony by putting it on "a scientific basis." To this glorification of sexual passion Beerbohm's entire life and work were opposed. "They were a tense and peculiar family, the Oedipuses, weren't they?" he once remarked.

His opposition arose chiefly from a quality of his mind rather than from a defect of his emotional nature. He had the rococo imagination—so much so that *Zuleika* is closer in spirit to *The Rape of the Lock* than it is to the work of fantasists today, with the exception of Nabokov. Beerbohm saw things as small, discrete, sharply defined, existing in a world that was inexorably finite. From this here-and-now vision came, for one thing, those opinions of his which, often penetrating, sometimes fatuous, are frequently quoted. He objected, for example, that the modern theater lives always in its presumptive future rather than in its present. This opinion is still exemplary. He said of William Morris, "Of course he is a wonderful all-round man but the act of walking round him has always tired me." Amusing but not so exemplary. One is tempted to say that Beerbohm tired rather easily, like a child at an all-day picnic; that his life-long obsession with the tedium of bigness—the bigness of Morris, Shaw, Gibbon, of whomever or whatever, was a kind of childishness or envy. No one else, surely, has ever given so much crafty energy to scaling bigness down, as Beerbohm did, for example, in the thin dummy volume entitled *The Complete Works of Arnold Bennett* which he was at pains to fabricate and which was found in his library at Rapallo. The fifty-odd volumes of Bennett's actual work appalled him. Shaw's reputation struck him as outrageously extensile. But Bennett's literary bulk would no doubt have appalled him regardless of its quality. And he was so oppressed by Shaw's reputation that, as a reviewer, he occasionally missed the point of Shaw's plays.

His opinions are one thing; the imaginary world projected by his rococo imagination and realized in his fiction and drawings is another. In his fiction, if ever in literature, style and substance live in wedded bliss, the perfect midget couple. The English sentence is for him distinctly "an unit," to quote one of his instructively correct phrases. He explores the possibilities of the sentence as thoroughly as Pope did those of the heroic couplet. All known devices of rhetoric and syntax are set to performing for us with unobtrusive gaiety. Thus is bigness mocked by triumphant littleness—bigness and solemnity and the "tragic sense of life." Not that the *materials* of tragedy are lacking in his work. Misery is everywhere potential in it. Throughout *Zuleika Dobson* the strains of the *Liebestod* can be heard swelling, only to dissolve into dissonance. The rococo ethos has been defined by Egon Friedell as a "last craving for illusion," illusion to assuage the painful mysteries of loving and dying. Max Beerbohm had no such craving. For him, loving and dying were mysteries too inscrutable to be encompassed by the slap-happy word "tragedy." Assuagement lay in the contemplation of beauty and folly and in the act of laughter.

[1966]

Notes

1. For the remarks that follow I am much indebted to these books as well as to J. G. Riewald's *Sir Max Beerbohm, Man and Writer*.

2. See J. G. Riewald, "Max Beerbohm and Oscar Wilde," reprinted in this book.—*Editor's note.*

3. S. C. Roberts, *Zuleika in Cambridge* (Cambridge: Heffer, 1941).—*Editor's note.*

4. I learn that an agreeable musical version of *Zuleika* was produced in 1954 at Cambridge and then, briefly, in London. It seems, however, to have been more of a "period piece" than a satire.

5. See Edmund Wilson, "An Analysis of Max Beerbohm," reprinted in this book.—*Editor's note.*

John Felstiner

MAX BEERBOHM AND THE WINGS OF HENRY JAMES

I

Marcel Marceau's terrifying dance, "The Mask Maker," is above all
a parable of his own art as pantomimist. The man, his countenance
pure, tries on comic and tragic masks, becoming more and more
caught up with his fluency in changing them. After awhile he chooses
to wear the comic mask: it takes him dancing around the stage. He
comes finally to pull it off, but cannot. Underneath the laugh, his
body revolts, his fingers wrench at his face. At last, he spends himself in a total agony and rips off the mask. The gesture leaves his
arms stretched out strengthlessly. During the applause, his face is
empty.

Pantomime is imitation of everything. Condensed into an image
of mask making, it holds as well for the writer capable of assuming
any style, *disponible* to the extent that he parodies everything: *Who's
Who*, Regency memoirs, Victorian diaries, parliamentary reports,
American and English journalese, Midwestern slang, Walter Pater's
talk and essays, Samuel Johnson's, the speech of Whistler, Carlyle,
Rossetti, George Moore, Ibsen, Einstein, John Bull, Labour, and the
verger of Westminster Abbey, the poetry of Wordsworth, Byron,
Landor, Yeats, Hardy, Housman, dialect verse, Latin elegiacs, Surrey
proverbs, phonetic spelling, crossword puzzlers, Slavophiles, Baconi-

John Felstiner, "Max Beerbohm and the Wings of Henry James," *The Kenyon Review*, 29 (1967), 449-471. With this essay the author won the Kenyon Review Award
in Criticism. The text has been slightly changed and enlarged for this edition. Reprinted by permission of John Felstiner.

ans, letter-writing manuals, authorial inscriptions, popular romance, classical scholarship, Shaw's prefaces, the stories of Kipling and Conrad, the novels of Wells, Bennett, Galsworthy, James, the plays of Shakespeare, neo-Shakespearean tragedy, W. S. Gilbert, Pinero, Wilde, Queen Victoria's handwriting, and—once, with no success—himself.

Max Beerbohm's parodies form a kind of freehand circle of voices, drawn without reference to a fixed center. There seems to be no more of Beerbohm in his parodies of Henry James than in his model letter for an offended bride. This absence of an obstinate self, a ruling motive, will trouble anyone who thinks such absence should have put Beerbohm in despair. Of course, the literary motive was always amusement, no matter what threatening implication "The Mask Maker" may have.

In writing that is mainly parodic, such as Beerbohm's "A Defence of Cosmetics," the author is distanced or not present at all. Still, the major part of Beerbohm's work is in his own voice. The style of the essays and stories is reflexive, and they deal in private sentiment. Beerbohm brought himself into them so easily that one gets the illusion of a dependable personality. (Beerbohm would disarm the suspicion of insincerity in various ways—most simply, for instance, in an essay on the beauty of Whistler's *The Gentle Art of Making Enemies:* "The book lies open before me, as I write. I must be careful of my pen's transit from inkpot to MS.") Even in the thin atmosphere of fantasy, in *Zuleika Dobson,* the author is immediately present, discussing the action with us, revealing his role as part-historian, part-novelist. As long as these open assurances of sincerity do not cloy, *Zuleika Dobson* and many shorter pieces are the more convincing for Beerbohm's intrusion.

The temperament in the books of essays (*The Works, More, Yet Again, And Even Now*) and the actor in his own stories (*Seven Men*) is consistently modest, charming, under control. Critics in need of a point of balance against the self-destructiveness of Wilde, the assertiveness of Shaw, the intensity of Lawrence, turn to Max Beerbohm. He is coolly in touch with himself, his point of view makes no demands. Given this comfortably dispensable "Max," parodies will seem to be the exercise of one more literary talent, amid essays, fairy tales, criticism, biography, and poetry. But the element of parody pervades Beerbohm's art, as much as it does that of Joyce. It is too habitual for merely the "cleansing, exorcising" function that Proust mentioned in *Pastiches et Mélanges*; and too instinctive for the usual satiric effect of parody. Instead, so much good parody points to an end in itself: an idea of what literature is, including what is lost and gained between the writer and himself, between one writer and others.

Beerbohm's only familiar parodies are the deliberate ones in *A Christmas Garland*. These are confined to late Victorian and Edwardian writers, several of whom are now forgotten. Yet, taken together with all the casual and momentary parodies, they define an essential literary motive that amounts to philosophical principle. Keats, thinking of Shakespeare and of himself, described the character of "the camelion Poet": "it is not itself—it has no self—it is everything and nothing . . . continually in for—and filling some other body." For Keats this ideal was an expectation; it is nearly realized in the parodist, who plays equally with slang or elegiacs, Oscar Wilde or Queen Victoria.

Less generously explained, the habitual parodist is an actor or obsessed clown, mimicking anyone, innocent because he can always drop the role and because he will not learn or suffer from it. He may in the extreme be disinterested and obsessed at the same time, like Felix Krull, a quintessential figure of parody. In any event, the more immersed he is in his craft, the sooner the parodist may turn into a man without ideas, like.Beerbohm and Nabokov. Keats recognized this tension between philosophic onlooking and actual human single-mindedness—or, to bring it into the literary sphere, between parody and any man's engaged rhetoric. "It is a wretched thing to confess," he wrote in an often omitted section of the "camelion Poet" letter, "but is a very fact that not one word I ever utter can be taken for granted as an opinion growing out of my identical nature . . ."

Max Beerbohm is sometimes charged with lacking a primary vision of life, a staunch identity in face of world wars, technological and psychological revolution. Even worse, the catalogue of his parodic impersonations suggests that Beerbohm's imagination was not given over to "the dark side of things," as Keats's letter put it. He said there was only word play, for example, in Oscar Wilde's catharsis, *De Profundis*. Nevertheless, Beerbohm is not much like any other artist, and for just that reason compels interest. Though he was essentially uninfluenced and influenced no writer of importance, Beerbohm reveals as much about the nature of fiction as many of its more powerful innovators. And thanks to a certain gusto he had for nearly all literature before 1920, Beerbohm's peculiar critique of literature rises fully from the attentions he gave to other writers. Wilde was more or less his presiding spirit during the '90s. However, Beerbohm's maturest values start in the comic dispute made up by his caricatures and parodies of Henry James.

II

Contemporaries of Max Beerbohm sensed everything from cruel ferocity to kindly banter in his attitudes. "*On se moque de ce qu'on aime*" is the phrase his favorable critics borrowed from him. The phrase is misleading, since Beerbohm saw through what he liked or disliked—through James's fastidiousness or Kipling's vulgarity. But the range of estimates between cruelty and banter is understandable. Beerbohm's typical outlook was part satire, part nostalgia. And though he styled himself after Wilde at first, his deeper preferences were orthodox. They left him more and more at odds with his time: his traditionalism and quiescence, abraded by Labour, by the motor car; a liking for small endeavors, failed endeavors, along with his thorough distaste for any corpulent person or institution; his impatience with new forms of art that gave away his own delicate little work. All this begins to describe someone more complex than "sprightly, incomparable Max," someone who could publish a gross, unforgiving caricature of Wilde at the height of his success and at the same time happily imitate Wilde's wit in essays and letters.

Cruelty and kindness vary somewhat with the mode in which Beerbohm criticized Wilde. For, in Beerbohm, a precocious artist with narrow but highly developed skills, the act of drawing called forth different emotions from the act of writing. The caricature of Wilde is as cruel as a later one of Sir Edward Carson, who brutally cross-examined Wilde during the 1895 trial. Generally Beerbohm's caricatures tend to ridicule, while his judgments in writing are less direct—the rough distinction is between satire and irony. (The drawings in *Rossetti and His Circle*, emphasizing incongruities of Pre-Raphaelitism, are an exception. Apart from the fact that it is futile to satirize the past, this collection is conditioned by Beerbohm's nostalgia for the period, and by his affinity for artists born out of their "proper time and place.") For one thing, Beerbohm's virtual presence in stories and essays, as character or self-conscious stylist, inhibits outright satire. And a comment Beerbohm himself often made clarifies the distinction further: he insisted that drawing figures was delightful and natural for him, compared to the labor of writing prose.

The public spectacle of such labor probably first attracted Beerbohm to Henry James, in sympathy and amusement. There is an early caricature, drawn (as Beerbohm often drew) on the title page to a presentation copy of *The Aspern Papers*. The caricature shows James doubled up in pain, with the caption below: "Mr. Henry James in the act of parturiating a sentence." The glibness of the caption and the pastime of decorating title pages point to an ultimate disparity between the two men that calls in question Beerbohm's whole scattered critique of James. Beerbohm loved to notice James's strengths, yet they are totally unlike his own comparable qualities: James's passionate absorption in the art of fiction, and Beerbohm's disengagement from it (publishing his *Works* at age twenty-three, he promised to retire to a villa somewhere and write no more); James's great formal culmination, and Beerbohm's versatility dwindling to a piece every few years; James's thick swaddling of human action, and Beerbohm's lightness; James's self-effacement, and Beerbohm's insinuations—the break looks too wide for what Melville called the shock of recognition among great writers.

The question, after all, is not one of parity or even ruling influence. Though Beerbohm's stories of failed writers compare remarkably with James's, the two men share very little in method and material. The relation between them is instinctual, something like that between Whistler and Manet. Beerbohm's direct comment on James takes place throughout sixty years—from some early notes ("very literary . . . never smiles—rather appalled by life—cloistral") to the last thing Beerbohm ever wrote, "An Incident," which recalls his decision one day to read James rather than walk through London with him. The caricatures, reviews, letters, poems, essays, and parodies suggest in themselves that Beerbohm's criticism of certain aims and inadequacies in James was indirect self-evaluation, a kind of literary transference. In light of his preoccupation with James, Beerbohm's own qualities—such as versatility—seem not so much deliberate achievements as fallings short of the primary passionate task of art. Perhaps disengagement from the total duty of writing is only a resource against misgivings that art is not worth it. Perhaps versatile, sporadic production is a failure of concentration and energy; light treatment of human dealings makes do for inexperience; self-insinuation in one's works admits they

196

have no other true subject. These are suppositions, at best. They deepen, they do not alter what most makes Beerbohm's critique of James worth studying—its ironic discoveries of both men.

Plenty of writers have criticized other writers suggestively without revealing deep self-questioning: James on Flaubert, Thackeray on Sterne, Eliot on Dante. The particular value of Beerbohm's case is that he belongs to a different order of seriousness from James; that Beerbohm's best criticism, "The Guerdon," is itself a comic form, certainly the finest parody in English; and that his judgments have unexpected overtones, coming from one who had committed much less to literature than James had. Beerbohm's greatest attentions were to James, but other artists also drew specially qualified criticism from him. An article on Whistler in 1897 begins with a gay verbal caricature, then sinks into unironical analysis, as close to brooding as Beerbohm ever came:

> Mr. Whistler has never tried conclusions with life . . . he has never essayed actuality. His nocturnes are beautiful as fantasies, beautiful as decorations. . . . When, nowadays, art critics prate of his "marvellous knowledge of the limitations of his medium," they mean really that marvelous knowledge of his own limitations, that divine caution, which has ever withheld him from (perhaps) higher tasks and has left him content with absolute monarchy in his own sphere. . . . I doubt whether Mr. Whistler has ever suffered greatly in the pursuit of his art.

Hard sayings, and they deepen if taken as requirements of Beerbohm himself.

It is worth locating this kind of submerged identification for what it reveals mutually in Beerbohm and in the more influential writers he addressed himself to. In one year, for instance, he advertised his independence of Oscar Wilde in four essays: an ironical eulogy, an imitation, a parody, and a satiric hoax. Later, by parodying George Moore's fascination for the Mona Lisa, Beerbohm rid himself indirectly of the afflatus of Walter Pater. What emerges is that the artists about whom Beerbohm was equivocal—Pater, Wilde, Whistler, James—are notably those who made the strongest claims for artistic autonomy. Beerbohm only partly dissociated himself from these claims, having it both ways in the fin-de-siècle issue of art for art's sake. He made fun of Wilde for dismissing morals from art, but took over from him the literary genres least capable

197

of a direct, moral vision of life—fairy tale, fantasy, paradoxical essay.

To find such clearly ironic identification in Beerbohm's relation to Wilde, James, and others is to see why his parodies are extraordinary. They are more than an apprenticeship in style. Parody is the perfected form of ironic identification, and it developed in Beerbohm as a natural comic vision. For several reasons, the vision of James is most significant: Beerbohm's excellence lies in parody and caricature; his best parodies are of James; there are at least fifteen caricatures of James, two of them with miniature parodies ballooning from his mouth.[1] All Beerbohm's writings and caricatures make up a fairly random group, but they come back again and again to James. His peculiar example locates the central value of Beerbohm's art, and fixes another point of view to the study of James. Generally taken, this parodic relation also begins to explain points in the evolution of literature as a whole, such as *Sir Gawain and the Green Knight, Don Quixote, Candide, Northanger Abbey, Ulysses, Doctor Faustus.*

Few artists have practiced both parody and caricature. Where the drawings of Thackeray, Lear, Lewis Carroll, and Thurber only illustrate their writing, Beerbohm in effect created a small genre. The change in the art of caricature, especially in *The Poets' Corner* and *Rossetti and His Circle*, was profound. Beerbohm's innovation, one that only he was capable of making and sustaining, was to bring the dynamics of parody into caricature. That is, he began to place his subjects in plausible circumstances (Henry James in a "to him so very congenial" blind London fog) and then let them react with characteristic excess (James's sudden dismay that he *can*, "with an almost awful clarity," see his hand in front of his eyes). Beerbohm's parody, transmuting situation and thought as well as style, has an integrity that burlesque and travesty have not.

Of course, Daumier and the satirists of *Punch* had been drawing cartoons with ironic quotations in the caption. But *Punch's* art, forebear of the *New Yorker* style, is radically different from Beerbohm's. First of all, it lacks what Beerbohm simply called "beauty." Beerbohm's water colors are beautiful. More important, the situations, the settings of Du Maurier do not transmute circumstance, they reproduce it. Beerbohm's parodic caricatures create a new, quintessential situation that might almost happen to the subject, in dream or in a slight failure of conscience—thus, James kneeling with his ear to the keyhole of a hotel bedroom, his eyes glaring at two pairs of men's and ladies' boots.

Before Beerbohm started to create background and situation in caricature, he already had the habit of inventing significant hoaxes about British writers. One of his first articles, "A Peep into the Past,"[2] imagines Oscar Wilde as a Victorian gentleman rising at 4:30 a.m and "bending over the little spirit-kettle" for hot cocoa. In his reviews and letters, Beerbohm often used physical description to sketch some hypothetical predicament for Whistler, Conan Doyle, and others. So his best literary caricatures are a logical development for him: fantasies such as "Mr. W. B. Yeats, presenting Mr. George Moore to the Queen of the Fairies," or Mrs. Tennyson interrupting the sculptor Woolner to ask *when* he will begin modeling Tennyson's halo. If these caricatures owe something to the beautiful anti-portraits of Pellegrini and to Hogarth's expressive situations, their astonishing invention is that of the utter parodist.

Beerbohm continued to use traditional forms of caricature—personification, metaphor, parody of the fine arts; many of his drawings of James, in fact, show only a large head on a small, portly body. In the earliest published version, James is bearded, stout, strongly contained, severe. For in 1895, Beerbohm wrote, James "had looked rather like a Russian Grand Duke." After the '90s, he looked more like "a lay Cardinal," and Beerbohm began to design James's body in a way that suggests what he thought of James's aesthetics: almost corpulent; ungraceful but not flabby, like Wilde, nor letting itself go, like Rossetti; the eyes always bulging.

Sometimes the double selves of James, bearded and beardless, appear in Beerbohm's caricature. One set, in Beerbohm's copy of James's *Notebooks*, is now printed in the soft cover edition of that book. The other is probably the most ingenious fusion of parody and caricature Beerbohm ever managed. It appears in a book by Constant Coquelin, *Art and the Actor* (1915)—one of the many books in Beerbohm's library that he could not help improving.[3] Since the introduction to the book, by Henry James, had appeared as an essay years before, the publishers added a note on the first page: "The substance of this paper appeared in the *Century Magazine* for January, 1887." Beerbohm, seeing more to it than that, made another addition in pencil: "and was very obviously—or, rather, deviously and circuitously—revised in the great dark rich fulness of time, for republication in 1915." Leading away from that brief parody, Beerbohm drew an arrow pointing to a caricature on the facing page. There, in pale blue wash and dark ink, two portraits confront each other—on the right a thickset, bearded, early James; on the left a heavy-chinned, balding, clean-shaven later James with backhair trailing over his collar. The old man is making a gesture of reproof, the young man is stubborn. Their words to each other share one balloon containing the phrase, "How badly you . . ."—completed by early James with "write!," by later James with "wrote!"[4]

In Beerbohm's private game of judgment, the caricatures sometimes indulge in what now seem outworn ironies about James. Even in 1915, the later James's "How badly you wrote!" looks trivial beside James's grandiose apology for revision—"the act of seeing it again"—in the preface to *The Golden Bowl*. It happens that Beerbohm found the prefaces to James's collected edition more confusing than elucidating, and he compared the revising to "patching pale gray silk with snippets of very dark thick brown velvet. It was a strange sad aberration: and a wanton offense against the laws of art." His objection is to the principle of tampering with early works, not to James's later manner, which Beerbohm called "his greatest achievement." But, as the notebooks show, James had more reasons to revise than Beerbohm. When Beerbohm published his own collected edition in 1922-28, he changed a few punctuation marks, but delicately respected the "young coxcomb in the distance" by not changing "the *style* of the punctuation."

"The Old and the Young Self," a series of double caricatures by Beerbohm, contrasts youthful pretense with the form of eventual success. James was not included. About him Beerbohm was divided, sometimes praising the fine strength of the earlier prose, sometimes the "lyrical conscience" in *The Wings of the Dove* and *The Golden Bowl*. In any event, Beerbohm had neither the privilege nor the desire that William James had, demanding the novelist's return to a "directer manner." He liked the rich difficulties of the later novels. But Beerbohm did not care greatly about James's "act of seeing it again," about the long crisis that led James through theatrical failure, tales of ghostly disaster and the artist's isolation, toward a new mode of perception—what James's persona in "The Middle Years" called the "splendid 'last manner,' the very citadel, as it would prove, of his reputation." There is an inescapable contrast between the careers of Beerbohm and James. None of Beerbohm's youthful pretension was belied by his later success, which corresponded simply to his precocity. And at age fifty-six, when James had just entered upon that "greatest and richest achievement," Beerbohm had long since ceased to write or draw regularly.

In itself the dwindling of Beerbohm's production during the '20s (he lived until 1956) is no more damning than if he had died then or turned to missionary work. But it does mark the limitations of a primarily nostalgic vision of history, and of a satiric aloofness that stems from what Beerbohm called his Tory Anarchism: the desire for "every one to go about doing just as he pleased—short of altering any of the things to which I have grown accustomed." Again, Beerbohm's openness to James is impressive, given the disparity in their artistic energies and devotion. That openness may have been reserved for James. Beerbohm had no critical or even comic grasp of another greatly developing writer, W. B. Yeats. Yeats's early verse worried Beerbohm; he could find nothing in it, though he wrote a weirdly accurate parody of its vague colors and wavering tempo.[5] He made even less, apparently, of Yeats's maturity, and the reason is not merely Beerbohm's indifference to poetry. In 1954, he broadcast an essay on Yeats, an essay written in 1914. The fact that he did not care to revise it expresses Beerbohm's view of his own critical—and Yeats's creative—process. So does the essay's relaxed conclusion:

> As years went by, the visual aspect of Yeats changed a little. His face grew gradually fuller in outline . . . those very long, fine hands did seem to have lost something of their insubstantiality . . . I found it less easy to draw caricatures of him. He seemed to have become subtly less like himself.

Less like himself: a purely visual intuition of Yeats's mask, his impulse toward common themes and public language. This was too strenuous for Beerbohm's taste. He had doubts about change of any sort. Reviewing De Profundis in 1905, Beerbohm discounted Wilde's alleged rebirth as a man of sorrow and nature: "He was still precisely himself. He was still playing with ideas, still playing with emotions." De Profundis was only Wilde's final mask, an art of suffering.

201

James's mask—at least, the one Beerbohm attributed—was a sentence Beerbohm loved from *The Art of Fiction* (1888): "Be generous and delicate and pursue the prize." To judge from the prefaces, twenty years later, James's "beautiful incentive" was a more complex enterprise than this. By 1906 Beerbohm had seen clearly enough the depth of James's fictional analysis as well as its frustrations. Otherwise, he could not have written "The Mote in the Middle Distance," which embodies the difficult grace of a method that tries to be at once generous and delicate in portraying experience. Beerbohm's parody stretches apart art and life; it tests imitation against what life actually offers. Yet, if that tension between image and fact animates his parodies, he would not recognize a similar tension in the life of Yeats.

Skeptical about Wilde and Yeats, involved but not identified with James—these critical relations are not incidental; they define Beerbohm more reliably than all the explicit self-reference of his sentimental essays. Through parody, caricature, any means of comic criticism, Beerbohm fixed himself in relation to other, more salient forces in literature and in society. For that reason, he was unwilling to see those forces modified. The point is, it was harder to caricature Yeats because Yeats became subtly *more* like himself. So Beerbohm's pleasure in drawing the James of both 1895 and 1905 is a measure of more than usual tolerance. Self-transformation is disquieting to watch, and a risk for the artist; Beerbohm ignored it in Yeats, denied it in Wilde, urged it innocently in Whistler. For himself, it was never an option.

The vision of James in Beerbohm's caricatures alone is fairly complete, with two on the problems of James's prose and one on the Jamesian narrator's keyhole psychology. On the Anglo-American James, Beerbohm published three caricatures: James in a London fog, James revisiting America, and James returning to Europe. He also based one caricature on "The Jolly Corner," James's story of an exile returning to New York to confront the American self he might have been. James's expatriation was totally unlike that of Beerbohm, whose voluntary returns from Rapallo to England were mainly to set up exhibitions of caricatures, and who neither learned Italian in forty-six years nor wrote much about Italy. Before he had moved away from England, however, Beerbohm was drawn to James's "complex fate" of being an American. One of the published caricatures, "Mr. Henry James revisiting America," appeared in the same year as *The American Scene* (1907), and begins to reach into the thickly qualified attitudes that make the book so strange. Beerbohm's drawing has James confronting a group of stereotyped Americans, all welcoming the novelist in their peculiar idioms—among them, an Indian with his eyes shut ("Hail, great white novelist! Tuniyaba—the Spinner of fine cobwebs!") and an Aunt Jemima with open arms ("Why, it's Masser Henry! Come to your old nurse's arms, honey!"). The rest of the figures are as wildly unlike James's American types; they seem to come from Oscar Wilde's tour of the United States in 1882 and Beerbohm's short, sheltered trip in 1895. This burlesque group implies part of James's dismay at American vulgarity and vernacular; it does not quite reach the awkward bias of *The American Scene*, against Jews, "tatterdemalion darkies," and other aliens. At best, it suggests an uncertainty that permeates James's book—whether James can understand just who and what these people are. Standing opposite Beerbohm's improbable American scene, James holds back, musing:

> . . . So that, in fine, let, without further beating about the bush, me make to myself amazed acknowledgement that, but for the certificate of birth which I have—so very indubitably— *on* me, I might, in regarding, and, as it somewhat were, overseeing, *a l'oeil de voyageur*, these dear good people, find hard to swallow, or even to take by subconscious injection, the great idea that I am—oh, ever so indigenously!—one of them. . . .

James called himself an "ancient contemplative person" in *The American Scene*, but he never brought himself to say what Beerbohm puts in his mouth. Beerbohm could not after all associate James seriously with the United States. When James became a British subject and received the Order of Merit, it was not the change of citizenship Beerbohm stressed in his parody, "The Guerdon," but the tribute. And in 1947 Beerbohm wrote an elaborate note in his copy of James's *Notebooks*, regretting that books of primarily English interest should be published in America first. In fact, nothing in Beerbohm's work suggests he had a sense of any element in American character. Apart from Whistler and Frank Harris, who were as much expatriates as James, Beerbohm wrote convincingly of no American, real or created. Essentially, Beerbohm was affected only by the working of James's mind.

"Mr. Henry James revisiting America" is cleverly fashioned, but there and in other caricatures of James the drawing is not particularly beautiful, compared to the water colors of *The Poets' Corner*. James's stolid body is less striking than the micro-parodies joined to him. The only brilliant traits in Beerbohm's James are his eyes. Whether James had his face toward America or Europe or was in the fog or kneeling at a keyhole, his eyes were always bulging with apprehension. In a 1908 sonnet "To Henry James,"[6] Beerbohm called them "your fine eyes, blurred like arc-lamps in a mist." Above all the eyes are perception, awareness, the felt life of the man on whom nothing is lost. James called the writer "a figure with a pair of eyes" standing at one window in the house of fiction. His vision was his moral reference—and in Beerbohm's caricatures the eyes look both angry and perplexed.

James's greed for life is a form of what Pater urged—to be present at the focus where vital forces unite. However, Pater was "an old woman" and "a hump-back *manque*," as Beerbohm called him privately. The caricature of James snooping at a bedroom door is equally skeptical, and antedates Freudian inquiries into the course of James's narrative vision. Beerbohm's caricature is a direct satire on *The Sacred Fount*, whose narrator, curious about the flow of vitality between men and women, says that while psychological diagnosis is acceptable, "what's ignoble is the detective and the keyhole." In making a caricature of voyeurism, Beerbohm was also using against James an essay on D'Annunzio in which James says that a novelist can tell us nothing distinctive about human passions by merely conducting us vulgarly among "the boots and shoes that we see, in the corridors of promiscuous hotels, standing, often in double pairs, at the doors of rooms." Usually Beerbohm's sexual ironies were subtler than in this caricature. Thus Wilde, in "A Peep into the Past," is said to employ "a constant succession of page-boys" because "he is something of a martinet about punctuality in his household." Indirection makes the freest, inescapable satire.

A skit Beerbohm wrote on James's seclusion in Rye shows the beauty of indirection, in contrast to later, heavier exposures of James's sexual neurosis. It involves an imaginary work, *Half Hours with the Dialects of England*, for which Beerbohm wrote a specimen chapter on Rye.[7] His example of Rye dialect is a sonnet by Miss Peploe, Dressmaker, introduced and annotated in every line by the parodic "Editor." The sonnet, number 153 of JAËMES: A ZONNET-ZEQUENCE, begins, "Jaëmes! Thou dost be för bein' egregious/To never discommode the heärt o' me," then chides him "för bein' damsel-coy," and ends:

> . . . As thou dost be för bein' ztrong,
> Do be för bein' merciful. Ahoy!
> Wings o' the Dove! No dove do be för bein'
> Möre dove than me when I do thee be zeein'.

The editor surrounds Miss Peploe's sonnet with notes on the cautious, roundabout speech of Rye people, and on Shakespearean influences in the couplet. He remarks only briefly that apart from the sonnet's importance as an example of dialect, he hopes "it may chance to meet the eye of Mr. James, and so, perhaps, pave the way to Miss Peploe's future happiness."

Ridicule of James's vital deficiencies is not deeply meant. So much absurd editorial paraphernalia suggests that Beerbohm was indifferent to the artist's privation, as long as the art was complete and convincing. Before the three last novels, Beerbohm had not been convinced. He had noticed James's "fastidious coyness" as a writer, his "fear of penetrating into the passions" of his highly civilized world. But in 1909, when Beerbohm wrote Miss Peploe's sonnet, he also published a short appreciation of James, stressing the superb moral conscience of his novels rather than their avoidance of primitive emotion. What is more, Beerbohm never published the dialect hoax on James's celibacy, or "A Peep into the Past." And he had only a vague posterity in mind when he improved the books in his library with caricatures and spurious "Opinions of the Press." In these unpublished drawings and parodies, Beerbohm's critical agency is elusive. To identify is to alter it, since the conditions it depends on are privacy and free play. Beerbohm plays with his judgment of James, putting it in the words of a Rye dressmaker. The advantage in this irony is a dramatic one, where Miss Peploe's sonnet makes both James and itself ridiculous, while Beerbohm remains innocent. Yet, there is a loss. If Beerbohm's comic vantage looks like that of the self-sufficient child, there is in it a disengagement not felt by the child at play—a loss of motive that James, whatever his defects, does not exhibit. In a large sense, it might be said that the frivolousness of Beerbohm is an ultimate criticism of James's sacred, misplaced passions. Still, Beerbohm was drawn and obliged to James.

He was obliged chiefly for the inspiration of his best writing— the parodies, and parts of *Seven Men*. When Beerbohm conceived the idea of his first *Christmas Garland* in 1896, he meant to parody "Henry James never mentioning Xmas by name," but did not. Ten years later he wrote "The Mote in the Middle Distance," which is an index of Beerbohm's growth since 1896 as well as James's. Beerbohm also wrote that James's amazing method, the slow full revelation of life, would perish with him because no one else could handle it. The prediction is amusing, coming from a parodist, who helps to make excessive styles obsolete. "The Mote in the Middle Distance" is both a mockery of James and an opening, an explica- tion, unlike the disengaged hoax of JAëMES: A ZONNET-ZEQUENCE. Beerbohm's parody keeps the technical quirks of James bound into James's central care in characterization. It also points to a certain moral radiance in James's scene, a radiance that Beerbohm achieved only within his parody.

"The Mote in the Middle Distance" is a fetish for those who love and those who disparage James. All the turns of style Beerbohm invents for the hypersubtle innocents, Keith and Eva Tantalus, wondering whether to investigate their Christmas stockings, can be found in *The Wings of the Dove* and *The Golden Bowl*. They are sometimes better, sometimes less well done by Beerbohm: the broken- ly qualified sentences, roundabout simplicities, syntactical quibbles, colloquialisms made genteel by inverted commas, italics for deli- cate intonation, stunning double negatives, accumulated homely adjectives, abruptly placed, vague adverbs, banal metaphors worried and reworried, the narrator's unsettling glances into the future, and his intimacy with the fine central intelligence of "our friend," the exasperating, magnified scruples, and, at last, the vibrant moral renunciation, "One doesn't even peer." Keith's choice not to seize the prize twists only slightly the great choice of Merton Densher at the end of *The Wings of the Dove:* "I won't take the money." However, parody cannot cope with one thing in James's method: the slow evolution of character and atmosphere, the scenario structure James saved from his ordeal in the theater. What the parody does give is an odd Jamesian predicament—Keith's boyish uncertainty in face of Eva's clear beauty. Compared to Beerbohm's treatment of Kipling and Shaw, "The Mote in the Middle Distance" is benign. Sharp criticism focuses only in the name of Eva Tantalus and in the title—one implying that some kind of sexual frustration animates James's art; the other recalling Jesus' scorn for people who were aware of everything but their own flawed perception.

Beerbohm was involved enough in James's art to come back to his parody in 1922 and write a new passage for it, which he meant to come closer to "the great dark glow of the later manner." Keith and Eva are talking about the unknown contents of the stockings:

> "In respect, you mean, of what's in either of *them?*"
> "In respect," she rose at it, "of what's in *both* of them."
> Well, he had got, *tout bonnement*, the measure of it now. But he had not yet covered, as was to appear, the span of his insistence. "You know, then, by blest induction, what there *is* in them?"
> "I know," she had a high gesture for it, "*only* that."
> He hardly hesitated. "*What's* in them?"
> "Everything," she gave back to him. She had closed her eyes. "More than everything," she passionately, she all but inaudibly now breathed.

And she resists Keith's vision that they might look into their stockings:

> "Ah, the vision!" It was as though, with a courage that matched his, she could hang and brood over that too. But she presently turned from it. "What we have to hold on to—but with a tenacity!—is not so much what you perhaps saw as what you have all along, *caro*, foreseen—the impossibility, simply, of our *not* being able not to. *That's* all that counts. It's the lamp in our darkness and the seal of our good faith. It's the end of the journey and the garland at the feast."

It is hard to imagine anything closer to the toils and renunciations of James's moral consciousness. You have in Beerbohm's parody the sense of being present at the first few cell divisions of *The Wings of the Dove*.

Beerbohm never used this passage in later editions of *A Christmas Garland*. By the time he had an opportunity to do so, "The Mote in the Middle Distance" was a recognized work of art. Revising it would have called into question the integrity of the parody. Although his parodies are indeed criticism, he did not think of them as tools that might be improved. "The Mote in the Middle Distance" is a form of discourse in itself with Henry James for a theme, along with the theme of knowledge and renunciation. In fact, Beerbohm's addition has totally assimilated James. The finest parody may only erase its original, like dubbing over an entire tape.

An informal caricature by Beerbohm contains his ironic view of the relation between James and himself. He has James in profile with flattened forehead, thick chin and angry eyes; James's mouth is moving and his hand makes a remonstrative gesture. Opposite him, a slighter figure of Beerbohm—the hands gently, partly raised, eyes bland and attentive, tiepin in place.[8] Actually, James admired him, which is a tribute to Beerbohm, given the novelist's deep sensitivity to criticism. Edith Wharton wrote, in *A Backward Glance*, that James was fastidious in his dress and even more particular about his figure: "He resented any suggestion that his silhouette had lost firmness and acquired volume." Still worse, she says it was disastrous to let James know that his writing had been parodied. Beerbohm's letter to James in 1908, praising "The Jolly Corner," must have convinced James that caricature and parody could be a form of reverence, unlike H. G. Wells's damaging parody in *Boon*. James responded generously to "The Mote in the Middle Distance" when it appeared in *A Christmas Garland*. He said that Beerbohm had destroyed the trade of writing, because "no one, now, can write without incurring the reproach of somewhat ineffectively imitating—you!" No criticism could be more flattering, short of James's eventually believing the parody to be his own work.

When Beerbohm learned that James was to be given the Order of Merit, in 1916, he wrote "The Guerdon," without thought of publication. Although "The Mote in the Middle Distance" has been reprinted more than any other parody of Beerbohm's, "The Guerdon" is finer; almost too fine. The rhythms and movement of thought in it are articulated, the phrasing precise enough to be sheer communion with James. "The Guerdon" does not broaden once into farce, as other skits on James always do. Its fine intelligence is "poor decent Stamfordham," the Lord Chamberlain, on his way to the King with a prospective Honors list containing one name that he has omitted to identify.

This omission so loomed for him that he was to be conscious, as he came to the end of the great moist avenue, of a felt doubt

as to whether he could, in his bemusement, now "place" anybody at all; to which condition of his may have been due the
impulse that, at the reached gates of the palace, caused him to
pause and all vaguely, all peeringly inquire of one of the
sentries: "To whom do you beautifully belong?"

In 1909 Beerbohm had reviewed a play of James's, and, though he
thought the drama was no vehicle for James's genius, he was
gratified by Forbes-Robertson's speaking of one line: "I mean, to
whom do you beautifully belong?" Beerbohm described the actor's
intense rendition as "irony kneeling in awe" of James, and the
same holds for "The Guerdon." Stamfordham's six words, which
belong to James, purify the parodic substance of Beerbohm's
language; and they also ask, as Beerbohm was aware, to whom the
parodist belongs.

"The Guerdon" is an ecstasy of tact, doubt and release from
doubt, all in the vulnerable conscience of Stamfordham. In letting
a phrase from James blend with the parody, Beerbohm implies
that anything in James is potentially ridiculous. At the same time,
"To whom do you beautifully belong?" admits an allegiance between Beerbohm and James that is like the parodic narrator's
sympathy with "our poor harassed friend," Stamfordham. In
James's fiction there is usually a consonance between narrator
and central intelligence that is richer in irony and sympathy than
either remote or first person narration could be. So Beerbohm's
parody, without losing its purchase on James, gains by verging on
imitation. One thing about "The Guerdon" saves it from turning
into flattery: it deals with the precarious fame of Henry James. The
Lord Chamberlain's delicacy keeps him from giving away to the
King "his whole dim bland ignorance of the matter in hand," and
he fears but won't expose the King's dimness. What is dim, throughout "The Guerdon," is precisely the identity and accomplishment
of "Henry James." As the Honors list comes down to this name,
Stamfordham wonders if the King, living also "on the great grey
beach of the hesitational and renunciational," will be afraid to
look in *Who's Who.*

> Our friend held, as for an eternity, his breath. He was to form,
> in later years, a theory that the name really *had* stood in peril
> of deletion, and that what saved it was that the good little man,
> as doing, under the glare shed by his predecessors, the great
> dynastic "job" in a land that had been under two Jameses

and no less than eight Henrys, had all humbly and meltingly resolved to "let it go at that."

The joy of this climax is that it gathers and rises on the perfected idiom of James, with only a hint, a fantastic hint, that James was given the Order of Merit solely because of his affiliation with Britain.

III

The great enabling impulse of James's writing was self-consciousness, freed in the notebooks and controlled in the prefaces. Given this shaping power along with James's study of fiction, one asks why the writing of a conscious self-parody was alien to him. An answer lies in the notebooks: self-consciousness was not a critical act but an inspirational, a generative one. And, in any case, James's sentences build literally by exaggeration; he would have had trouble knowing where self-parody began. Surprisingly, Max Beerbohm's only explicit self-parody, "A Vain Child" (1896), is not very enlightening, though his late self-caricatures are simple and clever. "A Vain Child" is shallow, emphasizing only preciosity. Self-parody in Beerbohm was bound to be unenlightening, for his style was already naturally parodic. Unfortunately, the natural parodist can seem a con-man. Beerbohm's other writings during the '90s confused or annoyed the public. His best critic, Oscar Wilde, wrote to a woman about Beerbohm: "When you are alone with him, does he take off his face and reveal his mask?"

The rare moments in which James can be said to parody himself are when he is immensely gratified, often about some small matter. Beerbohm, writing to James about "The Jolly Corner," evoked a letter of thanks that blooms with incipient self-parody: "I can only gather myself in and up," wrote James, "arching and presenting my not inconsiderable back—a back, as who should say, offered for any further stray scratching and patting of that delightful kind." On the other hand, during his worst period of distress James did more than parody himself; his own fiction involved the role of the artist. Nearly all the short stories about novelists were written between 1888, when James was "staggering" under the evil failure of his last two novels, and 1896, when he began to recover from the opening-night catastrophe of his play, *Guy Domville*. James never appears in his fiction, as Beerbohm does throughout *Seven Men*, and the closest figure of himself is Dencombe in "The Middle Years." Yet, the stories of writers and artists constitute a fuller exposure of James's predicament than *The Sacred Fount*. Beerbohm praised them for their loving, cunning analysis, and noted that James had a wonderful way of imagining paintings or sculpture. But it remains to be said that in "The Death of the Lion," "The Figure in the Carpet," "The Middle Years" and others, James does not at all recreate his authors' writings. He does not, in effect, parody them. We take Vereker's "finest fullest intention" and Dencombe's "fine talent" to be very much like James's. That James will not parody his artist-heroes to demonstrate their fineness agrees with his dramatic ideal: the value of their art must be felt by someone else—by the public or by an admiring narrator. In contrast to this beautiful restraint, Beerbohm takes every chance for parody in " 'Savonarola' Brown" and "Enoch Soames," the best stories of *Seven Men*. He could do this, not humbled as James was by the sacred exclusiveness of his Muse. Beerbohm's pseudo-erotic poem about rotted flutes and cymbals rouged with rust is primarily a fair and careful presentation of Enoch Soames. It makes him more believable than James's writers. As a parody of remnant *decadents* in England, as a dimwitted lyric, it also guarantees Beerbohm's independence in the fin de siècle.

After *The Wings of the Dove*, Beerbohm was most attracted in James to the stories about writers. In a 1914 essay, "Books within Books," he carefully discusses the nonexistent canon of these imaginary novelists—Ray Limbert's *The Hidden Heart*, for instance, " 'the shortest of his novels, but perhaps the loveliest,' as Mr. James and I have always thought." Later in 1914, Beerbohm began to write the brilliant fantasy "Enoch Soames," which stems mainly from his attachment to James. Soames is the nerveless replica of a British imitator of Verlaine. He has published a book of poems (*Fungoids*) and a collection (*Negations*), and is acquainted with Beerbohm, who is actor and narrator in "Enoch Soames." Because Soames makes a pact with the Devil to travel into the future and observe his own fame, Beerbohm's story reminds one of *Faust* and *The Time Machine*. It has also been linked with Pater's *Imaginary Portraits*, but there is no room for Pater as a character in what are mostly veiled self-portraits. The real source of "Enoch

Soames" is the mixture of literary friendship, ambition, neglect, failure, and death in the stories James wrote before his last period.

Yeats's image of the Tragic Generation in the mid-'90s—Dowson, Wilde, Beardsley, John Davidson—does not insist that these artists died from the world's vulgar neglect. But, in James's stories, the real aesthetic failure *is* the world's. This makes the difference between Beerbohm's pathetic characters—Soames, Brown, Maltby, and Braxton—and most of James's heroes, who are as good as they try to be. James's "The Middle Years" (1893) is a subtle example of the artist's private as against his public worth, since Dencombe has to hear from a queer young admirer that he is a success. "Poor Dencombe," who faints when caught revising his own new book ("The Middle Years"), dies before reaching the certain splendid "last manner." But the evocation of his death, in Beerbohm's view, is a triumph—"it rises and glows and gladdens," he wrote in "Books within Books." "It is more exquisite than anything in 'The Middle Years.'" Dencombe's own triumph is ambiguous at best, and he is the most fortunate of all James's superb failures, as well as the closest to his creator. The others either die unreconciled or go on in painful circumstances. Enoch Soames's fate is even more perverse: he disappears with the realization that he is not only a dismal writer but a phantasmal one, a creature of Beerbohm's parodic imagination. Soames as a man is barely apparent, and not only because Beerbohm wanted him dim. His poems, Beerbohm's parodies, are livelier than he is.

To present the person of the artist, rather than his accomplished work, James chose as subject "the artist deluded, diverted, frustrated or vanquished." That is, unless Henry St. George failed as a novelist, in "The Lesson of the Master," James's irony about his marital doings would be lost. But James's principle of bringing his authors out above their work does not after all apply to Beerbohm. Nothing is lost if Soames vanishes behind his poems, because Max Beerbohm is the real protagonist and subject of all the stories in *Seven Men*. As he tries gradually to see through Soames's weary attitudes, it is not Soames we come to know but Beerbohm. Soames was a fool all along. In *Seven Men*, Beerbohm takes roughly the same role as the young disciple or critic in James's stories. So, in "The Figure in the Carpet," Hugh Vereker's perfection is taken for granted, while the first-person critic-narrator toils toward the prize through moments of self-analysis that might almost be James parodying himself. But entries in James's notebooks of the '90s show how sedulously he kept himself out of his stories, filtering them through a privileged observer. The contrast with Beerbohm is fundamental. He was his own persona in *Seven Men*, conniving playfully with himself as James could not have done. James, in settling his point of view, took more precautions with the stories of novelists than with any others. Among the major stories of this sort, only the narrator of "The Middle Years" is the author himself, the tragic hero.

Care and grace and irony in presenting the artist "vanquished" do not free James's stories from their preoccupation with literary failure. Although Beerbohm welcomed James's serious literary themes, he left alone the technical and personal sources of James's narratives of failure, not liking to see James obsessed, unfree. Yet, the narratives are an example for Beerbohm's own, with these differences: Beerbohm conceived his imaginary failures at the height of his own success; and he was free enough—at least, of James's sacred obligations—to implicate himself immediately in his fiction. "As to the craftsmanship" of Soames's poetry, wrote Beerbohm, " 'rouged with rust' seemed to me a fine stroke." The enabling impulse here is not self-consciousness but two-edged parody, innocent and noncommittal.

James was an example in many ways for Beerbohm. Reading *Daisy Miller* in 1937, Beerbohm had "pangs of longing for the dear delicate un-panic-stricken world of sixty years ago." But the parodic analogy he sensed as early as 1896 brought Beerbohm into a continuum with James where their disparities of background, temperament, demeanor, calling, and expectation could be justified in comic forms. Beerbohm took James partly as a warning against the expense of absolute self-expression in art. In another sense, James stood for the whole of fiction, and parody for its possible criticism. "The Mote in the Middle Distance" asks of James: How is life rendered in that scrupulous manner? What is lost and gained? Are emotions generated by the style alone or do they start in the writer? Then taken generally, as the natural parodist takes them, these are the radical questions of literature.

[1967]

John Felstiner

Notes

1. In his *Catalogue of the Caricatures of Max Beerbohm* (London: Macmillan, and Cambridge, Mass.: Harvard University Press, 1972) Sir Rupert Hart-Davis lists nineteen caricatures of James.—*Editor's note.*

2. Now published in *A Peep into the Past and Other Prose Pieces by Max Beerbohm*, ed. Rupert Hart-Davis (London: William Heinemann, and Brattleboro, Vermont: The Stephen Greene Press, 1972), pp. 3-8.—*Editor's note.*

3. Now in the Harvard College Library.

4. This drawing is now reproduced in John Felstiner, *The Lies of Art: Max Beerbohm's Parody and Caricature* (New York: Alfred A. Knopf, 1972, and London: Victor Gollancz, 1973), Plate XXI.

5. See *Max in Verse: Rhymes and Parodies by Max Beerbohm*, ed. J. G. Riewald (Brattleboro, Vermont: The Stephen Greene Press, 1963, and London: William Heinemann, 1964), p. 73.—*Editor's note.*

6. Published in *Max in Verse*, p. 19.—*Editor's note.*

7. Published in *Max in Verse*, pp. 21-25.—*Editor's note.*

8. This drawing is now reproduced in John Felstiner, *The Lies of Art: Max Beerbohm's Parody and Caricature* p. 145.

Bruce R. McElderry, Jr.

MAX BEERBOHM: ESSAYIST, CARICATURIST, NOVELIST

This essay might well be entitled "How to be famous at twenty-one, retire at thirty-eight, and continue to be famous for forty-five years longer." That is what Max Beerbohm managed to do. For sixty years there was only one "Max" in the English-speaking world, and when in 1956 he was in his last lingering illness the London *Times* ran daily bulletins, as if for a great statesman or a member of the royal family. Without ever taking a course in journalism, he became one of the best journalistic writers of his time. Without drawing lessons after the age of thirteen he achieved some of the best-remembered cartoons of his day. By writing a single novel he assured himself a permanent place in any adequate history of the English novel.

How did he do it? It helped, of course, that he had a half-brother twenty years older who was one of the most successful actor-managers of the late nineteenth century: eventually Sir Herbert Beerbohm-Tree, who knew all the famous people of the day. It also helped to be sent to a good school—Charterhouse (though of course Charterhouse was hardly Eton). It helped still more to go to Oxford, even if young Beerbohm left at twenty-one without bothering to take a degree. Yet many men have had such advantages and remained nonentities. Beerbohm knew how to use the advantages that came his way.

Bruce R. McElderry, Jr., "Max Beerbohm: Essayist, Caricaturist, Novelist." From *On Stage and Off: Eight Essays in English Literature Presented to Dr. Emmett L. Avery*, ed. John W. Erstine, John R. Elwood, and Robert C. McLean (Pullman: Washington State University Press, 1968), pp. 76-86. Reprinted by permission of the author and Washington State University Press.

Beerbohm's uneventful but interesting life I shall compress to a thumb-nail sketch, since it is his work that chiefly interests us. Even before he left Oxford he attracted attention by his caricatures and by essays in undergraduate magazines. As a result, he was asked while still an undergraduate to contribute to that famous avant-garde magazine *The Yellow Book*, which flourished in 1894-1897. Meanwhile he was selling his caricatures and his essays to many other magazines. Partly through his half-brother Herbert, but even more by his sophisticated wit, he could number among his friends writers like Oscar Wilde and George Bernard Shaw and such rising young artists as Aubrey Beardsley and William Rothenstein. A series of free lance contributions to *The Saturday Review* made him known to the readers of that leading paper. When Shaw, its dramatic critic, decided to resign his post in 1898, Shaw himself urged Beerbohm to succeed him. For twelve years Beerbohm was the most brilliant of a talented group of dramatic critics at a lively period of the English theater. Then, abruptly, he resigned, married, and retired to Italy. Settling near Rapallo, a beautiful town on the Mediterranean coast, he remained there from 1910 until his death in 1956. He made frequent trips to London to exhibit his drawings and publish his various books; and he lived in England for extended periods during the two world wars. In 1939 he was knighted. His marriage bothered everybody except Max and his wife; Florence Kahn, the American actress he married after a long courtship, did not fit in with Max's brilliant friends, but she suited him. They seem to have been ideally happy until her death in 1951. Then nearly eighty, Max was looked after by an old family friend, whom he married during his last illness in order to make sure that she would inherit what small property he had. When Max Beerbohm died, he had published fifteen volumes of prose, including his novel *Zuleika Dobson* (1911) and a collection of narrative sketches called *Seven Men* (1919); he had published ten collections of caricatures. His bibliographer has listed more than four hundred uncollected magazine and newspaper articles,[1] and a gentleman in England has listed some fourteen hundred drawings aside from more than three hundred in the well-known published collections.[2] Yet Beerbohm early adopted the pose of dilettante, and kept it to the end. He always seemed the observer, sometimes placid, sometimes supercilious, rarely malicious; he never seemed the doer that he actually was.

216

I

It was under the influence of Oscar Wilde and Oxford that Beerbohm's earliest essays were written. "I was a modest, good-humoured boy. It is Oxford that has made me insufferable."[3] "Dandies and Dandies," the first in the 1896 volume entitled *The Works*, celebrates the importance of clothes because they give pleasure. Dress is an art too little valued for the simple reason that what is a daily routine is for most people dull. How strange it is, he remarks with condescension, that the philosophy of clothes should have been described in *Sartor Resartus* by a writer—Thomas Carlyle—who dressed so badly. The highest praise is accorded to a fictitious gentleman who for fifty years kept a daily record of his dress: "Yes [Beerbohm ruminates], fifty springs have filled his buttonhole with their violets; the snow of fifty winters has been less white than his linen; his boots have outshone fifty sequences of summer suns and the colours of all those autumns have faded in the dry light of his apparel."[4]

The pleasure principle leads in another essay to a defense of King George the Fourth against the earlier moral strictures of Thackeray. George was, indeed, a great voluptuary, but he gave as well as received pleasure. Sinning greatly, he was yet more greatly sinned against, and he brought to the throne a grace sadly lacking in his predecessors, the first three Georges.

In later essays, Beerbohm is less affected, but he remained individual, an adroit opponent of popular taste, a defender of neglected quality. He expressed a hearty dislike for Madame Tussaud's wax works (they were ingenious, but abortive and depressing); for serious music (he did not enjoy it); for sculpture (it is a lost art); for the over-affectionate attitude toward children; for bicycles, especially for women bicyclists; for knighthood (it is much too common now). On the other hand, he professed a liking for seaside resorts in winter, when deserted; for the unabashed vulgarity of old-time music halls; for such a popular novelist as "Ouida," whom no one would ever think of calling artistic.

One of his best essays has the forbidding title "A Clergyman."[5] This essay, which I found in a collection by that old Oxonian, Christopher Morley, is a special one for me because it is the first piece by Beerbohm that I ever read. Since my own college and graduate studies had been restricted to authors dead at least thirty years, I knew nothing of Beerbohm. But I did know a little about Boswell's Johnson, and that is what the essay is about. Beerbohm describes the clergyman thus:

> Fragmentary, pale, momentary; almost nothing; glimpsed and gone; as it were, a faint human hand thrust up, never to reappear, from beneath the rolling waters of Time, he forever haunts my memory and solicits my weak imagination. Nothing is told of him but that once, abruptly, he asked a question, and received an answer.

The question, Beerbohm explains, occurred at the home of the Thrales, whom Johnson and Boswell often visited. On this occasion, Boswell questioned the great doctor about the best writers of sermons. Atterbury, Tillotson, Seed, Jortin, Sherlock, Smalridge and Ogden were approved by Dr. Johnson with those nice distinctions of compliment of which he was master. Then said Boswell:

> What I want to know is, what sermons afford the best specimen of English pulpit eloquence.
> JOHNSON: We have no sermons addressed to the passions, that are good for anything; if you mean that kind of eloquence.
> A CLERGYMAN, whose name I do not recollect: Were not Dodd's sermons addressed to the passions?
> JOHNSON: They were nothing, sir, be they addressed to what they may.

"The suddenness of it," says Beerbohm. "Bang!—and the rabbit that had popped from its burrow was no more." Beerbohm then speculates about this mysterious clergyman. Who was he? Why had Boswell not mentioned him earlier? Why did he not remember his name? He must have been a shy young man, probably the curate from the church nearby. The question, carefully inspected, is one which must have been uttered in a high thin voice that grated on the slightly deaf Dr. Johnson. "Were not Dodd's sermons addressed to the passions?" Hopeful of praise for his suggestion, the young clergyman probably never recovered from Johnson's rebuff. "He sank into a rapid decline. Before the next blossoming of Thrale Hall's almond trees he was no more. I'd like to think that he died forgiving Dr. Johnson."

One of the slyest touches in the essay is a parallel imaginary scene about 1920. The discussion with some nameless pundit would then center about novelists, not sermon writers:

"Yes, Sir," the pundit may be telling a disciple at this moment, "Wells is one of the best. Galsworthy is one of the best, if you except his concern for delicacy of style. Mrs. Ward has a very firm grasp of problems, but is not very creational—Caine's books are very edifying. I should like to read all that Caine has written. Miss Corelli, too, is very edifying.—And you may add Upton Sinclair." "What I want to know," says the disciple, "is, what English novels may be selected as specially enthralling." . . . "We have no novels addressed to the passions that are good for anything, if you mean that kind of enthralment." And here some poor wretch (whose name the disciple will not remember) inquires: "Are not Mrs. Glyn's novels addressed to the passions?" and is in due form annihilated.

In such a piece as "A Clergyman" the full possibility of the essay is realized. There is a sharp recollection, there is discovery, there is satiric juxtaposition; pathos is checked by a laugh at human folly; and the laugh is checked before it sours into cynicism.

For a variety of reasons Beerbohm became dramatic critic for *The Saturday Review* when he was not yet twenty-six. He had published a collection of essays and a volume of drawings. His name was familiar in a dozen magazines, and through some twenty-five free-lance contributions it was familiar to readers of the *Review*. When Shaw decided to resign, Harris, the editor, was out of the country. That Shaw himself picked Beerbohm is suggested by a letter in the Shaw collection at the British Museum; it is a first draft of Beerbohm's first article, entitled "Why I ought not to have become a Dramatic Critic." He considered himself a poor substitute for the brilliant Shaw. He took, he said, "neither emotional nor intellectual pleasure" in drama. He had no critical theory. He could, he admitted, recite backwards most of the successful plays of the past ten years, and had (through his half-brother Beerbohm Tree) an acquaintance with many actors. His lot as critic, he concluded, would at least be better than that of railway porter.

He approached plays as a man of intelligence and taste. A good dramatic idea, he thought, was one that enabled the playwright to show fresh observation of a human situation. The freshness was important. "If a man is dull, rightness in him does not conciliate me," he observed.[6] In his own independent way, Beerbohm carried on the war with the nineteenth-century theater that Shaw had begun. They were both against melodrama and stereotyped characters. They both derided lavish spectacles designed to minimize interest in character and idea. When a French playwright produced a play about Robespierre he seemed unable to function with the mere trestles, planks, and passion required by Dumas. Instead, the author of *Robespierre* said in effect: "Give me an exciting period, two hundred supers and sixty-two speaking parts, and Sir Henry Irving shall do the rest."[7]

Beerbohm, though sympathetic to many of Shaw's ideas, was thoroughly independent with regard to Shaw's plays. This is well illustrated in his review of *The Devil's Disciple* in October 1899. The play, I remind you, is about a young atheist who offers to sacrifice himself for a minister involved in the American Revolution, all because of a hopeless love for the minister's wife. Beerbohm congratulates Shaw on having written a superb melodrama (such as Shaw himself would have condemned) and turning it to farce in the last act. The young atheist is Shaw's "first really human and convincing character." Shaw, who, Beerbohm says, "imagines emotion to be an unfortunate and not inevitable nuisance," probably had other intentions, but they miscarried. The review closes with a paragraph parodying what Shaw would probably say in his preface to the published play.[8]

Beerbohm's eighteen reviews of Shaw's plays raise most of the questions that subsequent critics have wrestled with. He thought Shaw wrong when he was serious, successfully funny when his comic imagination took over. The reviews have the liveliness of contemporary impression and the attractions of good talk. Beerbohm omits the obvious, he exaggerates and parodies for effect, and he is content to say part of the truth well. Moreover, he is willing to admit errors. In 1903 he considered the published version of *Man and Superman* as merely a series of dialogues, and not a play at all. Later he branded this judgment as a howler, since on stage the play had proved highly amusing.[9]

Like Shaw, Beerbohm was no bardolator. He was apprehensive when Shakespeare was revived. Shakespeare has been so enshrouded with literary and theatrical tradition that his plays are the signal for reverential and undiscriminating praise. When "every head in the auditorium is a casket of reminiscence," he said, it is impossible to get a fresh response. *Hamlet, Macbeth,* and *Romeo and Juliet* he thought were revived much too often. *The Tempest* he welcomed because it was unhackneyed. *Richard III* and *Henry V* he dismissed as the mere hack-work of genius. *Coriolanus* he thought a bad play. *The Merchant of Venice* was "a particularly sad instance of the way in which Shakespeare wasted so much of his time." *The Merry Wives of Windsor* is "the wretchedest piece of hack-work ever done by a great writer, and is by us condoned for the sake of the love we bear him." In Falstaff's "facile coarseness" Beerbohm discerned "hardly one gleam of genuine humor."[10]

In the numerous comments on Shakespeare (thirty reviews in all) there are the insistent questions: Is the play relevant and dramatic? Despite our familiarity with it, does the new production create a genuinely fresh response? Does the poetry, however lovely, get in the way of dramatic effect? Can the actors read the lines appropriately, with due allowance for the verse and proper accent of its dramatic values? These are the questions wholly pertinent today as they were in Beerbohm's time. Like Beerbohm, we must all too often answer no. Because he raises them so well, Beerbohm's dramatic criticism is still interesting, whether he discusses Shakespeare, Shaw, or some forgotten playwright of the 1890's.

In 1912 Beerbohm published a volume of parodies generally considered to be the epitome of the parodist's art. But to explain the parodies one must first explain the works parodied, and this would take too long. I mention only the one on Henry James, "The Mote in the Middle Distance," which many of you have encountered. (James, by the way, greatly enjoyed the parody.) There is another one, "The Guerdon," written when James received the Order of Merit; but since James died within weeks, this parody remained unpublished for many years. The tone of these parodies is anticipated in the captions of some caricatures of James.[11]

II

Of Beerbohm's caricatures it is difficult to speak—and, I may add, difficult to write. I am frustrated by the impossibility of conveying in words the charm of the drawings that delight the eye even when one does not know the person caricatured. Arthur Balfour in the 1896 volume may be a very dim name from the period before and after World War I, but when we see Beerbohm's drawing we recognize the type. Beerbohm shows his tall slender body as a reversed figure

S, a tiny head perched at the top, and a long thin arm carrying a dispatch case. He is the intellectual in politics, remote from the beefy concerns of ordinary people.[12]

In 1901 Beerbohm did a series of drawings on John Bull under the impact of the Boer War, a badly managed and unpopular war, though ultimately successful. John Bull is shown taking comfort from the presence of a jut-jawed and bespectacled Rudyard Kipling, the poet of empire and the thin red line of 'eroes:

> "Yes [says John Bull], I've took a fancy to you, young feller. 'Tain't often I cottons to a Pote neither. 'Course there's Shakespeare. 'E was a wonder, 'e was . . . Swan of Avon,' *I* calls 'im. Take 'im for all in all we shall not look upon 'is likes agin. . . . But most potes ain't like that. What I say is, *they ain't wholesome*. . . . Got your banjo with you to-night? Then empty that there mug and give us a toon."[13]

Beerbohm, by the way, had a high opinion of Kipling's talent, but felt that he sacrificed himself too much for popularity. Kipling remained a favorite target for caricature.

The caricatures that have survived best are those dealing with literary figures, like Kipling, who are still familiar. In *The Poets' Corner* of 1904 is the memorable drawing of Browning, taking tea with the Browning Society. The poet, seated on a pink-upholstered chair, is surrounded by fifteen unsmiling figures reflecting in a variety of expressions, reverence, mystification, polite boredom, and even querulous indignation. Beerbohm assumes, of course, that Browning's actual aversion to the formation of a Browning Society is known to the viewer of his drawing.

In the same volume the romantic self-indulgence familiar in Fitz-Gerald's Rubáiyát is ridiculed. Omar, so fat that he must be shown lying down, reads from a tiny pink book numbered one. Other items in the famous stanza are duly identified by number: the bough, loaf of bread, jug of wine, Thou (an unattractive female yawning in neglect), and "Wilderness," the endless monotonous desert.

In 1907 Henry James is shown visiting America, and an extract from his unspoken thoughts is a trial flight for the parodies published several years later:

> . . . So that, in fine, let, without further beating about the bush, me make to myself amazed acknowledgement that, but for the certificate of birth which I have—so very indubitably—*on*

me, I might, in regarding, and, as it somewhat were, over-
seeing, à l'oeil de voyageur, these dear good people, find hard
to swallow, or even to take by subconscious injection, the great
idea that I am—oh, ever so indigenously!—one of them. . . .

Nine figures in the background represent American types as different as possible from James. A girl calls out, "My! Ain't he cree-ative?"
A Red Indian welcomes James. And a group of four give an American
college yell: "What's—the matter with—*James?*" "*He's* all—right!"[14]
In 1913 appeared the most memorable of many caricatures of Shaw.
The bearded playwright is shown standing on his head, quizzically
observed by Beerbohm in self-caricature. The caption reads "Mild
surprise of one who, revisiting England after long absence, finds
that the dear fellow has not moved."[15]
In 1922 came the series called *Rossetti and His Circle,* esteemed by
connoisseurs as Beerbohm's finest drawing, but requiring too much
explanation for discussion here. In 1923 Beerbohm exhibited a
number of drawings of the late King Edward VII, father of George
V. Edward, as everyone knew, had led a very gay life as a young
man, and a pretty gay life even as an old man. The gross figure of
Edward, twanging a lyre in heaven, and some other drawings,
grated on public taste. There were protests in the papers, and in a
dignified letter Beerbohm authorized managers of the gallery to
withdraw the offensive caricatures. They were likewise omitted
from the volume based on that exhibition. One milder drawing of
Edward was retained. It is entitled "The rare, the rather awful
Visits of Albert Edward, Prince of Wales, to Windsor Castle."
Edward, who was sixty when his mother died in 1901, is shown
as a grown man standing in a corner like a naughty boy. Queen
Victoria, in black, sits in the foreground, sadly pensive over the scold-
ing she has presumably administered. On the wall is the lower part
of a portrait, showing only the legs of some royal person, no doubt
the saintly Prince Albert, Edward's father.[16]
Beerbohm's last book of caricatures appeared in 1925, and though
he continued to draw, it was for his own pleasure. He spent an unreasonable amount of time and energy "improving" books by satirical marginal decorations. One such is a worshipful biography of
Shaw. The volume, now in the Berg Collection of the New York
Public Library, is profusely illustrated. Beerbohm has altered most of
the illustrations, and supplied new captions. On a picture of Shaw
himself is written a one-line parody of the biographer's pedantic

style: "A merrier man, within the limits of becoming mirth, I never spent an hour's talk withal." A more famous volume is Queen Victoria's *Leaves from a Journal of our Life in the Highlands*. Beerbohm imitated the Queen's handwriting and made the book appear to be a presentation copy. On the title page is inscribed: "For Mr. Beerbohm, the never-sufficiently-to-be-studied writer whom Albert looks down on affectionately, I am sure—From his Sovereign Victoria R. I. Balmoral, 1898."[17]

Critics of the art of caricature point out, with justice, that Beerbohm was an imperfect draughtsman. He could not draw feet, and he never mastered shadows. Increasingly he depended on captions and text to underline his idea. If you turn from Beerbohm to the great caricaturists who preceded him—to Hogarth, to Gillray, and to Rowlandson, to the Ape and Spy of *Vanity Fair*—you find more finished and more powerful use of the drawing pencil. Yet these greater artists will never remind you of Beerbohm nor he of them. He achieved in caricature what he achieved in writing, a manner and a point of view that were unique in the literal sense. There has been only one Max.

III

Beerbohm's one novel, *Zuleika Dobson*, was begun perhaps as early as 1898, but not completed and published until 1911. Indeed the desire to complete this novel was a minor motive in Beerbohm's retirement in 1910. The novel is one of those special books, not central in a syllabus of the English novel, but for those who discover it more interesting than some of the major landmarks.

A brief synopsis is likely to be more than usually discouraging to an intending reader. The plot is deliberately preposterous. Zuleika Dobson, a young woman who has made a brilliant success as performer of magic tricks, comes to visit her uncle, the Warden of Judas College, Oxford. (This college, of course, is fictitious.) She meets the Duke of Dorset, who immediately falls in love with her. But when he enumerates his titles—fourteenth Duke of Dorset, Marquis of Dorset, Earl of Grove, Earl of Chastermaine, Viscount Brewsby, Baron Grove, Baron Petstrap, and Baron Wolock—and the many estates Zuleika will share as his wife, that young lady says indignantly: "I think you are an awful snob." The Duke, having de-

meaned himself first by falling in love at all and then by being refused, forms the idea of dying for his love. "Death was the one true
bridal." It even seemed to him that by dying for her, he might cause
her to love him. "He saw her bending over his tomb, in beautiful
humble curves, under a starless sky, watering the violets with her
tears."[18]

When the Duke tells Zuleika his determination to die for her, she
does not believe him. They quarrel, and the Duke changes his mind.
But at this point he receives a telegram from his ancestral estate:

> Deeply regret inform your grace last night two black owls came
> and perched on battlements remained there through night
> hooting at dawn flew away none knows whither awaiting
> instructions.[19]

Realizing that his death is fated, the Duke goes through with his
suicide, which he carries out by throwing himself into the river during the annual boat race, when the river is crowded with spectators.
Meanwhile, all the other undergraduates have fallen hopelessly in
love with Zuleika, and have resolved, each one of them, to die for her.
So they *all* throw themselves in the river. (Beerbohm deftly passes
over such realistic problems as undertaking and coroners' inquiries.)
The Warden of Judas, when Zuleika informs him of this disaster,
agrees that she had better leave Oxford. Perhaps she could pay him
another visit later—but not in term time. Next day, by special train,
Zuleika departs for Cambridge.

How did Beerbohm sustain interest in so preposterous a story,
and why? Both questions can be answered if the book is regarded as a
caricature in fantasy. Just as a caricature bears a recognizable relation
to reality, no matter how great the exaggeration, so the story of Zuleika reflects real life in the very act of distorting it. The highlights of
the Oxford scene are reassuringly there: the Broad, the portals of
Balliol and Trinity, the Ashmolean, and the Sheldonian, with its
crumbling busts of Roman emperors. Oxford's beauty is recurrent.
As the Duke looks out his window the morning after he met Zuleika,

> Some clock clove with silver the stillness of the morning. Ere
> came the second stroke, another and nearer clock was striking.
> And now there were others chiming in. The air was confused
> with the sweet babel of its many spires, some of them booming
> deep, measured sequences, some tinkling impatiently and out-
> witting others which had begun before them.[20]

Against these last enchantments of the Middle Age—the phrase is Matthew Arnold's, introduced in Beerbohm's first paragraph—how contemporary is the theme of the story. The Duke of Dorset is the epitome of ancient privilege at the very time when ancient privilege was being challenged, not only in Parliament, but more insidiously by The New Woman. Zuleika *is* The New Woman. She is aggressively charming; she has so little respect for tradition that she is unimpressed by the Duke's titles and estates. In 1881, Henry James—Beerbohm's favorite novelist—had treated the same theme seriously. In *The Portrait of a Lady*, when Isabel Archer refused Lord Warburton's proposal, that nobleman had too much sense to throw himself into the river, but he seems to have had but a sad life ever after. The New Woman of the 1890s modified permanently not only the concept of hereditary privilege, but also the concept of romantic love inherited from the Pre-Raphaelites and the Wildean aesthetic movement. The Duke's love for Zuleika, and that of every other undergraduate, is spontaneous and complete in the old inherited and literary way. Since there is no room for it to grow, its perfect expression is death, and in the preposterous death of the Oxford student body it is duly satirized. Beerbohm himself had experienced a hopeless, ideal love for a music hall girl while he was at Oxford; and a realistic novel of Oxford life which he greatly admired, Compton Mackenzie's *Sinister Street* (1913-14), has a similar episode of hopeless immature love.

A reader of *Zuleika Dobson* will find many subordinate beauties to choose from. I am fond of Zuleika's uncle, the venerable Warden of Judas College, who alludes to London and such far-away places as "the outer world." The history of the fictional Judas College is a wonderful parody of guidebook solemnities. Mr. Abimilech V. Oover of Trinity College, an American Rhodes Scholar, begins a long speech: "Like most of my countrymen, I am a man of few words." Then there is Mr. Pedby, a mathematician of international renown, who at a college dinner reads a Latin grace with numerous false quantities. Beerbohm comments: "Summers and winters would come and go, old faces would vanish, giving place to new, but the story of Pedby's grace would be told always. Here was a tradition that generations of dons yet unborn would cherish and chuckle over."[21] There are portents and preternatural events. The Roman emperors on the Sheldonian are apprehensive from the very arrival of Zuleika, and perspiration glistens on their brows. When Zuleika passes by, Corker, a dog, growls like the mastiff in

Coleridge's *Christabel*. Zuleika's pearl earrings and the Duke's pearl shirt studs change color from pink to black, signaling the hope and despair inherent in the love story. The skill with which such details are fitted into the structure of the novel, and the style which touches satire into beauty can be admired more readily than analyzed.

Why did Beerbohm never write another novel? Apparently no one ever asked him that question. One can only guess that he doubted his ability to write another one as good. He did do some narrative sketches which interlock and approach a loose, episodic unity. These are found in a book called *Seven Men* (1919). There are five sketches dealing with six men; Beerbohm appears in each and is thus the seventh man. The best of these is the first, called "Enoch Soames." Soames is represented as a minor author of the 1890s so unsuccessful in his own time that he thinks posterity must accord him some notice. He makes a bargain with the Devil (like Dr. Faustus). He is allowed to spend a day at the British Museum a century hence. He is crushingly disappointed to find not one of his volumes of poetry preserved there. The only allusion to him is in a book of literary history which refers condescendingly to Max Beerbohm's very labored essay about him.

Beerbohm reached the peak of his fame in the 1920s, though in the late thirties, the years of World War II, and even in the 1950s his popularity was revived by a series of radio broadcasts, chiefly reminiscent of London life at the turn of the century. As he recedes into the literary history of those remote times, how relevant is he to the rebellious, frustrated present? For those who will read him and look at his drawings, he stands for leisure, intelligence, and taste. His active years show that amalgam of independence and conformity best represented in America in *The New Yorker*—a journal almost inconceivable without the precedent of Beerbohm's writing and drawing. His retirement has about it something of Thoreau's sojourn at Walden, except that Thoreau stayed at the Pond for only two years; Beerbohm stayed at Rapallo most of forty-six. Beerbohm was independent, yet well-mannered. He gained wisdom, yet he remained lively. To those who will give time to his drawings, to his writings, and to the pattern of his life, he will remain what Shaw so appropriately called him early in his career: the incomparable Max.

[1968]

Notes

1. J. G. Riewald, *Sir Max Beerbohm, Man and Writer: A Critical Analysis with a Brief Life and a Bibliography* (The Hague: Martinus Nijhoff, 1953, and Brattleboro, Vermont: The Stephen Greene Press, 1961), pp. 271-294. Most of these articles and essays have now been collected.—*Editor's note.*

2. The total number actually amounts to 2093; see Rupert Hart-Davis (comp.), *A Catalogue of the Caricatures of Max Beerbohm* (London: Macmillan, and Cambridge, Mass.: Harvard University Press, 1972).—*Editor's note.*

3. "Going Back to School," *More* (London, 1899), p. 155.

4. *The Works* (London, 1896), p. 26.

5. *And Even Now* (London, 1920), pp. 233-241.

6. *Around Theatres* (London, 1953), p. 46. The remark appeared in *The Saturday Review,* 9 December 1899.

7. *The Saturday Review,* 22 April 1899, pp. 491-492. Reprinted in *More Theatres* (London, 1969), pp. 133-137.

8. *Around Theatres,* ed. cit., pp. 38-41.

9. Riewald, in his *Sir Max Beerbohm, Man and Writer,* lists 17 reviews of Shaw (p. 341). There is another, of "Mrs. Warren's Profession," in *The Saturday Review* of 14 and 21 May 1898, before Beerbohm became the official drama critic of that journal. (This review is listed by Riewald on p. 274.—*Editor's note.*) Twelve of the reviews of Shaw appear in *Around Theatres,* ed. cit., which includes the comments on *Man and Superman,* pp. 268, 472.

10. *Around Theatres* includes only eight of Beerbohm's comments on Shakespeare. The quoted passages appear in *The Saturday Review,* 19 January 1901 and 14 June 1902 (*More Theatres,* pp. 342-345 and 470-474).

11. "The Mote in the Middle Distance" first appeared in *The Saturday Review,* 8 December 1906; it was the first item in *A Christmas Garland* (London, 1912). "The Guerdon" was privately printed in New York in 1925. Beerbohm first included it as the seventh item in *A Variety of Things* (New York, 1928), with a contemptuous note (p. viii) on the previous pirated edition.

12. *Caricatures of Twenty-Five Gentlemen* (London, 1896). The drawing of The Right Hon. Arthur James Balfour is the seventh.

13. *Cartoons "The Second Childhood of John Bull"* (London, 1911). The Kipling drawing is the thirteenth of a series of fifteen, exhibited in 1901 but not published until 1911.

14. *A Book of Caricatures* (London, 1907). "Mr. Henry James (in America)" is the last of forty-eight plates.

15. *Fifty Caricatures* (London, 1913). The Shaw drawing is the eighth.

16. *Things New and Old* (London, 1923). The drawing of Edward is the tenth of forty-nine.

17. The biography of Shaw is that by Archibald Henderson (1911). S. N. Behrman, *Portrait of Max* (New York, 1960), pp. 89-97, describes the volume by Queen Victoria.

18. *Zuleika Dobson: or, An Oxford Love Story* (London, 1911), pp. 64, 87, 90.

19. Ibid., p. 217.

20. Ibid., p. 39.

21. Ibid., pp. 308-309.

David Cecil

THE MAX BEERBOHM ENTERTAINMENT

"The incomparable Max," Shaw called him. The phrase has stuck. Indeed it is apt; from the first Max's work was too individual profitably to be compared with that of anyone else. Not that it was always the same. Max the impertinent exquisite of the 1890s changed gradually into Max the mature and subtle humorist of the 1920s. His style altered along with his spirit: the florid Rococo of the essay on "Dandies and Dandies" sobered and refined itself into the classic Chippendale of the essay on "Going Out for a Walk". All the same the difference between the two is far less than their likeness. From the beginning to the end of his career Max's work is homogeneous; an expression of the same personality and the same attitude towards his art.

This is that of the entertainer. From the start of his career Max thought it the first duty of an artist to be true to the nature of his talent and to refrain from writing on subjects that did not inspire it. "It is curious," he writes, "how often an artist is ignorant of his own true bent. How many charming talents have been spoiled by the desire to do 'important' work. Some are born to juggle with golden balls, some are born to lift heavy weights." He was not ignorant of his own bent. He knew he was a juggler and he devised his work accordingly. Though as capable as anyone of serious views and deep feelings he recognised that these did not stir his artistic impulse: so that very rarely does he allow them to appear openly in his work.

David Cecil, Introduction to the Bodley Head *Max Beerbohm* (London: The Bodley Head, 1970), pp. 7-18. Title supplied by Editor. Reprinted by permission of Lord David Cecil and The Bodley Head, Ltd.

Deliberately he writes not to disturb or to instruct but to please: and more particularly to amuse.

For—and this is the second distinguishing characteristic of his work—his genius was a comic genius. The aspects of experience that stimulated him to create were the aspects that made him smile or laugh: the balls he juggled with were jokes: the Max Beerbohm entertainment is a comic entertainment. But it is one of a special and superior kind, for it is the expression of a special and superior man. Max was very intelligent, with a sharp, searching intelligence, continually at work noticing and concluding. Half his jokes are also penetrating comments on human nature. Well-informed comments too! Max liked to make out that he was imperfectly educated. In fact every page he wrote reveals him as the heir to an ancient culture which has furnished his mind, enriched his imagination and refined his taste, disclosing itself in his every casual allusion and in the unobtrusive, graceful confidence of his tone of voice. Finally culture and intelligence alike are strengthened by the fact that they are under the direction of a shrewd judgment. Unlike some intelligent people Max was extremely sensible. He surveyed the world with a realistic gaze that made him as impervious to nonsense as Dr. Johnson himself, however much it was accepted by respectable or fashionable opinion. Listen to him talking about the opponents of woman's suffrage in the 90s:

> Two or three years ago, other ladies, anxious to vote, came forward and have gone around literally shrieking; and the result is that already their desire is treated as a matter of practical politics, and a quite urgent one at that. What a pretty light all this throws—does it not?—on a world governed by the animals which distinguish themselves from the other animals by taking "reasonable animals" as their label! And yet the light does not seem to have enlightened the brilliantly reasonable animals which write for the press. Invariably, solemnly, at every fresh "raid" or other escapade of the suffragist ladies, those newspapers which are friendly to the cause itself announce that "this has put back the clock of female suffrage by at least twenty years". Bless their hearts! The clock must now, by their computation, have been put back "at least" twelve centuries.

Or commenting on the gospel of Marinetti, the prophet of the Futurist movement in art:

With the best will in the world, I fail to be frightened by
Marinetti and his doctrines. . . . When he asks why we "poison ourselves" by "a daily walk through the museums," I assure
him that his metaphor has no relation to fact. There are a few ped-
ants who walk daily in museums; but even they don't poison
themselves; on the contrary, they find there the food that best
agrees with them. There is a vast mass of humanity which never
sets foot in a museum. There are the artists who go now and
again, and profit by the inspiration. It must be a very feeble
talent that dares not, for fear of being overwhelmed and atro-
phied, contemplate the achievements of the past. No talent,
however strong, can dispense with that inspiration. But how
on earth is anyone going to draw any inspiration from the
Future? Let us spell it with a capital letter, by all means. But
don't let us expect it to give us anything in return. It can't,
poor thing; for the very good reason that it doesn't yet exist,
save as a dry abstract term.

The past and present—there are two useful and delightful
things. I am sorry, Marinetti, but I'm afraid there is no future for
the Future.

Anti-suffragists were old-fashioned; the Futurists were *avant-
garde*. Max was as unimpressed by the one as by the other. His
formidable good sense made him formidably independent. Even the
great brains of his time could not stampede him into accepting their
views against his better judgment:

Take them seriously? Ah no! If they happen to be artists expressing themselves through some art-form, through poems or
novels, let us delight in their concentration, the narrowness that
enables them to express just what they can feel, just what they
can understand, so much more forcibly than if they had a sense
of proportion and a little of the modesty that comes of wisdom.
Our Ibsens and D'Annunzios and Bernard Shaws and Gorkis—
let us harken to them and revel in them. But let us mix up all
their "messages" together, and strike an average, and not suppose even then that we are appreciably one whit nearer to the
truth of things.

Sceptical about "messages," Max, as this quotation shows, never
questioned the value of art. Indeed the impulse behind the work, in
so far as it was not comic, was aesthetic. The Beerbohm entertainment
set out to entertain by its beauty as well as by its fun. Max grew up
during the period of the Aesthetic Movement; and though he laughed

at it—as at most things—he shared its views. For him, art was the most important and most precious of human activities: and the distinguishing mark of a work of art was its beauty. Even a caricature, he thought, should aim at beauty—"beauty to be achieved by the perfect adjustment of means to ends." Max's feeling for beauty, apparent in his unsleeping sense of form, also showed itself in his taste. This was in keeping with the general character of his genius. Though he could recognise grand or primitive types of beauty, he preferred it light, delicate, elegant; beauty in its humbler, gayer manifestation as prettiness. Mingled with his sense of fun, this sense of beauty often incarnated itself in the form of graceful extravagant fantasy, the fantasy of wicked "Lord George Hell" converted to a saintly life by wearing a saintly wax mask, of the busts of the Roman Emperors outside the Sheldonian Theatre at Oxford bursting out in sweat at the sight of beautiful, fatal Zuleika Dobson. Yet—and this is one of the things that gives Max's work its unique flavour—his fantasy is always disciplined by his intelligence and his good sense. It is never silly: its charm comes largely from the fact that it is seen against an unwavering standard of realism and reason. The behaviour of the busts may be fantastic, but not the Oxford scene in which it takes place: Lord George Hell's conversion is described with a conscious, self-mocking affectation of manner which makes it quite clear that the reader must not take it too solemnly. Whatever clouds of fantasy may encircle Max's head his feet were always firmly on the ground.

The effect of this contrast running through his work is ironical. Irony is its most continuous and consistent characteristic; an irony at once delicate and ruthless, from which nothing is altogether protected, not even the author himself. Ruthless but not savage: Max could be made angry—by brutality or vulgarity—but very seldom does he reveal this in his creative works. His artistic sense told him that ill-temper was out of place in an entertainment, especially in an entertainment that aspired to be pretty as well as comic. His ruthlessness gains its particular flavour from the fact that it is also good-tempered. On the other hand it is not so good-tempered as to lose its edge. Max's irony is never that sort of "kindly" irony that softens and sentimentalises. His artistic sense tells him that softness, as much as savagery, would destroy the clear bright atmosphere needed for his entertainment to make its effect.

The Max Beerbohm entertainment takes various forms. First of all there are the parodies. Here Max is a supreme master. He manages

to parody his victim's sense as much as he does his style. Henry
James, once questioned about his next work, replied, pointing to
Max Beerbohm: "Ask that young man. He knows me better than I
know myself." Reading the James parody in this selection, one sees
what he means.[1] If Henry James had chosen to write about two children waking up to find their stockings on Christmas morning this
is what he would have said. And this almost is how he would have
said it. The exaggeration of style needed to make parody amusing is
all the more effective because it is so very slight. Sometimes Max
hardly seems to exaggerate at all. "If Euclid was alive to-day (and I
dare I say he is) . . ." Is this a phrase of Chesterton's or a phrase from
Max's parody of Chesterton? Once again the likeness is of sense
as well as of style. The sentence is an illuminating critical comment
on Chesterton's whole mode of thought. So is the parody on James
a profound and friendly criticism of James, so is the parody of Kipling a profound but devastating criticism of Kipling.

Max's entertainment took two other forms. The first is the
occasional essay. Of these there are four volumes: *The Works of Max
Beerbohm, More, Yet Again* and the last and best, *And Even Now.*
Max's essays are what may be called "pure" essays; that is to say they
are vehicles not for instruction or confession but designed simply
to fulfil his creative impulse, which is to amuse. If he does make a
serious point in them, it is in a playful tone; any imaginative moment
takes the form of a playful flight of fancy. For the rest they are deliberate exhibitions of personality. This personality is not a self-portrait.
Max the essayist is not the same as Max the man, but rather a fictitious
figure made up of those particular elements in his composition that
he judged would enhance his entertainment. He isolates some of his
own qualities—his humour, his fancy, his wit, his taste in style—
and uses them as material from which by means of an elaborate
process of arrangement and staging he creates the protagonist in
his one-man show.

Such a type of essay is hard to write successfully, as can be realised
by reading the essays of Max's imitators. On the one hand to keep the
tone so consistently light is to run the risk of making the whole thing
seem flimsy; on the other hand the writer who consciously exploits
his personality easily appears an exhibitionist all too obviously
anxious to show off his charm. Max walks the tightrope between
these dangers with confidence and ease. His essays do not seem flimsy because they are not built of flimsy materials; they are the prod-

uct of too lively an intelligence, too observant an eye. Such pieces as those on "The Naming of Streets" or "Hosts and Guests" are packed with enough fresh ideas and insights into human nature to furnish forth fifty average "serious" writers. If the reader fails to notice this, it is only because Max's tone is so carefree and throw-away.

Intelligence saves his essays from flimsiness; good sense saves them from self-admiring exhibitionism. No doubt Max is showing off; it is the function of the entertainer to show off. But he is far too sensible to be unaware of this fact and far too humorous not to be amused by it. In the essay entitled "Going Out for a Walk" he describes vividly how bored he has been by a fellow walker; but the climax of the piece is his unexpected revelation that he knows the fellow walker is likely to have found him equally boring. It is a secret of his strength that he is one of the very few writers whose irony is so impartial as to include himself.

Along with his "pure" essays we may consider Max's critical pieces, mostly drawn from his work as the dramatic critic of the *Saturday Review*. He wrote these reluctantly as a means of livlihood; and they do show his limitations. One cannot call them failures; they are too clever and too accomplished. But the critical mode, except in the form of parody, did not stimulate him. Criticism is not primarily a comedian's mode. Max knew it. "My whole position is uncomfortable," he remarked. "I have a satiric temperament; when I am laughing at anyone I am generally rather amusing but when I am praising anyone I am always dull." Here he goes too far; he did not know how to be dull. It is true, however, that only now and again in these criticisms does he seem vitally and unmistakably himself, and that is when he leaves off talking about a play to follow some comic or whimsical train of thought suggested by it, or to re-create with affectionate amusement some personality which has appealed to his fancy, like Irving or Dan Leno; when in fact he stops being a critic and reverts to being an entertainer.

The last category in his entertainment consists of his stories. These in their turn subdivide into two types. First come his two fables, *The Dreadful Dragon of Hay Hill* and *The Happy Hypocrite*. *The Dreadful Dragon of Hay Hill* is not included in this book; even more than his play reviews it exposes Max's limitations. Written after the First World War, it is designed to illustrate his conviction, taught him by the war, that mankind is incurably, congenitally quarrelsome. This is a bleak conviction and, for all that Max writes in his usual playful tone, it is a bleak tale. As such it does not suit his talent, for bleakness involves the eclipse of that good-humour which is an essential condition of his inspiration. At the same time he lacks the harsh force to drive his story's harsh moral home. Max cannot divest himself of his usual easy urbanity. This blunts the cutting edge of his attack on humanity. *The Happy Hypocrite* also points a moral, namely that by wearing a mask of goodness you may become good; for, as Max said: "I hold that Candour is good only when it reveals good actions or good sentiments, and that when it reveals evil, itself is evil." Here for once he is talking seriously. And wisely too; these principles, put into practice, are a good deal more likely to lead a man to live a satisfactory life than are all the hot gospels preached by the prophets of romanticism, from Shelley down to D. H. Lawrence. *The Happy Hypocrite* is charming as well as wise; with a fresh youthful charm that makes it impossible to omit it from any selection of its author's best work. Its only fault is that its charm and its wisdom do not completely harmonise. The mock-nursery-tale mode in which Max has chosen to tell his story is a little too childish to carry the weight of its mature moral.

There is no such fault in the second group of his stories, *Zuleika Dobson* and *Seven Men and Two Others*. These, along with his best parodies, are his masterpieces. They are best described as satiric fantasies and owe their peculiar flavour, even more than his other works, to the fact that they are a blend; on the one hand of humour and prettiness, on the other of fact and fancy. Most of them involve extravagant flights of fancy; yet each is founded on Max's personal experience of the real world and each derives substantial interest from the fact that it is sedulously true to it. Fantasy is at its prettiest and boldest in *Zuleika Dobson*. This tells how the most beautiful woman in the world arrived in what was then the exclusively male world of Oxford; how all the undergraduates fell in love with her and how they drowned themselves for her sake at the close of the boat races. This preposterous idea is exploited to its full preposterousness. No note of serious feeling checks the foaming flood of high spirits on which the tale sweeps along. It is consistently and audaciously heartless. Yet the fun is not "sick;" there is no question of the author taking an equivocal pleasure in pain. Our pleasure in it is unqualified by the smallest hint of horror or perversity. With all this, it is truthful too; the truest picture of Oxford in fiction. Dons and students and Rhodes scholars, Eights Week, Balliol concerts, exclusive dining clubs—every characteristic phase and fact of

David Cecil

University life is described with an extraordinary, perceptive insight. Finally it is written in a style which is a masterpiece of sustained virtuosity, a parody of aesthetic fine writing which is even finer than the manner which it mocks. As a blend of comedy and prettiness *Zuleika Dobson* has no equal in English literature but *The Rape of the Lock*.

Seven Men and Two Others, written in the full maturity of its author's spirit and manner, is an even subtler triumph. It is the most autobiographical of his works in that he appears himself in each piece and also in that each relates to a phase of his own experience. Of the stories from it selected here, "Enoch Soames" is about the London of the Decadent Nineties, "Argallo and Ledgett" is set in the literary world of the Edwardian age, " 'Savonarola' Brown" recalls Max's life as a dramatic critic, "James Pethel" is set in the Dieppe where he spent his youthful holidays. I have chosen these pieces for this collection partly because they are my favourites and partly because they are the most variously representative of his genius. "Enoch Soames" shows Max the satirist at his keenest. It is at once the truest and most amusing portrait that we have of the world of *The Yellow Book*. Equally true, equally comic, is the portrait of the Edwardian literary world in "Argallo and Ledgett." In " 'Savonarola' Brown" we get Max's gift for exuberant fun at its most infectious. Like Buckingham's *Rehearsal* and Sheridan's *Critic* it is a skit on pseudo-poetic tragedy. It is more laughable than either; and it rises at moments to be a parody not just of pseudo-tragedy but of Shakespeare himself.

"James Pethel" differs from the other pieces in the volume in that it is not, like them, a fantasy, but rather a straightforward realistic portrait of character, only differing from other portraits of the same kind in that it is conceived consistently in a comedy vein. It is a brilliantly convincing portrait, made substantial and alive by touch after touch of exact delicate observation of men and manners. But all through it maintains the comedy mood. It is noteworthy that though the story ends, as it should, with Pethel's death, this is mentioned as occurring painlessly and many years after Max's last meeting with him. Thus without falsification the smiling amenity of the entertainment is unbroken.

Two pieces in this selection do not fit into the categories I have named: "William and Mary" and "No. 2. The Pines". In form they resemble the stories in *Seven Men*; narratives about characters, related by Max in person, mainly in an ironic tone. But the intention behind them is different. "William and Mary," written late in Max's

236

career, is his only attempt at "serious" fiction. It ends sadly, and its dominant sentiment is a restrained pathos. Its irony is tender rather than satiric and the whole scene is bathed in a minor key which comes from the sense, bred in its author's heart by his advancing years, of the fleetingness of human life, the frailty of human happiness. The story does not leave a painful impression. Max still is out to please his readers, but this time by evoking agreeable tears rather than agreeable laughter. Yet he is not sentimental in the bad sense of that word. For the flow of tears is under the control of a vigilant sense of truth and a fastidious art. "William and Mary" is an example of how, if it is disciplined by discretion and style, indulgence in tender feelings can result in a charming work of art; and in one which genuinely moves the reader. In it Max's appreciation of reality did not desert him. He does not make too much of his emotion. His gracefully expressed sadness is sincere.

In "No. 2. The Pines" he adapts his fictional method to fact and uses it to give a portrait of the poet Swinburne in his later years. Max liked and admired Swinburne; but in this portrait his affection does not blind him or make him over-respectful. The portrait has a Boswell-like detailed vividness.

It is also exquisitely amusing. Memorable as the portrait of a famous writer, it is even more memorable as one more aspect of the Max Beerbohm comic entertainment. For in the end it is to Max's comedy one returns when attempting to analyse his achievement. It is its central pervading characteristic and that which gives him his place in literature. A distinguished place: Max is not a giant of the art of letters but still less is he one of its dwarfs—except to those who rate the comic element in human existence as of minor importance. For me, his work is the finest, richest expression of the spirit of comedy in all twentieth-century English literature, and the most varied, ranging, as it does, from the subtle satire of "Enoch Soames" to the extravagant fantasy of *Zuleika Dobson,* from the ironic moralising of *The Happy Hypocrite* to the ironic pathos of "William and Mary", from the psychological comedy of "James Pethel" to the sheer rollicking fun of " 'How Shall I Word It?' " It shines equally in a sustained passage of comic eloquence like the Duke of Dorset's proposal to Zuleika and in a concentrated epigrammatic phrase, as when Max says of the fashionable sages of his period: "It distresses me, this failure to keep pace with the leaders of thought, as they pass into oblivion."

It is in this variety of his humour that he surpasses his contemporaries. Others may rival him in one vein or other; Wilde in wit, for instance, or Firbank in the fantastic absurd. Max alone triumphs equally in every field. And two are all his own: parody and the comedy of human character as exhibited in himself. In this last his humour strikes deepest—though with how light a touch!

> In the course of my long residence in London, I did entertain friends. But the memory of those occasions is not dear to me —especially not the memory of those that were in the more distinguished restaurants. Somewhere in the back of my brain, while I tried to lead the conversation brightly, was always the haunting fear that I had not brought enough money in my pocket. I never let this fear master me. I never said to anyone "Will you have a liqueur?"—always "What liqueur will you have?" But I postponed as far as possible the evil moment of asking for the bill. When I had, in the proper casual tone (I hope and believe), at length asked for it, I wished always it were not brought to me *folded* on a plate, as though the amount were so hideously high that I alone must be privy to it. So soon as it was laid beside me, I wanted to know the worst at once. But I pretended to be so occupied in talk that I was unaware of the bill's presence; and I was careful to be always in the middle of a sentence when I raised the upper fold and took my not (I hope) frozen glance. In point of fact, the amount was always much less than I had feared. Pessimism does win us great happy moments.

It is impossible surely to be more finely, more enduringly amusing than this. Max may be only a juggler; but the balls he juggled with are of pure gold, and likely to be shining brightly long after most of the heavy weights lifted by his graver contemporaries have grown rusty and dull.

[1970]

Editor's note

1. The reference is to "The Mote in the Middle Distance by H*NRY J*M*S," one of the parodies in *A Christmas Garland* (1912).

CHRONOLOGY OF IMPORTANT DATES

Henry Maximilian Beerbohm
1872-1956

1872	Born August 24 at 57 Palace Gardens Terrace, Kensington, London, son of Julius Ewald Beerbohm and Eliza Draper.
1881-1885	Attends Mr. Wilkinson's day-school, Orme Square, London.
1885-1890	Attends Charterhouse, Godalming, Surrey.
1886	First publication: letter to the Editor of the *Carthusian*.
x890-1894	Merton College, Oxford. Leaves without taking a degree.
1891-1938	Correspondence with Reginald ("Reggie") Turner.
1892	Death of his father, August 30. Publishes thirty-six drawings, "Club Types", in *Strand Magazine*, September, November, and December.
1893	Spends summer term in London. Introduced to William Rothenstein. Meets Oscar Wilde and Aubrey Beardsley. Romance with the actress Cissy Loftus.
1894	Contributes caricatures and essays to the *Yellow Book* and other publications.
1895	Accompanies his half-brother Herbert Beerbohm Tree on a theatrical tour in the United States, January to April.

1895-1903	Unofficially engaged to Grace ("Kilseen") Conover, an actress in Tree's company. an actress in Tree's company.
1896	*The Works of Max Beerbohm* (essays), published June. First exhibition of drawings, The Fine Art Society, London, October. *Caricatures of Twenty-Five Gentlemen,* published December.
1897	*The Happy Hypocrite* (story), published April. Writes a weekly commentary for the *Daily Mail,* January 2 to April 17.
1898	Succeeds George Bernard Shaw as dramatic critic of the *Saturday Review;* first article dated May 28.
1899	*More* (essays), published April.
1901	First one-man show of drawings, Carfax Gallery, London, November, including the series *The Second Childhood of John Bull,* published in 1911.
1903-1904	Engaged to Constance Collier, an actress in Herbert Beerbohm Tree's company. Beerbohm Tree's company.
1904	Exhibition of drawings, Carfax Gallery, April, including the series *The Poets' Corner,* published in May. Meets his future wife Florence Kahn, an American actress, summer.
1906	Contributes series of articles on Italy to the *Daily Mail,* November 8 to December 27.
1907	Exhibition of drawings, Carfax Gallery, April. *A Book of Caricatures,* published November.
1908	Exhibition of drawings, Carfax Gallery, April-May. Engaged to Florence Kahn, November.
1909	*Yet Again* (essays), published October.
1910	Resigns from the *Saturday Review;* last dramatic criticism dated April 16. Marries Florence Kahn, May 4. Takes up residence at the Villino Chiaro, Rapallo, Italy, July.
1911	Exhibition of drawings at the Leicester Galleries, London, April-May. *Zuleika Dobson* (novel), published October. Cartoons *"The Second Childhood of John Bull",* published November.
1912	*A Christmas Garland* (parodies), published October. Exhibition of drawings at the Berlin Photographic Company, New York, October-November.

1913	Exhibition of drawings, Leicester Galleries, April-May. *Fifty Caricatures,* published October.
1915-1919	Residence in England during World War I.
1917	Death of Sir Herbert Beerbohm Tree, July 2. Exhibition of fifteen of the drawings that later formed part of *Rossetti and His Circle,* Grosvenor Gallery, London, November.
1918	Death of his mother, March 13.
1919	*Seven Men* (stories), published October. Returns to Rapallo, December.
1920	*Herbert Beerbohm Tree: Some Memories of Him and of His Art Collected by Max Beerbohm,* published October. *And Even Now* (essays), published December.
1921	Exhibition at the Leicester Galleries, May-June, including most of the drawings reproduced in *A Survey,* published in December. Exhibition of a series of eighteen drawings, "Rossetti and His Friends", that later formed part of *Rossetti and His Circle,* Leicester Galleries, September.
1922-1928	Publication of the Collected Edition of his writings in ten volumes, 1922, 1924, 1928. *Rossetti and His Circle* (caricatures), published September, 1922.
1923	Exhibition of drawings, Leicester Galleries, May-June. As a result of the general outcry of the newspapers against the Royal Family caricatures, Beerbohm decides to withdraw them. A number of the remaining drawings published in *Things New and Old,* October.
1924	*Around Theatres,* 2 vols. (a selection from his dramatic criticisms), published October.
1925	Exhibition of drawings, Leicester Galleries, April-May, including the series *Observations,* published in October.
1927	Introduced to Gerhart Hauptmann and his secretary companion Elisabeth Jungmann.
1928	*A Variety of Things* (essays and stories), published June. *The Dreadful Dragon of Hay Hill* (story), published November. Exhibition entitled "Ghosts", Leicester Galleries, November-Decem-

	ber, containing one hundred and nine caricatures of persons Beerbohm has known.
1929	Meets Evelyn Waugh, spring.
1930	Honorary Doctor of Laws, Edinburgh University, July 3.
1931	*Heroes and Heroines of Bitter Sweet,* five "sentimental" drawings of members of the cast of Noel Coward's play *Bitter Sweet,* published May (?).
1935-1936	Lives in London, August 1935 to October 1936, owing to threat of war.
1935	First radio talk, "London Revisited," December 29.
1936	Returns to Rapallo, October.
1938-1947	Decides to go back to England on account of the September crisis of 1938. Residence in England during World War II.
1939	Knighted, July 13.
1942	Inauguration of the Maximilian Society founded in honor of his seventieth birthday, August 24. Honorary degree D.Litt., Oxford University, November 21.
1943	Declines invitation to give Romanes Lecture at Oxford University. *Lytton Strachey,* the Rede Lecture for 1943, published June.
1944	Exhibition of drawings at the Grolier Club, New York, March, consisting largely of the collection of A. E. Gallatin, now in Harvard College Library.
1945	Exhibition of drawings owned by Philip Guedalla, Leicester Galleries, September-October. Honorary Fellow of Merton College, Oxford, December 21.
1946	*Mainly on the Air* (six radio talks and six "other things"), published September.
1947	Returns to Rapallo, September. Visitors between 1947 and 1956 include Thornton Wilder, Somerset Maugham, John Gielgud, Laurence Olivier, Robert Graves, and Truman Capote.

1951	Death of Florence, Lady Beerbohm, January 13. Elisabeth Jungmann becomes Beerbohm's companion and secretary.
1952	Exhibition of drawings "Max in Retrospect," Leicester Galleries, May. First visit of S. N. Behrman, the American playwright and biographer, June. Exhibition of drawings, books, and manuscripts, American Academy of Arts and Letters, New York, December 1952-January 1953.
1954	Visit of Edmund Wilson, the American critic, March 15 and 16.
1956	Attack of rheumatic asthma, March 10. Privately marries Elisabeth Jungmann, April 20. Dies May 20. Cremated at Genoa. Burial of ashes in the crypt of St. Paul's Cathedral, London, June 29.
1957	Memorial Exhibition, Leicester Galleries, June.
1960	Sale of his library and literary manuscripts, Sotheby & Co., London, December 12 and 13.
1962	Unveiling and dedication of the Memorial to Sir Max Beerbohm in St. Paul's Cathedral, London, April 12; address delivered by Sir Sydney Roberts.

Select Bibliography

Note. The titles listed below include publications in book form only. Privately printed and unauthorized editions are not included.

First Editions of the Writings

And Even Now. London: William Heinemann, 1920.

Around Theatres. 2 vols. London: William Heinemann, 1924.

A Christmas Garland Woven by Max Beerbohm. London: William Heinemann, 1912.

The Dreadful Dragon of Hay Hill. London: William Heinemann, 1928. [First separate edition.]

The Happy Hypocrite: A Fairy Tale for Tired Men. Bodley Booklets, No. 1. London and New York: John Lane, The Bodley Head, 1897.

Herbert Beerbohm Tree: Some Memories of Him and of His Art. Collected by Max Beerbohm. London: Hutchinson & Co., 1920.

Lytton Strachey: The Rede Lecture 1943. Cambridge University Press, 1943.

Mainly on the Air. London: William Heinemann, 1946.

More. London and New York: John Lane, The Bodley Head, 1899.

Seven Men. London: William Heinemann, 1919. [Enlarged edition, *Seven Men and Two Others,* by the same publisher, 1950.]

A Variety of Things. London: William Heinemann, 1928.

The Works of Max Beerbohm. With a Bibliography by John Lane. London: John Lane, The Bodley Head, and New York: Charles Scribner's Sons, 1896.

Yet Again. London: Chapman and Hall, 1909.
Zuleika Dobson: or, An Oxford Love Story. London: William Heinemann, 1911.

First Editions of the Drawings

A Book of Caricatures. London: Methuen & Co., 1907.
Caricatures of Twenty-Five Gentlemen. With an Introduction by L. Raven-Hill. London: Leonard Smithers, 1896.
Cartoons "The Second Childhood of John Bull." London: Stephen Swift & Co., 1911.
Fifty Caricatures. London: William Heinemann, 1913.
Heroes and Heroines of Bitter Sweet. London: Messrs. Leadlay, Ltd., 1931.
Observations. London: William Heinemann, 1925.
The Poets' Corner. London: William Heinemann, 1904.
Rossetti and His Circle. London: William Heinemann, 1922.
A Survey. London: William Heinemann, 1921.
Things New and Old. London: William Heinemann, 1923.

Collected Edition of the Writings

The Works of Max Beerbohm. 10 vols. London: William Heinemann, 1922, 1924, 1928. [*The Works of Max Beerbohm*, 1922; *More*, 1922; *Yet Again*, 1922; *And Even Now*, 1922; *A Christmas Garland*, 1922; *Zuleika Dobson*, 1922; *Seven Men*, 1922; *Around Theatres*, 2 vols., 1924; *A Variety of Things*, 1928.]

Posthumous Editions and Selections

The Bodley Head Max Beerbohm. Edited and with an Introduction by David Cecil. London: The Bodley Head, 1970, and Boston: Atlantic-Little, Brown, 1971, under the title *Max Beerbohm: Selected Prose*.

Caricatures by Max: From the Collection in the Ashmolean Museum. Oxford: Oxford University Press, 1958.

The Incomparable Max: A Selection. Introduced by S. C. Roberts. London: William Heinemann, 1962.

Last Theatres: 1904-1910. With an Introduction by Rupert Hart-Davis. London: Rupert Hart-Davis, 1970.

Max Beerbohm, Max's Nineties: Drawings 1892-1899. With an Introduction by Osbert Lancaster. London: Rupert Hart-Davis, 1958.

Max in Verse: Rhymes and Parodies by Max Beerbohm. Collected and annotated by J. G. Riewald. Brattleboro, Vermont: The Stephen Greene Press, 1963, and London: William Heinemann, 1964.

More Theatres: 1898-1903. With an Introduction by Rupert Hart-Davis. London: Rupert Hart-Davis, 1969.

A Peep into the Past and Other Prose Pieces by Max Beerbohm. Collected and introduced by Rupert Hart-Davis. London: William Heinemann, and Brattleboro, Vermont: The Stephen Greene Press, 1972.

Letters

Max Beerbohm: Letters to Reggie Turner. Ed. Rupert Hart-Davis. London: Rupert Hart-Davis, 1964, and Philadelphia: J. B. Lippincott, 1965.

Bibliographies

GALLATIN, A. E. *Sir Max Beerbohm: Bibliographical Notes.* Cambridge, Mass.: Harvard University Press, 1944.

GALLATIN, A. E., and L. M. OLIVER. *A Bibliography of the Works of Max Beerbohm.* The Soho Bibliographies, III. London: Rupert Hart-Davis, 1952.

RIEWALD, J. G. *Sir Max Beerbohm, Man and Writer: A Critical Analysis with a Brief Life and a Bibliography.* With a Prefatory Letter by Sir Max Beerbohm. The Hague: Martinus Nijhoff,

1953, and Brattleboro, Vermont: The Stephen Greene Press, 1961. [Bibliography pp. 213-343.]
Catalogue of the Library and Literary Manuscripts of the Late Sir Max Beerbohm. London: Sotheby & Co., 1960.
A Catalogue of the Caricatures of Max Beerbohm. Compiled by Rupert Hart-Davis. London: Macmillan, and Cambridge, Mass.: Harvard University Press, 1972.

Critical and Biographical Studies

LYNCH, BOHUN. *Max Beerbohm in Perspective*. With a Prefatory Letter by M. B. London: William Heinemann, 1921.

RIEWALD, J. G. *Sir Max Beerbohm, Man and Writer: A Critical Analysis with a Brief Life and a Bibliography*. With a Prefatory Letter by Sir Max Beerbohm. The Hague: Martinus Nijhoff, 1953, and Brattleboro, Vermont: The Stephen Greene Press, 1961. [Biography pp. 1-31; criticism pp. 32-212.]

BEHRMAN, S. N. *Portrait of Max: An Intimate Memoir of Sir Max Beerbohm*. New York: Random House, and London: Hamish Hamilton, 1960, under the title *Conversation with Max*.

CECIL, DAVID. *Max: A Biography*. London: Constable, 1964, and Boston: Houghton Mifflin, 1965.

McELDERRY, Jr., BRUCE R. *Max Beerbohm*. Twayne's English Authors Series. New York: Twayne, 1972.

FELSTINER, JOHN. *The Lies of Art: Max Beerbohm's Parody and Caricature*. New York: Alfred A. Knopf, 1972, and London: Victor Gollancz, 1973.

MIX, KATHERINE LYON. *Max and the Americans*. Brattleboro, Vermont: The Stephen Greene Press, 1974.

Notes on the Editor and Contributors

The Editor

J. G. RIEWALD, the Editor of this anthology, received his Ph.D. from the University of Nijmegen, Netherlands, in 1953. He is currently teaching at the University of Groningen, where he is Reader in English and American literature. In addition to some eighty articles and reviews in the field of English and American literature, he has published *Sir Max Beerbohm, Man and Writer: A Critical Analysis with a Brief Life and a Bibliography* (1953), *Reynier Jansen of Philadelphia, Early American Printer: A Chapter in Seventeenth-Century Nonconformity* (1970), and other studies. He is author or co-author of a number of standard textbooks on English and American literature and language, and editor of *Max in Verse: Rhymes and Parodies by Max Beerbohm* (1963), with a Foreword by S. N. Behrman.

Contributing Essayists

W. H. AUDEN (1907-1973), the leading poet of his time, made his reputation with *Poems* (1930), *Look, Stranger!* (1936), and *Selected Poems* (1938). Beginning his career in England, he became a naturalized American citizen in 1946. In 1956 he was elected Professor of Poetry at Oxford. He has published many volumes of poems and edited *Poets of the English Language* in five volumes (1952, with N. H. Pearson) and other anthologies. His *Collected Shorter Poems* were published in 1950 and 1966, his *Collected Longer Poems* in

1968. His major critical work is *The Dyer's Hand* (1962). In 1972 he returned to Christ College, Oxford, as an Honorary Student. His last book of poems is *Epistle to a Godson* (1972). *Forewords and Afterwords*, a collection of his essays and reviews, appeared in 1973.

S. N. BEHRMAN (1893-1973), one of America's leading writers of high comedy, was for long a star of the *New Yorker*. Achieving international fame with his play *The Second Man* (1927), he reached his peak with *Amphitryon 38* (1937) and *No Time for Comedy* (1939). In addition to film scripts for Greta Garbo films, he has written *Duveen* (1952), a biography, and *Portrait of Max* (1960), an intimate memoir of Sir Max Beerbohm. In 1962 he received the Theatre Medal of the Brandeis University Creative Arts Award. His last book, *Tribulations and Laughter*, a set of memories about people, appeared in 1972.

GUY BOAS (1896-1966) was Headmaster of Sloane School, Chelsea, London, from 1929 to 1961, Vice-President of the English Association, and General Editor of The Scholar's Library. His publications include *A Teacher's Story* (1963) and *The Garrick Club: 1831-1964* (1964). A good many of his books are edited anthologies, such as *A Punch Anthology* (1932) and *Selected Light Verse* (1964).

LORD DAVID CECIL, the son of the fourth Marquess of Salisbury, was appointed Goldsmith's Professor of English Literature at Oxford in 1948. He achieved a literary success with *The Stricken Deer* (1929), a life of Cowper, and published other literary and biographical studies, including *Early Victorian Novelists* (1934), *The Young Melbourne* (1939), *Hardy the Novelist* (1943), *Two Quiet Lives: Dorothy Osborne and Thomas Gray* (1948), *Poets and Story-Tellers* (1949), *Lord M.: or, The Later Life of Lord Melbourne* (1954), *The Fine Art of Reading* (1957), *Max* (1964), a biography of Sir Max Beerbohm, and *The Cecils of Hatfield House* (1973). In 1970 he edited *The Bodley Head Max Beerbohm*, an anthology of Beerbohm's writings.

F. W. DUPEE, Professor *emeritus* of English at Columbia University, New York, was on the editorial board of the *Partisan Review* from 1937 to 1941. His books include *Henry James* (1951) and *The*

King of the Cats and Other Essays (1965). He has edited *The Question of Henry James* (1945), a collection of critical essays, *Selected Letters of Charles Dickens* (1960), and (with George Stade) *Selected Letters of E. E. Cummings* (1969). His "Afterword" in the Signet Classics edition of Max Beerbohm's *Zuleika Dobson* (1966) was commissioned by the New American Library.

JOHN FELSTINER took his Ph.D. at Harvard University in 1965. He is currently teaching at Stanford University, where he is an Associate Professor of English. During the academic year 1967-68 he taught at the Universidad Nacional in Santiago, Chile. He has lectured on Pablo Neruda and published translations and articles on him in the *Yale Review*, the *New Republic*, and *Anales de la Universidad de Chile*. He has also published in *Kayak, Caterpillar*, the *Kenyon Review*, and in the *Princeton University Library Chronicle*. In 1967 he won the Kenyon Review Award in Criticism with his essay "Max Beerbohm and the Wings of Henry James." *The Lies of Art: Max Beerbohm's Parody and Caricature* appeared in 1972.

ROY HUSS is an Associate Professor of English Literature at Queens College of the City University of New York. In addition, he is editor-in-chief of *Psychology and the Humanities*, and is on the editorial staff of the *Psychoanalytic Review*. His (unpublished) doctoral dissertation is entitled "Max Beerbohm: Critic of the Edwardian Theatre" (University of Chicago, 1959). His publications on Max Beerbohm include "Max the 'Incomparable' on G. B. S. the 'Irrepressible'," in the *Shaw Review* for January 1962, and "Max Beerbohm's Drawings of Theatrical Figures," in *Theatre Notebook* (1966-67). He is co-author of *The Film Experience* (1968), editor of *Focus on "Blow-Up"* (1971), and co-editor of *Focus on the Horror Film* (1972).

LOUIS KRONENBERGER, the American writer, anthologist, and critic, has been a professor of theatre arts at Brandeis University and its librarian. His books, in addition to many excellent anthologies and editions in the field of English and world literature, include the novels *The Grand Manner* (1929) and *Grand Right and Left* (1952). Among his other publications are *The Thread of Laughter* (1952), an account of English stage comedy, and *Company Man-*

ners (1954), a cultural inquiry into American life. He has also contributed numerous articles to magazines. *The Republic of Letters* (1955) is a collection of literary criticisms.

BRUCE R. McELDERRY, Jr. (1900-1970) received his Ph.D. from the University of Iowa in 1925. He taught at several universities, and was a professor of English at the University of Southern California from 1950 to 1970. In 1965 he was given an award for Creative Scholarship and Research, and in 1968 the University of Southern California conferred on him an honorary degree of Doctor of Letters. The year before, friends had collaborated in a Festschrift in his honor, *Essays in American and English Literature*. His published works include books on *Thomas Wolfe* (1964), *Henry James* (1965), and *Max Beerbohm* (1972), and some eighty articles. He has also edited texts by Shelley, A. B. Longstreet, Mark Twain, Hamlin Garland, and others.

KATHERINE LYON MIX was graduated from Cornell University. As Katherine Lyon she had a career as a short story writer during the 1940s, which was terminated at the end of the war when she taught for five years in the English Department of the University of Kansas. Most of her stories appeared in the *New Yorker*, but she also had them in *Cornet*, the *American*, and several now defunct periodicals. For her writing on behalf of Norway's cause in the war she was awarded the Royal Order of Saint Olaf by King Haakon VII. After her husband's death in 1956 she returned to teaching, first at Kansas and then at Baker University. She has published *A Study in Yellow* (1960) and *Max and the Americans* (1974).

SIR HAROLD NICOLSON (1886-1968), British diplomat and author, was Parliamentary Secretary to the Ministry of Information from 1940 to 1941, and President of the Classical Association from 1950 to 1951. His works include literary studies and biographies —*Paul Verlaine* (1921), *Tennyson* (1923), *Byron: The Last Journey* (1924), *Swinburne* (1926), *Curzon: The Last Phase* (1934), and *King George V: His Life and Reign* (1952). His *Diaries and Letters: 1930-1962* were issued by his son, Nigel Nicolson (3 vols., 1966, 1967, 1968), who also published *Portrait of a Marriage* (1973), an intimate biography of Harold Nicolson and his wife Vita Sackville-West.

SIR SYDNEY ROBERTS (1887-1966) was Master of Pembroke College, Cambridge, England, from 1948 to 1958, Vice-Chancellor of Cambridge University from 1949 to 1951, and Vice-President of the International Association of Universities from 1950 to 1955. In addition to his books on Samuel Johnson and Sherlock Holmes, he is the author of the *History of Cambridge University Press* (1921) and *The Evolution of Cambridge Publishing* (1956). He has also written *Zuleika in Cambridge* (1941), a charming sequel to Max Beerbohm's *Zuleika Dobson*, and edited *The Incomparable Max* (1962), a selection from Beerbohm's writings. On April 12, 1962, he delivered the address at the unveiling and dedication of the Memorial to Sir Max Beerbohm in St. Paul's Cathedral, London.

SIR JOHN ROTHENSTEIN, the British art historian, is the elder son of Sir William Rothenstein, the painter. From 1938 to 1964 he was Director of the Tate Gallery, London. His books include *An Introduction to English Painting* (1933), *Modern English Painters* (2 vols., 1952-56), *Turner* (1960), *Augustus John* (1962), and *Francis Bacon* (with Ronald Alley, 1964). In 1943 he edited Max Beerbohm's *The Poets' Corner* for King Penguin Books. *Summer's Lease,* the first part of his autobiography, was published in 1965; the second volume, *Brave Day, Hideous Night,* appeared in 1966; the third, *Time's Thievish Progress,* in 1969.

DEREK STANFORD, the British poet, critic, and editor, was a Fellow of the Royal Society of Literature, 1956-60, and is now an Honorary Fellow of the International Poetry Society. He has written a number of books on contemporary authors, including *Christopher Fry* (1951), *John Betjeman* (1961), *Muriel Spark* (1963), and *Dylan Thomas* (1964). During the last ten years he has specialized in the literature and art of the second half of the Victorian period, particularly the 'nineties. His *Critics of the 'Nineties* (1970) contains a short study of Sir Max Beerbohm. Other books by him deal respectively with the poets and short storyists of the 'nineties and Aubrey Beardsley. His most recent book, *Pre-Raphaelite Writing,* an anthology, was published in 1973.

DAVID STEVENSON took his Ph.D. at the University of Michigan in 1954. His (unpublished) doctoral dissertation is entitled

"The Critical Principles and Devices of Max Beerbohm." As an Instructor of English he served in four colleges for various lengths of time and, as an administrator, in two more. He has written a number of reviews and catalogues, and an article on teacher training, "Who Will Teach the Teachers," in the *New Republic* for 13 January 1958. He is now Dean of Humanities and Social Sciences at Cuyahoga Community College, Cleveland, Ohio.

JOHN UPDIKE, the American novelist and short story writer, was a member of the staff of the *New Yorker* from 1955 to 1957. His novels include *Rabbit, Run* (1960), *The Centaur* (1963), for which he received the National Book Award in 1964, *Of the Farm* (1965), *Couples* (1968), *Bech: A Book* (1970), and *Rabbit Redux* (1971). In addition to his novels he has published a large number of stories, as well as numerous reviews, essays, parodies, sketches (many of which are collected in *Assorted Prose*, 1965), and a few volumes of verse. He was the winner of the O. Henry Prize Story Award, 1967-68. His most recent collection of stories and diversions is *Museums and Women* (1972).

EVELYN WAUGH (1903-1966), the distinguished British novelist, is the author of *Decline and Fall* (1928), *Vile Bodies* (1930), *Black Mischief* (1932), *A Handful of Dust* (1934), *Put Out More Flags* (1942), *Brideshead Revisited* (1945), *Helena* (1950), *The Ordeal of Gilbert Pinfold* (1957), and other books. His war trilogy *Men at Arms* (1952), *Officers and Gentlemen* (1955), and *Unconditional Surrender* (1961) was re-issued in 1966 under the title *The Sword of Honour*. His non-fiction books include *The Life of the Right Reverend Ronald Knox* (1959) and *A Tourist in Africa* (1960). His *Private Diaries* were published in the London *Observer* in 1973.

EDMUND WILSON (1895-1972) was one of the leading critics in the United States. He is the author of many influential books, including *Axel's Castle* (1931), a collection of critical essays on the symbolist movement, *The Triple Thinkers* (1938), *The Wound and the Bow* (1941), *Memoirs of Hecate County* (1946), *Classics and Commercials: A Literary Chronicle of the Forties* (1950), *The Shores of Light* (1952), *Patriotic Gore* (1962), and *The Bit Between My Teeth: A Literary Chronicle of 1950-1965* (1965). He has edited *The Shock of Recognition* (1943), an anthology of American writers' critical views of one another. *The Fruits of the MLA* (1969) is an account of his running battle with what he regarded as academic obfuscation. His last book *Upstate* (1972) contains records and recollections of Northern New York.